ASPECTS OF
THE THEORY OF
ARTIFICIAL
INTELLIGENCE

The Proceedings
of the
First International Symposium on Biosimulation
Locarno, June 29 - July 5, 1960

ASPECTS OF
THE THEORY OF
ARTIFICIAL INTELLIGENCE

The Proceedings
of the
First International Symposium on Biosimulation
Locarno, June 29 - July 5, 1960

Edited by
C. A. Muses, Ph.D.
Research Director, Barth Foundation
International Research Centre, Switzerland

Conference Chairman—W. S. McCulloch, M.D.
Head, Neurophysiology Group, Research Laboratory of Electronics,
Massachusetts Institute of Technology

Springer Science+Business Media, LLC
1962

Library of Congress Catalog Card Number 62-13474

ISBN 978-1-4899-6269-0   ISBN 978-1-4899-6584-4 (eBook)
DOI 10.1007/978-1-4899-6584-4

©1962 Springer Science+Business Media New York
Originally published by Plenum Press, Inc. in 1962.
Softcover reprint of the hardcover 1st edition 1962

PREFACE

This volume is the result of two experiments, one evident in the theme itself, which is designed to restore the unity of the forest enough so that it is no longer obscured by the albeit inviting trees of increasing and often uncoordinated published minutiae in the fields of artificial intelligence (wider than simply cybernetics), and biosimulation. We humans learn about objects best by trying to construct them ourselves, by building models. But how far can we go in this manner if the object we wish to learn about is ourselves? Hence "Man Build Thyself?" might have been a possible title for this volume.

The second experimental procedure adopted (unanimously seconding a suggestion of the Chairman) is that instead of presenting the reader with raw, uncut and often disjointed verbatim discussions, he is here presented with the mature results of those discussions after the mutual intellectual impact of the Symposium.

Dr. M. P. Schützenberger, though he had accepted the appointment as symposium editor, was later prevented by other duties from performing this task, and the responsibility finally reverted—after all the papers had been completed—to the present editor as publications and research director of the sponsoring organization, who takes this occasion to express thanks and debt to the wise counsel and guidance of the Conference Chairman, Doctor Warren S. McCulloch of the Massachusetts Institute of Technology.

As a result of the procedures adopted, the papers printed in the following pages represent and include all the beneficial results of the encounter, and also the continued individual thinking of the contributors as they worked out the final form of their monographs.

A joint enterprise such as represented by this volume makes one both sensitively aware and keenly appreciative of the ungrudging time and creative effort bestowed by one's fellow contributors on their results. To each of them goes sincere thanks for helping to make this book possible amid the pressures of very crowded schedules.

Finally, the unstinting help—despite a host of petty details and hindering circumstances—in preparing a difficult manuscript for the printer and seeing it through the press on the part of Mme Christiane de Montet and Miss Leah B. Drake is herewith acknowledged. Thanks are also due Mr. John Matzka, managing editor of the Plenum Press, and to Mr. J. F. O'Connor, editor.

C. A. Muses

Lausanne, September, 1962

LIST OF CONTRIBUTORS

(Institutional connections as of Symposium date)

A.M. ANDREW, Ph.D., B.Sc. Autonomics Division, National Physical Laboratory, Teddington, England

W.R. ASHBY, M.D., D.P.M. Burden Neurological Institute, Bristol England

R.L. BEURLE, Ph.D., B.Sc. English Electric Valve Co., Ltd., Chelmsford, England

H. von FOERSTER, Ph.D. Research Laboratory of Electrical Engineering, University of Illinois, U.S.A.

D.M. MacKAY, Ph.D., B.Sc. Department of Communication, University of North Staffordshire, England

W.S. McCULLOCH, M.D., M.A., A.B. Research Laboratory of Electronics, Massachusetts Institute of Technology, U.S.A.

C.A. MUSES, Ph.D., M.A., B.Sc. Barth Foundation International Research Centre, Switzerland

G. PASK, M.A. System Research Ltd., Richmond, Surrey, England

M. P. SCHÜTZENBERGER, M.D., Ph.D. University of Poitiers, France

K.R. SHOULDERS Stanford Research Institute, Menlo Park, California, U.S.A.

CONTENTS

CHAPTER I

LEARNING IN A NONDIGITAL ENVIRONMENT[*]

ALEX M. ANDREW

Machines which simulate animal learning have been described by Uttley [13, 14] with his conditional probability computer, Walter [16] with his conditioned reflex analogue, and many others including Selfridge [12] and Friedberg [5], who have programed digital computers to learn. When an attempt was made to apply the principles of these machines to process control, it became apparent that they were not readily adaptable, because they fail to utilize the continuity of their environment. A great many of the things which a person or animal can learn to do, particularly in acquiring manual skill, are rather like controlling a process. The deficiencies of the learning machines as process controllers are therefore also deficiencies if they are regarded as models of certain forms of biological learning. It is for this reason they seem worth mentioning in a symposium on biosimulation.

The signals which come from sense-organs are continuously variable, so that the raw data on which any form of biological learning must operate consist of continuously variable quantities. For some purposes these continuous signals are processed to provide discrete information. For instance, a driver recognizes that the traffic lights are red or green, and a dog recognizes the spoken commands "beg" or "sit." The discrete signals resulting from the recognition process (which may be either learned or innate) are entirely suitable to provide inputs to a system operating essentially like Uttley's conditional probability computer. In fact, one of the demonstrations of this machine which is frequently given to visitors simulates a dog learning to respond correctly to the commands "beg" and "sit."

---

[*]The author having had a prior commitment, his paper was read by Dr. MacKay.

In many situations, however, the learning process must take account of quantitative information in such a way that continuity is utilized. The mere recognition of discrete situations does not allow this. As an illustration, consider a person acquiring a well-known manual skill, namely the ability to ride a bicycle.

A person learning to ride a bicycle learns to turn the handlebars to the left if he is falling over to the left, and the appropriate amount of turning is a function both of his forward speed and of the angle to which he has fallen over. It is inconceivable that a person could get into the state of knowing what action to take for a speed of 10 m.p.h. and angle of 8 degrees, and also for 10 m.p.h. and 6 degrees, and yet have no idea what to do for 10 m.p.h. and 7 degrees. A person's learning is certainly not entirely based on the recognition of discrete situations. It is, however, extremely flexible, and could also adapt readily to a discontinuous environment in which the appropriate action for an angle of 7 degrees was quite different from an interpolation between the actions appropriate for 6 and 8 degrees.

To see how a learning process could utilize continuity, consider what an engineer might do if he wished to make a bicycle-riding machine, but was ignorant of the dynamics of cycling. He could make a versatile controller to be connected to the bicycle and adjusted while actually running. To make it he would probably proceed in one of two main ways. One would be to let the angle at which the handlebars were held be computed as a polynomial:

$$d = K + La + Mv + Na^2 + Pv^2 + Qav + \cdots$$

where d is the angle of the handlebars, a the angle of tilt of the bicycle, and v its forward speed. Then the parameters $K, L, M, \ldots$ could be adjusted for steadiest cycle-riding.

The other method which the engineer might use would be to select a number of pairs of values of a and v, and let a value of d be associated with each. Then a value of d for any other pair of values of a and v could be determined by an interpolation procedure from the values stored for the selected pairs. These might, for instance, be the 16 obtained by letting a have the values 4, 8, 12, 16 degrees for each of the values 5, 10, 15, 20 m.p.h. for v. Then the device could be adjusted for optimum performance by adjusting the 16 values of d associated with these pairs. The points in the phase space corresponding to the selected values will be termed "reference points."

For either of these methods it is possible to devise ways of making the adjustments automatically, and then the controller becomes a type of learning machine. The polynomial type has received more attention than the other in the literature. It is related to Kalman's [7] system (though in this the coefficients to be adjusted are in a difference equation and not a polynomial). Gabor's [6] learning filter does in fact optimize a polynomial expression. Intuitively, however, the reference-point method seems more likely to approximate learning processes in a person or animal.

Neither of these methods has a degree of flexibility approaching that of the brain. At least, they certainly do not if, in the first method, the terms to be included in the polynomial are selected in advance, or if in the second method the number and positions of the reference points are predetermined. The flexibility can be increased enormously by letting the learning process modify the *form* of the polynomial expression as well as find optimal values for parameters, or in the second case by letting the positions of the reference points be similarly adjustable.

Some principles which might allow the form of a polynomial expression to be modified during learning have been suggested by Andrew [1, 2]. It is assumed that the parameters K, L, M, . . . are made to move toward optimal values by superimposing fluctuations on their steady values, and attempting to correlate the fluctuations with some measure (termed "hedony," after Selfridge) of goal-achievement. If the correlation is positive, the value of the parameter is made to increase, or if negative, to decrease.

Let r_{Lh} be a measure of the correlation between fluctuations in the parameter L and the hedony h. Suppose r_{Lh} is indicated as a continuous or "running" value. Then if a significant correlation exists between r_{Lh} and a (where L is the coefficient of the a term in the polynomial) the conclusion can be drawn by the machine that the equation for d could profitably include a term in a^2. Similarly, if there is a significant correlation between r_{Lh} and b, the equation could profitably include a term in ab, and so on.

It is also possible to devise criteria by which a machine may decide which existing terms in the polynomial are serving no useful purpose. A learning machine using the polynomial method may therefore incorporate self-organization, since the computing elements which are released when a polynomial term is eliminated can be reallocated to compute new terms which have been shown to be desirable, and to adjust the coefficients of these terms to optimal values.

It would be uneconomical to compute continuously all the correlation measures, such as that between r_{Lh} and a, which might possibly be of interest. Instead, "wandering correlators" could be used to search randomly for correlations not previously known to exist.

In the case of the reference-point type of learning machine, it should not be difficult to devise procedures whereby new reference points would be instituted at points in the phase space at which interpolation from previously existing points was not giving satisfactory results. Also, reference points could be abandoned if the stored information associated with them indicated a control action very close to what might have been arrived at by interpolation from other points. Thus the possibility of self-organization exists in this case also, as the pattern of reference points is adjusted to suit the environment.

It is interesting to note also that this feature of self-organization can allow the machine to incorporate in its control function some signal which was not initially known to be relevant to its goal. For instance, in controlling an industrial process, a measure of atmospheric pressure might be made available to a learning controller. The controller might be able to incorporate this, advantageously, in its control function, even though there was initially no information as to how, if at all, the process would be affected by atmospheric pressure.

The facility of incorporating new signals in a computation is also shown by the machine described by Foulkes [4] for determining the statistical structure of a sequence of characters. Foulkes' machine contains units which compute the conditional probability of a 1-digit following a particular n-gram of digits. He incorporates in each of these units two further subunits which compute the separate conditional probabilities of a 1-digit following, for the two cases in which the n-gram was preceded by a 1-digit and where it was preceded by a 0-digit. If the probabilities computed by these two subunits are significantly different, the main unit splits into two new units which collect statistics for the two $(n + 1)$-grams obtained by putting 1 and 0 in front of the previously considered n-gram.

The computation carried out by the two subunits in a unit of Foulkes' machine is esentially the estimation of the degree of correlation between the digit preceding the n-gram and that succeeding it. If the correlation is significant the splitting of the main unit constitutes a modification of the machine's prediction function to take account of the preceding digit, which was not previously known to be relevant.

DISCUSSION

At first sight the learning systems discussed here appear to have more in common with self-optimizing systems for process control (Draper and Li [3], Kalman [7], and many others) than with systems inspired by biological studies (Von Foerster [15], Pask [11], Willis [17], and many others). Nevertheless I have ventured to introduce these ideas in a symposium on biosiumlation because I have myself been intrigued and pleasantly surprised by their versatility, and because they probably have more relevance to biological studies than is immediately apparent.

The two approaches to the study of learning systems are complementary, for although the most interesting simulation of animal learning would be one which used a network of neuron-like elements, its over-all behavior must have some of the characteristics of the learning systems discussed here. The model neurons of Von Foerster can certainly utilize the continuity of the environment, since they handle continuous signals; so can the deposited-thread systems produced by Pask. McCulloch-Pitts [10] neurons are certainly capable, in principle, of forming networks which utilize continuity, for they can be organized to do anything which can be done by a digital computer, including any arithmetical operation on binary numbers. It is, however, doubtful whether a biological growth process would organize them to do arithmetic with binary numbers, and they seem to be less well adapted to a continuous environment than neurons dealing with continuous signals. The neurons devised by Willis are an extension of the McCulloch-Pitts model and the same considerations apply to them.

MacKay [8, 9] has suggested learning models containing neuron-like elements which do not have a definite threshold of firing, as McCulloch-Pitts neurons do, and as Willis neurons do at any instant in time. MacKay considers statistical elements whose *probability* of firing in response to a stimulus depends on a stored quantity in the element. A network of MacKay's elements could certainly come to handle quantitative information in a way which utilized continuity, if the continuous variables were represented by pulse frequencies and there were sufficient parallel paths through the network to smooth out statistical fluctuations.

It is possible that the approach outlined in this paper may be relevant to the study of the *detailed* working of the nervous system as well as its over-all behavior. It is possible that each cell of the nervous system acts as a simple self-optimizing controller to compute an output signal which is a function of its inputs. The idea of self-optimization implies a criterion of goodness of control, or hedony function. Neurons may be interconnected, not only so that the output signal of one can become an input signal of another, but also so that the output signal of one can be used in computing the hedony function of another. Hence certain neurons can determine the goals toward which the activity of others is directed, and a hierarchical system is possible. The neurons higher in the system would make slower trial-and-error variations in their control policy than would the neurons occupying lower positions, whose goals are set by the higher neurons. This is because the higher neurons would be unable to assess the desirability of a trial variation in their mode of action until the lower neurons had had time to adapt to the variation in the goal specification transmitted to them. The goal specification for the highest neurons in the system must be the goal which is important to the animal.

Control systems with hierarchies of subcontrollers working toward goals set them by higher-order controllers have been discussed (Andrew [1]), though the idea that this provided a possible model for a nervous system only arose during subsequent discussion.

The ideas put forward here have not been related in any detail to the observed phenomena of learning in people and animals, but their consideration as models of biological learning is justified by the readily observed fact that humans and animals do exploit the continuity of their environments in certain forms of learning.

REFERENCES

1. A. M. Andrew, "Learning Machines," Symposium on the Mechanization of Thought Processes, Teddington, Nov. 1958. Proceedings published by Her Majesty's Stationery Office.
2. A. M. Andrew, "Self-optimizing Control Mechanisms and Some Principles for More Advanced Learning Machines," I. F. A. C. Congress, Moscow, June-July, 1960.
3. C. S. Draper and Y. T. Li, "Principles of Optimalizing Control Systems and an Application to the Internal Combustion Engine," A. S. M. E. publication, Sept. 1951.

4. J. D. Foulkes, "A Class of Machines Which Determine the Statistical Structure of a Sequence of Characters," I.R.E. Wescon Convention Record, Part 4, p. 66, 1959.

5. R. M. Friedberg, "A Learning Machine," I.B.M. Journal Vol. 2, p. 2, 1958.

6. D. Gabor, "Communication Theory and Cybernetics," Trans. I.R.E., C-T 1, No. 4, p. 19, 1954.

7. R. E. Kalman, "Design of a Self-optimizing Control System," Trans. A.S.M.E. Vol. 80, p. 468, 1958.

8. D. M. MacKay, "Mindlike Behaviour in Artefacts," Brit. J. Philosophy of Science Vol. 2, p. 105, 1951.

9. D. M. MacKay, "The Epistemological Problem for Automata," Automata Studies, p. 235, 1955.

10. W. S. McCulloch and W. Pitts, "A Logical Calculus of the Ideas Immanent in Nervous Activity," Bull. Math. Biophys. Vol. 5, p. 115, 1943.

11. G. Pask, "Physical Analogues to the Growth of a Concept," Symposium on the Mechanization of Thought Processes, Teddington, Nov. 1958. Proceedings published by Her Majesty's Stationery Office.

12. O. G. Selfridge, "Pattern Recognition and Learning," in "Information Theory," ed. Colin Cherry, Butterworths, London, 1956.

13. A. M. Uttley "A Theory of Learning Based on the Computation of Conditional Probabilities," 1st Int. Congress of Cybernetics (Namur, 1956) Gauthier-Villars, Paris, 1958, p. 830.

14. A. M. Uttley, "The Design of Conditional Probability Computers," Information and Control Vol. 2, p. 1, 1959.

15. H. Von Foerster, "Inaccuracy and Reliability in Biological Computers," 2nd Int. Congress of Cybernetics (Namur, 1958).

16. W. Grey Walter, "The Living Brain," Duckworth, London, 1953, p. 122.

17. D. G. Willis, "Plastic Neurons as Memory Elements," Int. Conf. on Information Processing (Paris, 1959).

CHAPTER II

THE SELF-REPRODUCING SYSTEM*

W. ROSS ASHBY

High among the interesting phenomena of organization shown by life is that of reproduction. We are naturally led to ask: How can a system reproduce itself? And we go headlong into a semantic trap unless we proceed cautiously. In fact, the answer to the question, "How does the living organism reproduce itself?" is "It doesn't."

No organism reproduces *itself*. The only thing that ever has had such a claim made for it was the phoenix, of which we are told that there was only one, that it laid just one egg in its life, and that out of this egg came itself. What then *actually* happens when ordinary living organisms reproduce? We can describe the events with sufficient accuracy for our purpose here by saying:

(1) There is a matrix (a womb, a decaying piece of meat, a bacteriological culture tube perhaps).

(2) Into it is introduced a form (an ovum, a fly's egg, a bacterium perhaps).

(3) A complex dynamic interaction occurs between the two (in which the form may be quite lost).

(4) Eventually the process generates more forms, somewhat like the original one.

In this process we must notice the fundamental part played by the matrix. There is no question here of the ovum reproducing *itself*. What we see is the interaction between one small part of the whole and the remainder of the whole. Thus the outcome is a function of the *interaction* between two systems. The same is true of other forms. The bacterium needs a surrounding matrix which will supply

*The work on which this paper is based was supported by the Office of Naval Research, Contract N 62558-2404.

oxygen and food and accept the excretion of CO_2, *etc.* An *interaction* between the two then occurs such that forms somewhat resembling the initial bacterium eventually appear.

So, before we start to consider the question of the self-reproducing system we must recognize that *no organism is self-reproducing*. Further, we would do well to appreciate that Rosen [2] has recently shown that the idea of a self-reproducing automaton is logically self-contradictory. He uses an argument formally identical with that used by me [1] to show that a self-organizing system is, strictly, impossible. In each case the idea of a *self*-acting machine implies that a mapping must be able to alter itself—*i.e.*, that it is within its own domain. Mathematics and logic can do nothing with such a concept. It is in the same class as the fantasy that can see a man getting behind himself and pushing himself along.

I make these remarks, not in order to confuse or to obstruct, but simply to make sure, by clearing away sources of confusion, that we do really find the right approach to our topic. Though the adjective "self-reproducing" is highly objectionable semantically and logically, it does of course refer to a highly interesting process that we know well, even if we sometimes use inappropriate words to describe it.

I propose, then, to consider the question re-formulated thus:

A given system is such that, if there occurs within it a certain form (or property or pattern or recognizable quality generally), then a dynamic process occurs, involving the whole system, of such a nature that eventually we can recognize, in the system, further forms (or properties or patterns or qualities) closely similar to the original.

I ask what we can say about such systems.

CAN A MACHINE DO IT?

Having got the question into its proper form, we can now turn to the question whether a machine can possibly be self-reproducing. In a sense the question is pointless, because we know today that all questions of the type "Can a machine do it?" are to be answered "Yes." Nevertheless, as we are considering self-reproduction, a good deal more remains to be said in regard to the more practical details of the process. Our question then is: Does there exist a mechanism such that it acts like the matrix mentioned, in that, given a "form," the two together lead eventually to the production of other forms resembling the first?

I propose to answer the question largely by a display of actual examples, leaving the examples to speak for themselves.

The first example I would like to give is a formal demonstration in computer-like terms showing the possibility. Let us suppose a computer has only ten stores, numbered 0 to 9, each containing a two-digit decimal number, such as 72, 50, 07, or perhaps 00. The "laws" of this little world are as follows: Suppose it has just acted on store S−1. It moves to store S, takes the two digits in it, a and b say, multiplies them together, adds on 5 *and the store-number S*, takes the right-hand digit of the result, c say, and then writes the original two digits, a and b, into store c. It then moves on to the next store and repeats the process; and so on indefinitely.

At first sight, this "law" might seem to give just a muddle of numbers. At store No. 3 say, with 17 in the store, it multiplies together 1 and 7, adds 5 to the product, getting 12, adds the store number 3, getting 15, takes the right-hand digit, getting 5, and puts 17 into store 5. It then goes on to its next store, which is No. 4. There seems to be little remarkable in this process. On the other hand, a 28 in a store has a peculiar property. Suppose it is in store 7. $2 \times 8 = 16$, $16 + 5 = 21$, $21 + 7 = 28$, 28 gives 8, so 28 goes into store 8. When we work out the next step we find that 28 goes again into store 9, and so on into store after store. Thus, *once a 28 turns up in the store it spreads until it inhabits all the stores.* Thus the machine, with its program, is a dynamic matrix such that, if a "28" gets into it, the mutual interaction will lead to the production of more 28's. In this matrix, the 28 can be said to be self-reproducing.

The example just given is a formal demonstration of a process that meets the definition, but we can easily find examples that are more commonplace and more like what we find in the real world. Suppose, for instance, we have a number of nearly assembled screw drivers that lack only one screw for their completion. We also have many of the necessary screws. If now a single complete screw driver is provided, it can proceed to make more screw drivers. Thus we have again the basic situation of the matrix in which if one form is supplied a process is generated that results in the production of other examples of the same form.

On this example, the reader may object that a great deal of prefabrication has been postulated. This is true, of course, but it does not invalidate the argument, because the amount of prefabrication that occurs can vary over the widest limits without becoming atypical; and some prefabrication *has* to be allowed. After all, the living things that reproduce do not start as a gaseous mixture of raw elements.

(The same scale of "degrees of prefabrication" sometimes confuses the issue when a model maker claims that he has "made it all himself." This phrase cannot be taken in any absolute sense. If it were to be taken literally, the model maker would first have to make all the screws that he used, but before that he must have made the metal rods from which the screws were produced, then he must have found the ores out of which the metal was made, and so on. As there is practically no limit to this going backward, the rule that a model maker "must make it all himself" must be accompanied by some essentially arbitrary line stating how much prefabrication is allowed.)

The two examples given so far showed only reproduction at one step. Living organisms repeat reproduction: fathers breed sons, who breed grandsons, who breed great-grandsons, and so on. This possibility of extended reproduction simply depends on the scale of the *matrix*. It can be present or absent without appreciably affecting the fundamentals of the process.

FURTHER EXAMPLES

The subject of self-reproduction is usually discussed on far too restricted a basis of facts. These tend to be on the one hand simply the living organisms, and on the other hand machines of the most rudimentary type, such as the watch and the motor car. In order to give our consideration more range, let us consider some further examples. Those I give below will be found to be sometimes unorthodox but every one of them, I claim, does accord with the basic definition—that the bringing together of the first form and matrix leads to the production of later forms similar to the first.

Example 3. A factory cannot start producing because the power is not switched on. The only thing that can switch the power on is a spanner (wrench) of a certain type. The factory's job is to produce spanners of that type.

Example 4. A machine that vibrates very heavily when it is switched on can be started by a switch that is very easily thrown on by vibration. Such a system, if at rest and then given a heavy vibration, is liable to go on producing further heavy vibrations. Thus the form "vibration," in this matrix, is self-reproducing.

Example 5. Two countries, A and B, were at war. B discovered that country A was a dictatorship so intense that every document bearing the dictator's initials (X.Y.Z.) had to be obeyed. Country B took advantage of this and ruined A's administration by bombing A with pieces of paper bearing the message: "Make ten copies of this sheet, with the initials, and send to your associates. X.Y.Z." In such a matrix, such a form is self-reproducing.

Example 6. A number of chameleons are watching one another, each affected by the colors it sees around it. Should one chameleon go dark it will increase the probability of "darkness" appearing around it. In this matrix, the property "darkness" tends to be self-reproducing.

Example 7. In a computer, if the order 0101010 should mean "type 0101010 into five other stores taken at random," then in this matrix the form 0101010 is self-reproducing.

Example 8. A computer has single digit decimal numbers in its various stores. It is programed so that it picks out a pair of numbers at random, multiplies them together, and puts the right-hand digit into the first store. In this condition, as any zero forces another zero to be stored, the zero is self-reproducing.

Example 9. Around any unstable equilibrium, any unit of deviation is apt to be self-reproducing as the trajectory moves further and further away from the point of unstable equilibrium. Thus, if a river in a flat valley happens to be straight, the occurrence of one meander tends to lead to the production of yet other meanders. Thus in this matrix the form "meander" is self-reproducing.

Example 10. A similar example occurs when a ripple occurs in a soft roadway. Under the repeated impact of wheels, the appearance of one tends to lead to the appearance of others. In this matrix, "ripple" is self-reproducing.

Example 11. (Due to Dr. Beurle) A cow prefers to tread down into a hole rather than up onto a ridge. So, if cows go along a path repeatedly, a hollow at one point tends to be followed by excessive wear at one cow's pace further on, and thus by a second hollow. And this tends to be followed by yet another at one pace further on. Thus, in this matrix, "hollow" is self-reproducing.

Example 12. Well known in chemistry is the phenomenon of "autocatalysis." In this class is the dissociation of ethyl acetate (in water) into acetic acid and alcohol. Here, of course, the dissociation is occurring steadily in any case, but the first dissociation that produces the acid increases the *rate* of the later dissociations. So, in this matrix, the appearance of one molecule of acetic acid tends to encourage the appearance of further molecules of the same type.

Example 13. In the previous example the form has been a material entity, but the form may equally well be a pattern. All that is necessary is that the entity, whatever it is, shall be unambiguously recognizable. In a supersaturated solution, for instance, the molecular arrangement that one calls "crystalline" is self-reproducing, in the sense that in this matrix, the introduction of one crystalline form leads to the production of further similar forms.

Example 14. With a community of sufficiently credulous type as matrix, the introduction of one "chain letter" is likely to lead to the production of further such forms.

Example 15. In another community of suitable type as matrix, one person taking up a particular hobby (as form) is likely to be followed by the hobby being taken up by other people.

Example 16. Finally, I can mention the fact that the occurrence of one yawn is likely to be followed by further occurrences of similar forms. In this matrix, the form "yawn" is self-reproducing.

REPRODUCTION AS A SPECIALIZED ADAPTATION

After these examples we can now approach the subject more realistically. To see more clearly how special this process of reproduction is, we should appreciate that reproduction is not something that belongs to living organisms by some miraculous linkage, but is simply a specialized means of adaptation of a specialized class of disturbances. The point is that the terrestrial environments that organisms have faced since the dawn of creation have certain specialized properties that are not easily noticed until one contrasts them with the completely nonspecialized processes that can exist inside a computer. Chief among these terrestrial properties is the extremely common rule that if two things are far apart they tend to have practically no effect on one another. Doubtless there are exceptions, but this rule holds over the majority of events. What this means is that when disturbances or dangers come to an organism, they tend to strike locally. Perhaps the clearest example would be seen if the earth had no atmosphere so that the organisms on it were subject to a continuous rain of small shotlike particles traveling at very high speeds. Under such a rain the threat by each particle is local, so that a living form much increases its chance of survival if replicates of the form are made and dispersed. The rule of course is of extremely wide applicability. Banks that may have a fire at one place make copies of their records and disperse them. If a computing machine were liable to sudden faults occurring at random places, there would be advantage in copying off important numbers at various stages in the calculation so as to have dispersed replicates. Thus, the process of reproduction should be seen in its proper relation to other complex dynamic processes as simply a specialized form of adaptation against a special class of disturbances. It is all that and nothing more. Should the disturbances not be localized there is no advantage in reproduction. Suppose, for instance, that the only threat to a species was the arrival of a new virus, that was either overwhelmingly lethal or merely slightly disturbing. Under such conditions the species would gain nothing by having many distinct individuals. The same phenomenon can be seen in industry. If an industry is affected by economic circumstances or by new laws, so that either all the companies in it survive, or all fail, then there is no advantage in the multiplicity of companies; a monopoly can be as well adapted as a multiplicity of small companies.

FUNDAMENTAL THEORY

After this survey we have at least reached a point where we can see "reproduction" in its proper nature in relation to the logic of mechanism. We see it simply as an adaptation to a particular class of disturbances. This means that it is at once subject to the theoretical formulations that Sommerhoff [3] has displayed so decisively. The fact that it is an adaptation means that we are dealing essentially with an invariant of some dynamic process. This means that we can get a new start, appropriate to the new logic of mechanism, that will on the one hand display its inner logic clearly, and on the other hand state the process in a form ready to be taken over by machine programing or in any related process. We start then with the fundamental concept that the dynamic process is properly defined by first naming the set S of states of the system and then the mapping f of that set into itself which corresponds to the dynamic drive of the system. *Reproduction is then one of the invariants that holds over the compound of this system and a set of disturbances that act locally.* If then f is such that some parts within the whole are affected individually, "reproduction" is simply a process by which these parts are invariant under the change-inducing actions of the dynamic drive f.

It must be emphasized that reproduction, though seeming a sharply defined process in living organisms, is really a concept of such generality that precise definition is necessary in all cases if it is to be clear what we are speaking of. Thus, in a sense every state of equilibrium reproduces itself; for if $f(x) = x$, then the processes f of the machine so act on x that at a moment later we have x again. This is exactly the case of the phoenix. It is also "self-reproduction" of a type so basic as to be uninteresting, but this is merely the beginning. It serves as a warning to remind us that processes of self-reproduction can occur, in generalized dynamic systems, in generalized forms that *far exceed in variety and conceptual content anything seen in the biological world.* Because they are nonbiological the biologist will hesitate to call them reproducing, but the logician, having given the definition and being forced to stick to it, can find no reason for denying the title to them. What we have in general is a set of parts, over some few of which a property P is indentifiable. This property P, if the concept is to be useful, must be meaningful at various *places* over the system. Then we show that "self-reproduction of P" holds in this system if along any trajectory the occurrence of P is followed, at the states later in the trajectory, by their having larger values for the variable "number of P's present."

It should be noted that because self-reproduction is an adaptation, which demands (as Sommerhoff has shown) a relation between organism and environment, and because the property P must be countable in its occurrences over the system, we *must* be dealing with a system that is seen as composed of parts. I mention this because an important new development in the study of dynamics consists of treating systems actually as a whole, the parts being nowhere considered. This new approach cannot be used in the study of reproduction because, as I have just said, the concept of reproduction *demands* that we consider the system as composed of parts.

The new point of view which sees reproduction simply as a property that may hold over a trajectory at once shows the proper position of an interesting extension of the concept. Reproduction, as I said, is a form of invariant. In general, invariants are either a state of equilibrium or a cycle. So far, we have considered only the equilibria, but an equally important consideration is the cycle. Here we reach the case that would have to be described by saying that A reproduces B, then B reproduces C, and then C repro-

duces *A*. Such a cycle is of course extremely common in the biological world. Not only are there the quite complicated cycles of forms
through the egg, pupa, imago, and so on that the insects go through,
there is of course also the simple fact that human reproduction itself goes regularly round the cycle: ovum, infant, child, adult, ovum,
and so on.

A further clarification of the theory of the subject can be made.
Let us define "reproduction" as occurring when the occurrence of a
property increases the probability that that property will again occur
elsewhere; this of course is positive reproduction. We can just as
easily consider "negative" reproduction, when the occurrence of a
property *decreases* the probability that the property will occur elsewhere. Examples of this do not appear to be common. We can of
course at once invent such a system on a general-purpose computer;
such "negative reproduction" would occur if, say, the instruction
00000 were to mean "replace all zeroes by ones." I have found so
far only one example in real systems—namely, if, under electro-
deposition, a whisker of metal grows toward the electrode, the
chance of another whisker growing nearby is diminished. Thus
"whiskers" have a negative net reproduction.

This observation gives us a clear lead on the question: Will
self-reproducing forms be common or rare in large dynamic systems?
The *negatively* self-reproducing forms clearly have little tendency
to be obtrusive—they are automatically self-eliminating. Quite otherwise is it with the positively self-reproducing forms; for now, if the
system contains a single form that is *positively* self-reproducing,
that form will press forward toward full occupation of the system.

Suppose now we make the natural assumption that the larger the
system, if assembled partly at random, the larger will be the number
of forms possible within it. Add to this the fact that if any *one* is
self-reproducing, then self-reproducing forms will fill the system,
and we see that there is good reason to support the statement that
*all sufficiently large systems will become filled with self-reproduc-
ing forms*.

This fact may well dominate the design of large self-organizing
systems, forcing the designer to devote much attention to the question: "What self-reproducing forms are likely to develop in my system?" just as designers of dynamic systems today have to devote
much attention to the prevention of simple instabilities.

SUMMARY

Reproduction has, in the past, usually been thought of as exclusively biological, and as requiring very special conditions for its achievement. The truth is quite otherwise: it is a phenomenon of the widest range, tending to occur in all dynamic systems, if sufficiently complex.

The brain may well use this tendency (for self-reproducing forms to occur) as part of its normal higher processes. The designer of large self-organizing systems will encounter the property as a major factor, as soon as he designs systems that are really large and self-organizing.

REFERENCES

1. W. Ross Ashby, "Principles of the Self-organizing System," Symposium on Self-organizing Systems, University of Illinois, June 7-10, 1960, Pergamon Press, 1962.

2. R. Rosen, "On a Logical Paradox Implicit in the Notion of a Self-reproducing Automaton," Bull. Math. Biophysics, Vol. 21, pp. 387-394, 1959.

3. G. Sommerhoff, "Analytical Biology," Oxford University Press, London, 1950.

CHAPTER III

STORAGE AND MANIPULATION
OF INFORMATION IN RANDOM NETWORKS

R. L. BEURLE

1. INTRODUCTION

Innumerable questions can be asked in relation to the brain. How does it work? How should a "thinking machine" work? How is it that there is in the universe the consistency which makes a "thinking machine" possible?

A line of thought that might lead to an answer to the first question was suggested in some earlier papers. The idea was to use our knowledge of cortical structure and of the properties of cortical material to derive a picture of the nature of corporate activity which could exist in a network of neuron cells, and to relate this to known behavior patterns. The model built up in this way was a bare framework, illustrating in principle that some important features of behavior could arise out of neuron networks having a large random factor in their structure.

The purpose of the present paper is to carry this idea a little further, and to suggest how various wider issues may fall into place in relation to the framework of the original model. Among the most important of these are the growth of the functional organization within the mass of cells and the logical structure of this organization. This logical structure links anatomy and physiology with the psychology of learning and behavior, and ultimately becomes much more important than the more topological structure of the cell mass.

2. THE BASIC CONCEPT

The concept on which this paper is based is the outcome of a number of earlier papers on the subject [1-3] and is illustrated in

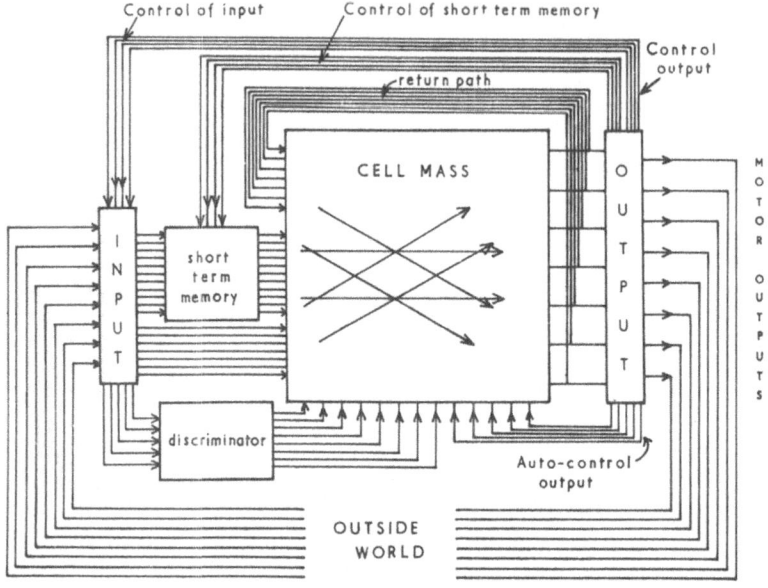

Fig. 1

Fig. 1. This shows, in diagrammatic form, the functional relationships between the various parts of a deliberately simple hypothetical organism. The heart of the matter is the cell mass. In the earlier
papers the cell mass was described as a hypothetical cell network
based as closely as possible on the known structure of the cortex
and on the properties of cortical neurons. Where the meager nature
of the empirical data on the interaction between cortical cells made
the arbitrary assumption of some property unavoidable, care was
taken to assume only biologically likely properties for these cells.

The cell mass is assumed to be randomly connected, but no virtue is made of this assumption other than that it is biologically
plausible. The networks requiring the minimum of information to be
carried by the chromosomes are, on the one hand, those having a
high degree of regular order and, on the other hand, those having no
order, i.e., randomly connected networks. There is no evidence of
a high degree of order, and it therefore seems reasonable to postulate a random network. It should be pointed out that randomness of
connection is not an essential condition for this network to show

the behavior discussed in what follows. The striking fact is that the network should be able to show such behavior in spite of its random connections.

Arising out of the cell properties of the individual cells, the mass of cells has certain bulk properties which allow it, in conjunction with the other elements portrayed in Fig. 1, to exhibit both goal-seeking behavior, and the ability to form associations. The most important bulk property is that the mass can be modified slightly, by any form of activity passing through it, in such a way that activity of that particular form or any similar form is favored in the future [1, 3].

It will be seen that there is a closed loop leading from the outside world through the input organs (and the short-term memory), to the cell mass, and thence to the output organs and the outside world. Goal seeking arises from the relationship in Fig. 1 between this loop and the subsidiary loop which embodies the "discriminator" and controls the activity in the main loop by excitation or inhibition according to predetermined characteristics of this discriminator. It is thus the reaction of the discriminator, corresponding to pleasure and pain in a real organism, which makes certain that the only motor responses permitted to continue are those which elicit a reaction from the outside world which is defined as satisfactory.

Until this steady state has been reached, the discriminators provide an output which permutes the excitation to the cell mass, thus providing a form of goal-seeking behavior which continues until some steady state has been found. It is the activity continually propagating through the cell mass when a satisfactory steady state has been reached, that builds up a path of low attenuation which makes certain that this particular activity will be more likely to occur in the future as a response to the same initial stimulus. The short-term memory is often an essential link in the chain as a means of preserving the initial stimulus while this goal-seeking operation is in progress.

In considering the first steps of goal-seeking behavior, we immediately come up against the importance of learning, as a factor determining the structure of the functional organization which is superimposed on the network. To start with we have a featureless mass of cells, the connectivity of which bears no relation to the incoming information or its meaning. It is only with the first attempts at interacting with the outside world, via the intermediary of the sensory input organs and the motor output organs portrayed schematically in Fig. 1, that a skeleton organization is gradually and laboriously built up. The form of this skeleton organization will color all subsequent interaction with the world in any similar circumstances, and will thus to some extent predetermine the final structure. In learning under tuition it is the tutor who, acting via the discriminators, provides the necessary reinforcement or suppression by encouraging or discouraging and rewarding or punishing. Thus tuition will also play a very important part in shaping this logical structure.

After the first few steps in goal-seeking learning, association becomes important. This arises out of bulk properties of the mass similar to those that made trial-and-error learning possible. This may be summarized by saying that, as a result of activity, the mass becomes modified so that activity of a similar form is favored in the future. The fact that similar activity is favored, even though it is not identical, not only allows some latitude in the form of the stimulus from one occasion to another, but actually provides a means whereby one stimulus can become associated with another, and whereby a response can be transferred from the one stimulus to another [3]. Association within the cell mass takes place as a result of interaction between the activity initiated by two simultaneous stimuli and the mass itself. If one stimulus already has a well-established response, and if a second stimulus occurs frequently in association with the first, the cell mass becomes modified in a characteristic manner as a result of their simultaneous occurrence. This modification of the mass (or "memory trace") can build up to a point where the second stimulus occurring in isolation will tend to regenerate activity within the mass, which bears a close similarity to the surge of activity which normally follows the first stimulus and is the internal representation of that stimulus. Eventually, when it becomes strong enough, this will initiate the response which previously followed the first stimulus, thus providing a basis for the conditioned response and the other familiar features of association.

Association thus provides a means of building up rapidly on the skeleton structure formed during the initial steps of trial-and-error goal seeking. From this point of view the coexistence of the two effects in one cell mass could be important. It has been pointed out elsewhere [2, 3] that a short-term memory may arise through reverberatory circuits forming within a random mass. This is of interest because a short-term memory, introduced between the input organ and the cell mass, makes possible the recording and regeneration of associations based on isolated incidents. These incidents may be temporarily stored in the short-term memory, and information regarding them may be fed continuously into the cell mass for as long as is necessary to establish a permanent memory trace.

A second aspect of association is introduced by any means which allows circulation of information within the cell mass, or which imposes a delay in an information path. The return path illustrated diagrammatically by the bundle of fibers above the cell mass in Fig. 1 is an example. Any such return path permits sequential associations to be established between events separated in time. These associations are formed in the same way as associations between simultaneous events, the time difference being accounted for by the delay in traveling round the return path.

To quote a simple example which has been given previously, let us assume that a series of events A, B, C, D, etc., occur in the outside world. Then activity caused by A, delayed by a short time, will record its simultaneous presence with activity caused by B. This gives a memory trace of the form "B follows A" which, when it has grown sufficiently strong, enables activity generated by A on some future occasion to cause the regeneration of the activity which is the internal representation of B. This regeneration can continue, so that we may have the internal representations of the whole sequence of events A, B, C, D, etc., following each other as though the events were actually occurring in the outside world. Here it is interesting to note that, by means of temporary storage in the short-term memory, associations can be formed between separate important incidents, and the mere uneventful passage of time in between can be ignored. This gives us the familiar "telescoping" of time in the recall of a series of incidents. For this to occur presupposes some mental control of the recording of events in the short-term memory (see Fig. 1), but this needs no justification.

We can thus have two different modes for the recall of events separated in time. Short sequences may be recalled as a continuous picture, while more widely separated incidents, each of which may itself comprise a short sequence of events, may be pieced together by association leaving imperceptible gaps where perhaps long strings of unimportant details have been ignored. This "editing" of excerpts happens so smoothly and subtly that we hardly realize it is taking place. We do not normally have anything to check it against, for it is itself the memory against which we normally check details of the past. Nor does it seem curious to us that much should be left out, for this is the only form in which we have ever been able to recall long sequences of incidents, and to think about them. It is only by trying to recall every detail of an experience and then reliving it in detail, as for example in watching a film for a second time, that we can realize how much is normally omitted in memorizing a long sequence.

Another interesting point arising out of this is that whereas one would expect short sequences to replay in the forward direction, there is no reason why separate incidents, which have been stored in the short-term memory and have subsequently been associated, should not be recalled in either forward or backward sequence. This accords with common experience. If one recalls, say, putting a coin into a slot machine, there is generally no question that one has inserted the coin rather than extracted it. If, however, one wishes to jump from that incident to another, neighboring in time, it is usually as easy to go backwards as it is to go forwards. It is as easy to recall walking to the slot machine as it is to recall receiving the chocolate, or cigarette, or whatever it may be.

The recall of a sequence of events or a series of incidents gives us retrospection. An even more important aspect of the association of sequential events is that the same basic mechanism can give us speculation. Speculation involves the recall of events in a most probable sequence which may not correspond in its entirety to any particular sequence of events that has occurred in the past. In a most probable sequence, each event is followed by the event that has most frequently followed it in past experience, and this, by its very nature, is a train of thought about the future. This provides a more powerful method than the simple conditioned response of eliminating the wastage involved in trial-and-error learning. A slight elaboration of this process can take into account not only the probabilities of pairs of events, but also more widely separate transition probabilities.

It will be evident that for such thought processes to have predictive value, they too must be subject to some form of mental control. The survival value of the ability to generate speculative trains of thought is obvious, but it is not sufficient to piece together one such sequence. In order to decide on a course of action it is neces-

sary to follow out the consequences of several alternatives. Moreover it will often happen that the most probable link at some point
in the chain will have a probability only marginally higher than
other possibilities. The introduction of a randomizing influence
would allow somewhat less than most probable sequences to be introduced, with a probability proportional to their frequency of occurrence as measured by past experience. The less probable the sequence, the less likely it is that it will be useful to examine it, and
it is only in dreams that we normally see grossly improbable sequences regenerated. Normally the regeneration of such sequences
will be under the control of the brain itself, and at least a part of
this autocontrol will be a learned aptitude. It is to symbolize this
that autocontrol paths have been shown in Fig. 1 returning from the
output region back to the cell mass itself.

Elaboration of the Basic Concept

We are now beginning to see that the illustration of Fig. 1 is far
too simple to be a complete model of the complex functions of the
human brain. Such a system would only deal effectively with the
simplest of situations. We have already added various control links
which allow the cell mass to regulate and control its own reactions,
but there is another way of increasing the complexity of interaction
without affecting in principle anything that has been said already.
That is to have more than one cell mass, the several being connected together so that each serves a different purpose.

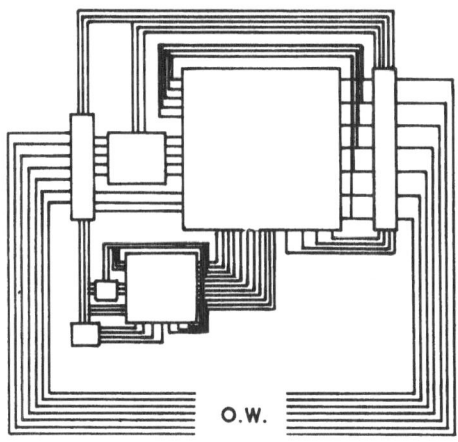

Fig. 2

For example, the discriminators of Fig. 1 may themselves be cell mass units capable of some adaptation (see Fig. 2). Another possibility is that one mass may be largely concerned with motor outputs, and another with control (see Fig. 3). The latter would "play the tunes" on the former. Then again, a second cell mass might be so arranged as to take as its input the activity in the output region of the original mass and would thus be able to take account of more abstract parameters in the environment (Fig. 4). The possibilities are endless, but one comes to a point where it is no longer fruitful to postulate more and more complex mechanisms without further reference to the biological system one is trying to simulate. For this reason it is not intended to follow the question of elaboration any further at present.

To summarize the main features of the model, we may say that it shows how various aspects of goal seeking, association, and short-term and long-term memory can arise largely out of random

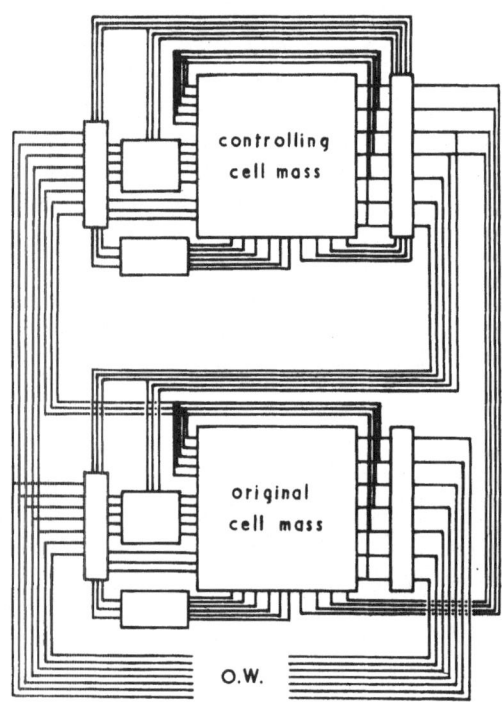

Fig. 3

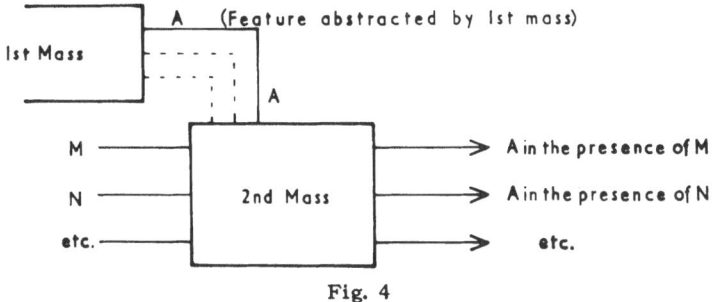

Fig. 4

connected networks. The growth of goal seeking and association within the same network plays an essential part in the development of both. The same is true of the juxtaposition of short-term memory and long-term memory. The former makes the latter practical, and the latter makes it possible to give meaning to the "scrambled" output of a short-term memory arising in a random network. It could be that in the brain the two might be even more closely related than in the model of Fig. 1; the reverberatory circuits of the short-term memory could arise within the same mass of cells that provides the long-term memory. However, Fig. 1 has been drawn as it is primarily to illustrate a logical relationship between the two; it is interesting to note that a similar diagram has been drawn by Broadbent [4] to illustrate conclusions drawn from behavioral observations.

3. THE ORGANIZATION OF THE CELL MASS
AS PART OF A BRAIN

The picture we have now built up is one of a basic "thinking material." This is a material which to begin with is logically formless and structureless, but which, given the opportunity to interact with the outside world, can build up within itself a replica of certain aspects of the outside world, namely those aspects related to well-being and needs and desires of the organism of which the material forms the adaptable part.

Does the adaptable part of the central nervous system actually work like this? We have not sufficient evidence to tell yet, but it is instructive to follow out the implications of the assumption that it does. We can then see how the functional organization might be expected to develop with experience, and we can see whether this is sufficiently plausible to support the assumption we have made.

The First Stages Of Learning — Self-Aligning Filters

The flow of information from the outside world through the sensory receptors must, at first, be completely meaningless. By experiencing this over a period and, in particular, by exploratory interaction with the world, certain features of the information flow gradually take on a meaning in terms of the action which appears to be called for. The physical change corresponds to the gradual development of an information-filtering action within the material. The material has, in effect, the ability to form a multitude of self-aligning filters which respond to familiar Gestalten. When major features are familiar, activity will occur readily within the material; when little is familiar, the opposite will be true. The question of some stabilizing influence has already been discussed. Familiarity and surprise find a direct parallel in the degree of inhibition or excitation required to maintain a given level of activity. Recognition is simply the reaction of the material together with its organism to something familiar.

Learning, in the early stages, involves a randomizing process which allows a continual modification of the filtering action until an appropriate response has been found. The selectivity of the filter then increases further and further, but only as long as the result is beneficial to the organism. Learning in later stages consists rather of the use of association to assist selection, from an existing set of filters, of the one that gives the best results, and of the adaptation of this filter to the purpose in hand. Thus, the filter structure established in the early stages plays an important part in determining the whole approach to new problems and places certain constraints on the choice of trial solutions, and it therefore influences the subsequent growth of the structure. The responses which act through the control fibers, shown in Fig. 1, to control the activity in various regions are probably among the most important in this respect. An autocontrol response structure will grow up concerned, for example, with the control and direction of attention, of interest and perseverance, and of contemplative processes. There is no doubt that these will constitute an important factor in predetermining the attitude to new problems.

Abstraction

When the growth of an operational structure in the material is viewed in this way, it seems only natural that the filters established to begin with will respond to a broad cross section of the environment. The stabilizing influence, which formed an essential part of the original model, impose an economy of the activity so that there is a tendency for activity corresponding to irrelevant background to be eliminated in the course of time. Thus, with experience, the filters gradually become modified to separate the relevant from the irrelevant with increasing efficiency. Eventually, particularly under the influence of education, language, and society, highly selective filters will become established which abstract particular objects or details which are of importance. Even then the response will in effect still be a Gestalt response in that a detail of the environment which calls for one response in one set of circumstances may call for a completely different response on another occasion.

The ability to concentrate on the important details, while ignoring a background which is usually unimportant, is useful in that it makes for economy of mental analysis. When such abstract features are taken as a guide for action, and the rest of the environment is temporarily ignored, we have generalization. Generalization contains an implied assumption that some feature which has been the important criterion on a number of occasions will continue to be important, irrespective of changes in the rest of the environment. This is often, but of course not always, true.

Once it has become possible to abstract individual details, there arises the possibility of a second mass of cells receiving as its input the abstracted information which comprises the output of the first, and thus enabling a second order of abstraction to take place. Then, in place of objects and details abstracted from the Gestalt we may have relationships between objects. Further developments along these lines would make it possible to take into account more and more abstract and complex relationships in a cascaded hierarchy of cell masses. Given appropriate mental control, the transition from one stage to the next may occur naturally as experience grows, but a far more powerful influence in insuring a smooth transition is deliberate tuition in which the environment is carefully controlled at each stage.

Tuition

In the early stages of tuition, problems are presented and techniques used which enable just those objects and details to be

isolated which will be of importance in establishing important relationships in later stages. Then, in the course of time, the first
simple relationships that are presented prepare the ground for more
complex relationships, and so on. By tuition we superimpose a tried
and tested structure on the functional organization. Over the centuries man has discovered a multitude of facts which enable him to
live in the world in which he finds himself. These are passed on to
successive generations both consciously and unconsciously, and
play a large part in establishing not only the response structure but
also the autocontrol structure of the brain. There is, of course, a
price to pay when we force a predetermined logical structure on to
the brain like this, in order to enable it to deal with very complex
relationships. We are prejudicing the issue by deciding for ourselves
what relationships are important, and we are inevitably destroying
some of the versatility with which the brain was originally endowed.
If we are right in our decisions all is well, but there is always the
danger that we are slowing the progress of understanding. We cannot evade this difficulty, because the collective knowledge and
understanding of a civilization is vast compared with what any one
individual personally discovers during his lifetime. In fact, an individual would be lost in our present-day world without the experience passed on to him by his fellows. If this knowledge is to grow
and change with experience it must be passed on, and while it is
true that mistakes may be made, this is an inevitable accompani-
ment to the search for knowledge. The best we can do in tuition is
to present our knowledge in a form which allows the recipient the
greatest freedom and gives him the greatest encouragement to add
to this knowledge.

Association

This is a convenient point to discuss the question of association, and the place of the conditioned response and inductive
and deductive logic. The individual is concerned with these in his
search for solutions to his own personal problems, and in view of
what has just been said, they concern civilization as a whole in
the development and accumulation of its collective knowledge.
Our concept of a thinking material based on a mass of neuron-like
cells has given us a basis on which to account for association,
and the factors which contribute toward the association of ideas

derived from past experience bear a surprising similarity to the parameters which enter the relationship given by Bayes' theorem on inverse probability. In terms of action this accounts for the conditioned response, and in terms of speculative thought it gives us a basis for inductive logic. At first sight it might appear that deductive logic, being formulated in terms of a set of precise rules, is of an essentially different nature. However, when we come to apply deductive logic to a practical problem, we find that there is always sufficient uncertainty in the premises, and in the practical interpretation of the conclusion, for the problem as a whole to resolve itself into one of inductive logic.

All the various aspects of association presented here—the conditioned response, inductive logic, and the speculative generation of a train of thought—have one factor in common. They provide a means of choosing a tentative response to a novel situation with a great economy of effort as compared with a random trial-and-error selection from the possible alternatives. This tentative nature of the conditioned response if often forgotten, but is clearly implicit in the method of generation. In fact, there will frequently be a choice between two alternative responses, each of which receives support from past experience. Here two conflicting surges of activity will arise and eventually one will swamp the other. Roughly speaking, in view of the relation between the criteria controlling association activity and the criteria of Bayes' theorem, the result will be related to inverse probability. Because the selection is subject to acceptance or rejection according to its success or failure, it must be regarded as tentative until reinforcement by success has built up into an almost automatic reflex.

In the composition of each step of a speculative sequence of thought there will frequently be a similar selection from a number of conflicting forms of activity, each corresponding to one of the many possible succeeding events. Again, the influence of criteria resembling those of inverse probability, will be such that the event that is most probable, in terms of the experience stored in the medium, will be the one most likely to be regenerated. It has already been pointed out that it would be of great value in forecasting future events to be able to introduce some randomizing process so that the consequence of other likely, but slightly less probable, sequences could be taken into account. It would obviously be very simple for some randomizing influence to serve this purpose.

A particularly interesting feature of the speculative sequence is that it may be generated while the corresponding sequence of real events is actually occurring in the outside world. It then provides a means of monitoring events in the outside world to see if the tentative predictions based on past experience do in fact fit the future as it occurs. This serves as a check on the validity of prediction in the speculative sequences, and at the same time it is an effective way of bringing to notice anything unexpected which may occur in the outside world. This is what one consciously does in formulating and verifying hypotheses, but it seems likely that the same process goes on subconsciously the whole time.

The Logical Structure

The logical structure of the functional organization that would grow up in an adaptable nervous system built on the principles we have been discussing will obviously be the most important single factor in deciding its behavior under a given set of circumstances. Let us look at the way in which such a structure would grow. It is important to realize that the logical structure is a dynamic one, based everywhere on previous exploratory interaction between the material and the outside world, through the intermediary of the input and output organs. Once the initial experimental period is over, and some sort of path for activity (or memory trace) has been established through the material, this path will form a foundation for further development. One possibility has already been mentioned. It is that the activity at the end of an established path of this nature, because it represents something that has already been abstracted from the background, may usefully be used as the input to a further mass of cells, where it may be combined with other incoming information so that further refined analysis and abstraction may be performed. For example, this might enable "A in the presence of M" to be recognized as different from "A in the presence of N," etc., and therefore discrimination is increased so that classification becomes more complete (Fig. 4).

A second possibility is that the basic path may, by means of association and reinforcement, grow multiple branches at the input end (Fig. 5). This means that a number of different entities are lumped together as meriting the same response, and it is, therefore, a further stage in generalization. The process of generalization reduces discrimination, and in terms of classification results in am-

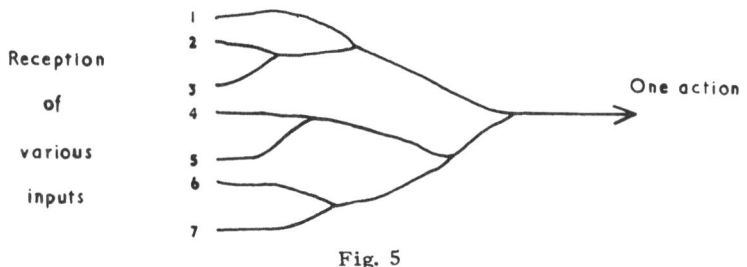

Fig. 5

biguity, for the various entities are merely recognized as members of one class and in the process their other attributes, which may qualify them for membership in other more discriminating classes, are ignored.

It may be, in fact, that these several entities have some feature or quality in common, but the criterion on which their association is based is one of action. They call for the same action, and generalization is therefore in relation to action. In practice this may be so far from our usual picture of generalization for, after all, the action may consist of naming the class of objects in question or their common attribute. In any case the action will be tantamount to recognition of the class or the attribute. A very simple example is that in which the different entities are merely different aspects of a particular object, for example, different sides of a letter box. These obviously all call for the same action. If we have a letter to post, we post it.

As with "association" and "generalization," it is true of the terms "classification" and "meaning" that their significance lies in the functional paths which become established. Meaning and classification are thus related to action during the formation of the pathway while it is in the tentative stage. Even if these pathways become an integral part of a much longer chain of tentative or speculative activity, it still remains true that the significance of each element of pathway derives partly from the associated action and other circumstances at the time it was formed. The success with which it is possible to absorb these original elements of pathway into a longer chain depends on the similarity of the conditions under which the original pathway was formed to the conditions under which the new tentative or speculative chain is being composed. It may happen, just from the nature of the world, that past experience can often be a good guide to action in the face of a new problem. If so, this is our good fortune, but in tuition we can be sure that past experience is a good quide to the future. Everything can be dealt with in such an order that each new step can be based on previous experience and appears to come as a logical sequence. Learning under tuition is learning in a world in which everything is presented in a quite unnaturally logical way. It is much quicker than learning from the world itself which knows no logic and is not prepared to adjust itself for the convenience of the pupil.

Generalized Memories

Returning again to our model, a combination of branching at both the input and the output ends of a pathway gives what one might describe as a generalized memory trace (Fig. 6). This is a memory trace which can recognize a number of different aspects of something and can initiate one of a number of alternative actions according to some other predetermined criterion or "set." Take our example of the letter box. Our multiple input enables us to recognize various shapes of letter box in various surroundings. Our multiple output means that if we know we have a letter to post, and this knowledge is represented by activity of input M, then as a result we post the letter. If we have no letter but expect to have one later, input N may result in a note being made of the position of the box and the times of collection. If we are unlikely to have need of a letter box, the chances are that it will be passed by completely unseen.

The importance of this form of generalized memory is twofold. First, it provides for great economy in storage, and second, it is very readily modified in the light of further experience. When we encounter a new letter box it is unnecessary to make any addition whatsoever to our existing generalized memory unless some feature is so unusual that the box fails to come within the span of the branched input to the generalized memory. If we are surprised by some such unexpected feature then, by the mechanism of association already discussed, the span of the input may be increased by addition to, or modification of, the input branches. Even then, these modifications will require far less storage than the formation of a completely new memory trace together with its reflex action. For example, if we have spent most of our time in one country we may expect our letter boxes to be all red, all yellow, or all blue as the case may be, and when we first visit another country we may be

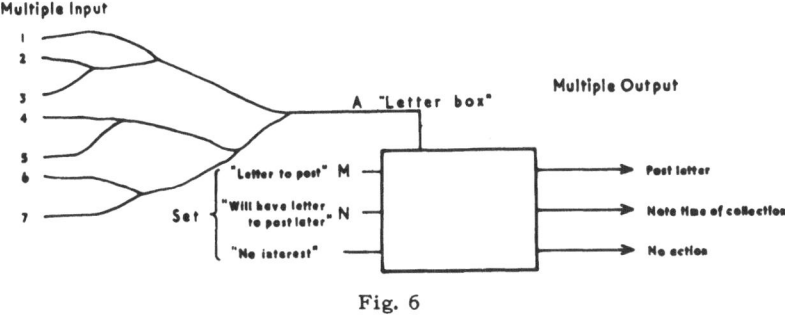

Fig. 6

mildly surprised to find an unfamiliar color. Such a difference can easily be assimilated within the generalized memory in the form of, say, "when in Switzerland look for yellow." One might find, in fact, that surprise could be defined as the subjective feeling accompanying the mental control that initiates modification of a generalized memory. It may be that the immediate reaction to something unexpected is to record the incident in the short-term memory, so that it can gradually be assimilated within an existing generalized memory trace by passing the information repetitively on to the long-term memory. One is sometimes conscious of reliving an unusual incident at leisure, some time after the event, and the same process may well go on subconsciously as well.

It is an important advantage that when an object is seen and recognized by means of a generalized memory no additional information is stored, and that if something unexpected happens it will often call only for a small modification of an existing memory trace. This gives us the utmost economy in the use of the information-storing medium, and accords closely with information theory. If something happens in accordance with expectations then, by definition, no information passes, and it is obviously appropriate that no change should be made. The more unexpected an occurrence, the more information is available and the more necessary it will be that there should be a change. Only in an extreme case will it happen that something is so uncommon and so unexpected that there is no existing memory trace to start from, and it is then necessary to start afresh.

The output end of the generalized memory can also be readily modified. Returning to our previous example, we may one day discover a letter box with a stamp-dispensing machine beside it. By the mechanism of association we can now add another branch at the output which is dependent on a predetermined set "I want some stamps," and the action of looking for a stamp dispenser may be added to the repertoire of alternative reactions to the generalized concept of "letter box."

The generalized memory is thus a very versatile element which serves as an interpretive link between the sensory input and the motor output. It is only seldom that one such link will act in isolation. More generally a large number of links of this type will combine to form a number of complete composite chains in parallel. Among them they sum up the important content of the environment. At the same moment that we recognize the letter box we may almost without realizing it recognize the station beyond it, a policeman directing traffic, the bus we have come to catch stopping on our left, a gust of wind, and a slightly anxious note in the voice of someone we have just met, which we guess is because we are late. We can take in all these diverse things almost simultaneously only because we are familiar with them and have the corresponding chains of generalized memories waiting to be triggered off by one or two slight clues from each.

Economy and Reliability —the Model and the Brain

To sum it up, one might say that if the brain works along the lines that have been discussed here, we should not expect it to provide perfect answers to the problems it encounters. Nevertheless, within the limitations set by a restricted information-storing and information-handling capacity, it will provide a means of making a passable attempt at choosing the best course of action. To make this point clear, it may be worth considering a simple analogy. The telephone system generally gives reasonably efficient service with reasonable economy of apparatus and it does so by sharing facilities on a very wide scale. Between two towns the telephone system only provides a few interconnecting cables and in normal circumstances these are adequate to cope with the number of callers. However, in the unlikely event of everyone in one town wanting to telephone someone in the other town at the same time, the system would break down completely. A universal telephone system designed to cater for every possible combination of calls that might arise in this way would require perhaps one thousand times the number of lines, and the telephone service would cost several hundred times as much as at present. Such a universal telephone system is clearly not the economically ideal telephone system. The telephone system in fact provides a service in which one accepts limited capabilities for the sake of reasonable economy in the apparatus required.

It is the same with a thinking machine. A universal thinking machine, able to take in and store all the information available to it, would need an enormous store of information. If there are, say, N sensory receptor elements, each of which can be either active or passive, this gives us N binary digits. If each of these can sense variations in input at the rate of n per second, the total information capacity will be Nn binary digits per second. Taking conservature estimates for the eyes, the information which could be accepted would amount to 10^{10} bits in a few days, more than the number of neuron cells in the cortex. Thus a machine which had to absorb and take into account all the information which could be accepted by the human eyes, would be quite impossibly large. In fact, the net information actually coming in is less than this because of redundancy, but even so the brain ignores the vast majority of information coming to it through the sensory organs. By ruthless selection it picks out just those few features it has learnt to take note of, and these constitute a minute proportion of the whole.

The model we have been discussing also selects information, in accordance with the dictates of the discriminators, and it thus provides for a versatility analogous to the sharing of facilities in a telephone system. The information capacity of the thinking material is available for the storage of any information of importance that may come along, and is in no way bespoke for a particular type or limited class of information. It merely stores information arising out of the exploratory interaction between the organism and the outside world. If the brain itself bears a resemblance to this model, this would readily provide an explanation of the versatility of the brain in sifting through a large amount of available information without overloading its limited information capacity.

The brain must necessarily fall very far below the concept of an ideal universal thinking or classification machine that stores and makes the best possible use of all the information available from the environment. It is only by being taught, and by learning to recognize just those things that are necessary for comfort and sustenance, that the brain is able to make a passably good attempt at ensuring survival. Nevertheless, when we look at the colossal wealth of information which is discarded out of hand, it will not surprise us how many centuries it has taken man to realize, for example, that many of the facts of nature could be expressed as scientific laws. We may well wonder how much is going on around us of which we are still as blindly ignorant as our ancestors were of the recent scientific knowledge of which we are so proud.

The model we have been discussing is an adaptive classifying network which would, like the brain, show memorizing and classifying ability very inferior to that of a universal classifying machine except in those matters to which its attention has been directed. Within this limited field, owing to the tendency to follow Bayes' theorem, the machine may show a high degree of competence in classifying and forecasting by inverse probability. Its limitation is that its field of competence is restricted to those objects, situations, percepts, and concepts which it has, through necessity, learned in the earlier stages of its encounter with the outside world. Outside this field, whether we measure the efficiency in terms of information storage or in terms of classification efficiency, we shall find the coverage very incomplete. Not only is it incomplete, resulting in a failure to recognize some situation that has been encountered before, but it may be ambiguous, resulting in a failure to distinguish between different objects or situations. This narrowness of outlook is something with which we are very familiar in the brain, and is inevitable with a memory having a limited capacity in relation to the incoming information.

We may ask how it is that we get by with mental equipment that is so inefficient by any absolute standards. The answer probably is that man is the child of his circumstances. It just happens that there has been sufficient consistency in the natural world in which we live to enable man to get by with the very small amount of knowledge he has been able to accumulate for himself, and with the knowledge he receives from his forbears and passes on to succeeding generations. Nor is this the only information passed on. Information is implicit in the adaptation of the human body to the environment in which man has lived for so long, and information for survival is passed on in the form of the predetermined reflexes and in the desires represented in our model by the discriminators. This information, passed on in the physiological and psychological make-up, is less easily changeable and provides a stability that would otherwise be lacking, while the adaptable side of the brain that we have been discussing allows the individual to learn directly from his environment, and allows civilization to absorb and pass on its new-found knowledge quickly without waiting for the slower process of physical adaptation to catch up.

4. CONCLUSIONS

The implication behind the model that has been discussed is that there is a possibility of explaining some of the adaptive behavior of living organisms on the basis of the bulk properties of networks which may have a very large random factor in their construction. This fits in very well with the facts of evolution and with the problem of storing the requisite information for the construction of the complete brain in the small compass provided by the chromosomes. The model discussed has deliberately been kept extremely simple in order to emphasize the important features with the minimum of complication but it would, of course, be possible to build up more complex structures from a number of units of this type, which would have a much richer behavior pattern. The reason for caution is that the whole of this has of necessity been based on very sparse empirical evidence. It would be desirable to await confirmation of some of the basic facts before extrapolating too far.

By looking on the model and its environment as a whole, we see how, by exploratory interaction, a functional organization can be built up which is in a way a replica of those features of the outside world which have played a part in its formation. The model may be regarded as a self-aligning or adaptive filter both in the dynamic and the static sense. Recognition, familiarity, and surprise find a direct parallel in the degree of excitation or inhibition required to maintain stability, and the progressive modification of the medium is directly related to the information received. The model is by no means an ideal thinking machine. In fact, one would expect it to show an intuitive type of behavior with a mixture of brilliance and fallibility which would be all too human.

From the point of view of comparison with human behavior, it is interesting to note the implication that thought is very closely bound up with action as well as with past experience, and this must have a very considerable bearing on the way we learn, on the way we should be taught, and on the way we build up concepts and generalize memories. Perception, thought, and action are all bound up together as different aspects of the same basic process. One can hardly overestimate the influence of past experience and education on the logical structure of the functional organization, and this in turn is the main factor determining the reaction to any situation. Looked at from this point of view, decisions and value judgments appear to be, if anything, more dependent on the way in which information is stored in the network, than on the activity at the time it is extracted at the moment of making the decision or giving the judgment.

The logical structure can also play a very important part in the communication of ideas and vice versa. Two people will only understand each other well if they have a somewhat similar background and education. The communication of ideas between them is then often merely a matter of triggering off lines of thought that are already largely preformed. Their common background and education will have a major influence on the form of the language by which they communicate, and the language will, in turn, place constraints on the form in which ideas are passed to and fro. The necessity for communication will have an overwhelming influence on the logical structure both because of the necessity of putting thoughts into a communicable form and because the majority of ideas are received by communication in the first place. In a complex society like ours, in which so much depends on education and communication, the logical structure and the language must develop in parallel and must match each other at each step as they do so. This applies both to the individual and to civilization as a whole.

A simple example is provided by scientific theories and laws, the nature of which is as much influenced by the mental outlook and needs of the observer, and of the scientific world of the day, as it is by the empirical data. A law or theory is, after all, merely a simple way of summarizing past experience in a condensed form, and this is most conveniently done by relating it to something already familiar, that is, by adapting the existing language and logical structure to suit the facts that have just come to light. In the early stages of investigation of a new field there is often a period during which one is overwhelmed with too many apparently unrelated facts. The information content of these is too great, and real progress is only made when someone discovers some simple theory serving as a "mnemonic" which is not only compatible with the facts, but is also closely enough related with existing patterns of thought, to condense the information content to an acceptable level and thus provide a simple method of remembering the facts.

The progress in a scientific field is liable to be very dependent on the discovery of such simple methods of assisting the memory. Without these the investigator is faced with assimilating such a vast amount of information that he is liable to be swamped by it. This difficulty has been very evident in the biological sciences, and has been reflected in the large number of alternative theories in existence at the same time in certain fields. Just as it is possible to devise alternative mnemonics to assist remembering a certain fact, so is it possible to have alternative theories compatible with given empirical data. It is only the advent of further empirical data that finally favors the one or the other, and subjects them to a process of natural selection and survival of the fittest.

It is not only in the scientific field that many complementary ideas may exist in the individual. We have a large number of generalized memory pathways in parallel and the success with which these are integrated into one composite, interlinked, logical structure will again depend to a great extent on experience and education. At any one time only a few of these memory traces will be active, sometimes one set and sometimes another, the rest being temporarily dormant. If these tend to form into exclusive groups or domains we have the possibility of explaining various features of the subconscious mind. Then again, the existence of multiple paths in parallel may provide confirmatory activity and this is a powerful factor in improving reliability by eliminating "noise" and giving independence of damage. Reliability is also improved by the very filtering action of the cell mass, but this involves decision making and thus sacrifices adaptability.

What can we get out of this picture of brain activity? The answer is that we have to wait and see. The earlier papers pointed out an apparent need for stability, and it is interesting to find that this subject is now being studied empirically. Perhaps by studying the brain we may learn how to use it better. By studying the integration of the brain we may be able to learn how a group of people should or could integrate their mental activity to the best advantage. Can it be that man does already subconsciously follow this example in his corporate activities?

The foregoing has been an attempt to find a tentative answer to the broad question "how does the brain work?" Whether or not the suggestions put forward are substantiated by further work, one conclusion is inescapable. Any decision which a practical adaptive brain system makes will not be based on the total situation in its environment. The information is too great. The decision will depend on what we have taught it and on the particular information that it has abstracted from the environment while it has been allowed to learn by exploratory interaction.

This raises the question of the general principles on which a thinking device should be based in order to get the best out of an unknown environment. This question is of particular interest in the field of control mechanisms. However, we must remember that the adaptive type of thinking mechanism we have been discussing is useful only if we are prepared to give it an education and experience in the environment of sufficient length and breadth to enable it to go through the slow process of building up its own concepts. In many control problems this is far from the most efficient way of dealing with things.

These two questions both contain, by implication, a third, "how is it that there is in the universe sufficient stability for a 'thinking mechanism' to be possible?" but this leads to deep philosophical waters. So also does the question of how far it is legitimate to seek an explanation in mechanistic terms. However, these issues are beside the point in the present context and have deliberately been avoided.

REFERENCES

1. R. L. Beurle, "Properties of a Mass of Cells Capable of Regenerating Pulses," Phil. Trans. of the Royal Society of London, Series B, Vol. 240, p. 55 (1956).
2. R. L. Beurle, "Storage and Manipulation of Information in the Brain," J. Inst. Electrical Engs. (New Series), Vol. 5 (Feb. 1959).
3. R. L. Beurle, "Functional Organization in Random Networks," paper presented at the Symposium on Self-Organization at the University of Illinois, June 1960.
4. D. A. Broadbent, "Perception and Communication," Pergamon Press, Inc., New York.

CHAPTER IV

CIRCUITRY OF CLUES
TO PLATONIC IDEATION*

HEINZ VON FOERSTER

First of all, I wish to apologize for this somewhat pompous title, but I hope that at the end of my talk you will have forgiven me for having invoked Plato's esoteric ideas in order to embellish the thoughts behind a few mundane gadgets. Perhaps you will grant me extenuating circumstances if I am going to make a confession at once, namely, that I believe the time has come when one may conceive of a happy marriage between philosophy and hardware. Since most of the functions of the hardware I am going to discuss in their concepts date back to the famous *Dialogues*, I felt obliged to give the proper reference.

To my knowledge, the first who clearly pointed out the distinction between the *a priori* and the *a posteriori*, that is, the distinction between that which we know before experience and that which experience teaches us, was—if we can believe Plato—Socrates. Many references to this distinction can be found in the *Dialogues*; to me, however, two instances are most impressive. The one appears during Socrates' discussion with Menon about problems in education. In order to make clear his point that education is in many cases not a transfer of knowledge from teacher to student but an awakening of the awareness of the knowledge already possessed by the student, Socrates calls upon one of Menon's servants, who is—one can be sure—not a mathematician, and demonstrates that this man is able to prove the Pythagorean Theorem, if only asked the right questions.

*This work was sponsored in part by U.S. Office of Naval Research, Contract Nonr 1834(21) and U.S. Air Force WADD, Contract AF 6428.

43

The other instance occurs in the dialogue with Phaedon which took place, as you may recall, in Socrates' death cell one hour before his execution. His friends have everything prepared for an escape. A ship is waiting in the Piraeus harbor and the guards are bribed; but Socrates refuses to leave, because he is not afraid to die. Since there is knowledge before birth and experience, he argues, there must be existence beyond death. He proves his assertion by showing that certain "forms" or "ideas," for instance the idea of "equality," can never be gained through experience, because there are no two equal objects in this world. One may make two sticks, two stones, two pieces as similar as one is able to do, there will be always some detectable differences, and thus "equality" cannot be experienced. Hence, this idea must come before experience and must have been gained before birth.

These ideas are "remembered"—as it is usually put in an English translation—and thus some implications as to a "life" before birth and after death are derived. Moreover, I would like to draw to your attention that in the original text Plato uses consistently the form "$ανα$-$μιμνῄσκομαι$," for this kind of remembering instead of the common usage "$μιμνῄσκομαι$," indicating, so to say, one level up ($ανα$-) in this memorization process, a twist we are unfortunately unable to express either in Latin or English or German.

Whether or not this little linguistic tidbit has any significance at all, the points I wanted to make in this brief introduction are (1) that essentially all the concepts about a fabric, without which experience cannot be gathered, as "Gestalt," "Archetype," "a priori," etc., go back to Plato, and (2) that ontologically this fabric cannot be explained, but requires ontogenetic argumentation. It is precisely the train of thought that is given in (2) which is used by Socrates in order to support his immortality assertion. Today, of course, we would adopt the terminology of evolution and would refer to this fabric as some genetically determined structure which evolved in the more successful mutants by the process of natural selection.

Since the gadgets I am going to talk about later are simple examples of just this fabric without which experience cannot be gathered, or—to put it into twentieth-century jargon—since these gadgets are simple examples of information-reducing networks which extract from the set of all possible stimuli a subset which is invariant to specified transformations, I have to stop for a moment in order to clarify a point which seems to me essential in all further arguments. This point deals with that fabric *per se*, namely with the question, "What are these structures or what are these invariants which permit us to gather the kind of experience we gather?" Perhaps my question will become a bit clearer if I add to Plato's philosophical examples the delightful neurophysiological examples which Lettvin and his co-workers recently reported in an article entitled "What the Frog's Eye Tells the Frog's Brain" [1]. Measuring with micro-electrodes in single fibers of the optic stalk in the frog, they confirmed and extended the observations of Hartline [2,3] and others [4], namely, that already highly reduced information is transmitted to the brain. In conclusion they wrote: "The output from the retina of the frog is a set of four distributed operations on the visual image. These operations are independent of the level of general illumination and express the image in terms of: (1) local sharp edges and contrast; (2) the curvature of edge of a dark object; (3) the movement of edges; and (4) the local dimmings produced by movement of rapid general darkening."

Since adaptation or learning is excluded in retinal and immediate post-retinal nets, it is clear that these nets are genetically structuralized in a manner which enables them to compute those invariants—or "properties"—which have a decisive survival value for the frog. This enables me to rephrase my earlier question by asking what should these properties be which have this "decisive survival value" for the frog. Of course, the question may be shrugged off by answering that a set of other properties may define another species—what's good for the elephant may be bad for the frog—a point which can be further supported by property-detector (2), the one which detects the curvature of the edge of dark objects. Clearly such a detector is a "bug-detector" and since frogs live on bugs it is quite natural that frogs should be able to detect their food.

My question, however, aims at the existence of the bug. If we are given a bug, I claim, a detector can be devised, or can evolve, which detects just this bug. In other words, if there is some structure in the environment—and clearly a bug has plenty of structure—a system may evolve which can detect this structure. Or, to put this in still another way, the ontogenetic argument—may it be immortality or evolution—hinges on a tacit assumption that the universe in which we live possesses structure. Maybe for the Greeks this assumption was not so tacit after all, since their universe was the representation

Fig. 1. Globular star cluster NGC 5272, in *Canes Venatici*, photographed
through the 200-in. telescope on Mount Palomar, Cal.

of order κατ'ἐξοχήν, the "Kosmos," in contrast to the "Chaos" which
prevailed before the gods cleaned up that mess in the successful
battle against the giants.

In spite of the somewhat trivial appearance of my assertion of
the ordered universe, I would not dare to prove this assertion to you.
It may lead to chaos. Instead, I shall give you two examples of the
magnificent order in our universe which, I hope, speak for themselves. The one illustrates order on the macroscopic scale. Here,
order is produced by the gravitational forces acting upon the 10^5
stars making up the globular star cluster shown in Fig. 1. Since a
force is a directed quantity, the presence of forces renders space

anisotropic, i.e., the properties of space depend upon the direction into which one looks. The weak gravitational interaction between the individual elements of this cluster accounts for the simple spherical symmetry. The other example is on the microscopic scale. It shows the complex symmetries which result from the much stronger electrostatic interaction between the atoms of water molecules which arrange themselves under the influence of these forces into the beautiful hexagonal pattern of snow crystals (Fig. 2). Unfortunately, we do not have pictures yet of the structure of an atomic nucleus. I venture to say that because of the extraordinarily strong nuclear exchange forces, the structure of the nucleus is so bizarre that our best brains in physics have not yet come to grips with its complexity.

From an information theoretical point of view it is obvious that the intrinsic order of our universe accounts for a tremendous reduction of information, because owing to the high conditional probabilities of certain state transitions—the "laws" of physics—not everything happens with equal probability.* With this observation, I hope, I have answered the question I asked earlier, "What is that fabric without which we cannot gather experience?" It is now clear that this fabric must represent some of the intrinsic regularities of our universe and that the more of these regularities are woven into this fabric, the better it is for that organism, because: (1) states which are meaningless in this universe are incompatible with the structure of the organism, and (2) states which are favorable or detrimental can be "instinctively" approached or avoided, and thus the survival of the organism is increased.

With these remarks I have concluded my "philosophical" exposure and shall turn now to a description of the "hardware" which is supposed to give us some clues to Platonic ideation. The justification of this hardware in engineering language is, of course, quite different from the one I have just given. Here, the systems I am going to describe serve a particular purpose, namely to perform as much information reduction as possible on the inputs of adaptive devices, learning machines, self-organizing systems, etc. [5-7], because it would be foolish not to simplify their task by "building in" as much information as is known about the environment in which they have to perform their task of adaptation, learning, or self-organization.

*A point independently considered by Dr. Muses.

Fig. 2. Hexagonal symmetries in snowflakes.

I will first give you a brief summary of what these systems are about, and then develop from a few simple examples the general idea of such information-reducing networks.

In the following I will deal mostly with sets of active elements which can perform certain arithmetic or logical operations on their inputs. Since the inputs to each element can come either from elements in the same set or from elements in other sets, I will distinguish between interaction phenomena or elements within a set and phenomena resulting from the stimulus activity of one set upon another. Furthermore, I will consider the implications which arise if the size of the individual elements is reduced to infinitesimal extension, so that in the limit one may define arithmetic or logical operations performed by a point in a continuous medium.

Since most of these considerations can be demonstrated with the aid of an extremely simple example, let me for the moment turn your attention to the scheme given in Fig. 3.

We have here an infinitely extending one-dimensional array of photosensitive cells in layer L_1 which are connected to active cells carrying out a certain logical operation. These cells are located in a second layer L_2. Using McCulloch's notation, whereby a loop around the spike indicates inhibition (-1), and a dot on the cell indicates excitation (+1), we easily see that a cell in L_2 will show no response if the two neighbors of its associated photocell are both stimulated $[+ 2 + 2 \times (-1) = 2 - 2 = 0]$. Hence, as long as the stimulus intensity over layer L_1 is uniformly distributed (independent of its intensity) no response will result in layer L_2. If, however, an obstruction is placed in the light path, the edge of this obstruction will be detected at once, since the cell associated with the photocell nearest to the edge will not be inhibited by the photocell in the dark region and thus will respond $[+ 2 + 1 \times (-1) = 2 - 1 = 1]$.

This simple scheme consisting of two layers could be termed an "edge detector," since the presence of edges only will give rise to a response of this system. If one wants to make use of the topological property that any finite obstruction must have two edges, the total output of the system, divided by 2, gives the number of obstructions in the visual field of the system. Hence, this simple scheme may be termed also a one-dimensional "N-seer" because it will extract N, the number of disconnected one-dimensional objects,

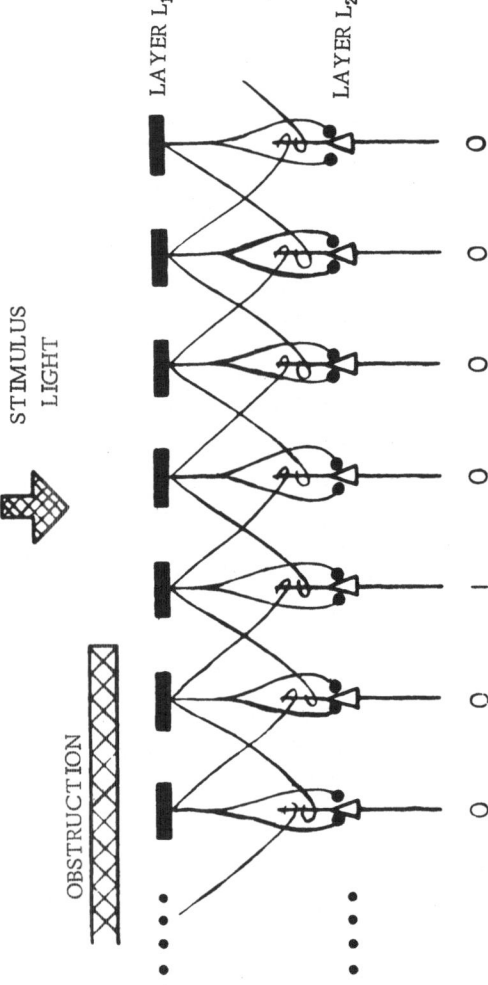

Fig. 3. Net of parallel channels computing an "edge" in a discontinuous stimulus distribution and computing the second derivative in a continuous distribution.

independently of their size and location, and independently of the strength of illumination in the visual field of the "retina."

Already these few remarks suggest some generalities. First, we may note that, owing to particular connections of elements in layer L_1 with elements in layer L_2, particular properties of the stimulus pattern of layer L_1 are detected. Hence, one may conclude that, in general, specification of connections may specify the properties to be detected. Thus, such structures may be termed "property-detector nets." Furthermore, we may note that owing to the identical operations performed on any element along this net, the concept of a discrete field of property detection arises. No conceptual difficulties are encountered in letting the individual cells become very small in comparison to any changes in the stimulus pattern so that, instead of speaking of a stimulation S_i or response R_i of cell i, we may refer to a stimulus density $\sigma(p)$ or response density $\rho(p)$ at a point p in an n-dimensional continuum:

$$\sigma(p) = \lim_{\Delta V^n \to 0} \frac{\Delta S(p)}{\Delta V^n}$$

$$\rho(p) = \lim_{\Delta V^n \to 0} \frac{\Delta R(p)}{\Delta V^n}$$

(1)

where ΔV^n stands for the n-dimensional volume-element (length: $n = 1$; surface: $n = 2$; etc.) in this continuum. Referring to this limit operation, we are now in a position to make legitimate use of the term "field" or "point function" to describe the ubiquitous capability of such a continuum to extract certain properties of the stimulus distribution.

Another generalization that we may draw from our simple scheme of Fig. 3 is the observation that there is no need to assume that one of the layers should be a "sensory layer" while the other one would be a computational network. The layer L_1 in our drawing could easily be preceded by a layer L_0 which, in turn, could have been preceded by another one, and so on, until finally one would arrive at a sensory layer. In other words, the stimulus for any layer L_j can be the response of a preceding layer L_{j-1}.

Furthermore, there is no reason why elements of layer L_j should not interact with elements of the same layer. We will see later, however, that the mathematical formulation of these two affairs,

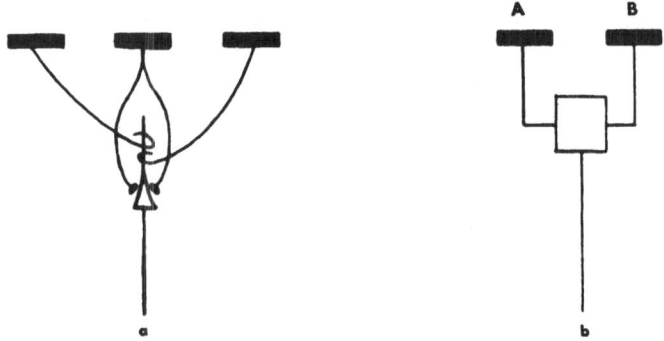

Fig. 4. Equivalence of the nonlinear binomial action function
(a) with a logical function with two inputs and one output (b).

namely the action of one layer upon another and the interaction of
elements within one and the same layer, will require quite different
approaches.

Presently, however, we will turn our attention to the modes of
description of the logical operations the elements are supposed to
perform.

If we turn our attention again to the "logics" performed by our
simple system in Fig. 3 we can easily see that the basic structure
of its performance as repeated in Fig. 4a can be replaced by a
"logical box" as seen in Fig. 4b which would compute, of all the
16 truth functions which can be computed from two variables A, B,
the one which reads:

A	B	Logical box
0	0	0
0	1	1
1	0	1
1	1	0

i.e., "A or B, but not both." Clearly, such a system would detect
edges as well as the original one. This indicates that by specifying
some other logical operations to be performed on inputs descending
from a defined set of cells in a previous layer, one may be able to
extract some other properties from a stimulus pattern than the ones
just discussed.

For illustrative purposes the 16 logical functions are listed in Table I and the corresponding response functions are sketched in

TABLE I

A	B	1	2	3	4	5	6	7	8	9	10	11	12	13	14	15	16
0	0	1	0	0	0	1	1	1	0	0	0	1	1	1	0	1	0
0	1	0	1	0	0	1	0	0	1	1	0	1	1	0	1	1	0
1	0	0	0	1	0	0	1	0	1	0	1	1	0	1	1	1	0
1	1	0	0	0	1	0	0	1	0	1	1	0	1	1	1	1	0

Fig. 5. From Fig. 5 we see that essentially four useful properties can be extracted by considering all 16 functions, namely, a left-edge detector (#2), a right-edge detector (#3), our edge detector (#8), and various modes of obtaining replicas of the original stimulus (including negatives, etc.).

The number of logical functions at our disposal goes up very fast indeed if one proceeds into manifolds of higher dimensionality. If only the immediate neighbors in an n-dimensional cubic lattice are considered as inputs to our "logical box," one has

$$2^{2^{2^n}}$$

logical functions available,* since the number of neighbor lattice points is 2^n. Table II lists the number of these possible functions for dimensions from 1 to 4. It is not inconceivable that with this

TABLE II

Dimension	No. of logical functions
1	16
2	65536
3	6×10^{76}
4	10^{1800}

stunning increase in possible functions the number of "useful" functions is also increasing. I wish I could tell you more about this intriguing problem, but presently I would like to leave the approach to property extraction via logical functions and discuss in more

*There is a notational ambiguity here; what is meant is $2^{\left[2^{(2^n)}\right]}$—Ed.

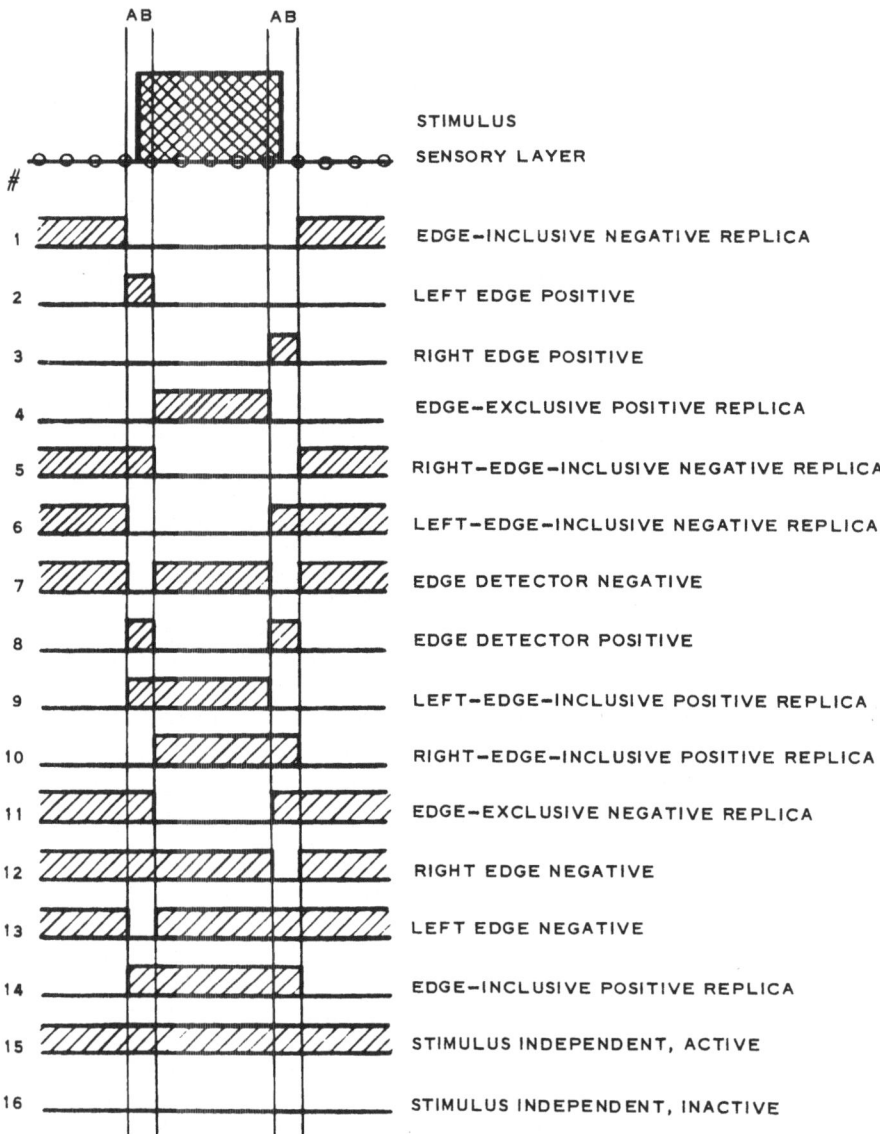

Fig. 5. Exhaustive enumeration of all "properties" computable by a logical functor with two inputs and one output.

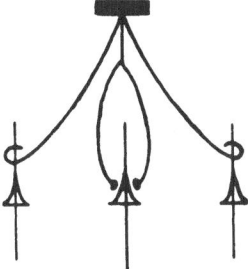

Fig. 6. Structure of binomial
action function
$(-1)^p \cdot (1-1)^{2p}$
for $p = 1$: $-1+2-1 = 0$.

detail another approach which is based on geometrical consider-ations.

Let us again turn to our simple scheme in Fig. 3 and consider the way in which a cell in layer L_1 is acting upon cells in layer L_2. One can express the situation as indicated in Fig. 6: double excitation for the cell located at the corresponding place in the next layer, and single inhibition for the neighbor cells.* Let us define an "action function" which specifies how much activity of cell i in layer L_s is passed on to a corresponding cell i and all its neighbors in another layer L_{s+1}. If all cells are a unit distance apart, a graph-ical representation of this "action function" for the specific case above has the form sketched in Fig. 7. This representation allows definition of action in terms of stimulus strength as a function of distance, which makes it particularly apt to be used in the contin-uous case, where the discrete step function of Fig. 7 may be re-placed by an appropriate continuous function.

Of course, there are an infinite number of continuous functions which would, e.g., approximate the step function pictured above. Considerations of convenience or suggestiveness give preference of one over other possible choices.

*It may be noted that this sequence consists of the binomial coefficients which result when expanding the expression $- (1 - 1)^2 = - 1 + 2 - 1 = 0$. Indeed, this action function is a special case ($p = 1$) of a general class of discrete action functions:

$$K_{p,i} = (-1)^i \binom{2p}{p+i}$$

$$i = 0; \pm 1; \pm 2; \ldots \pm p$$

the "binomial action functions." They are of particular interest insofar as a response layer connected to a primary layer via this action function will display the $2p$th derivative of the stimulus function present in the primary layer.

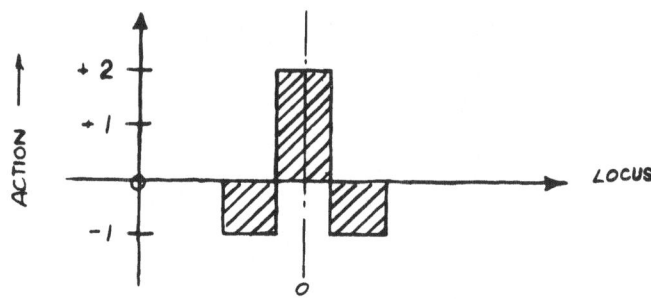

Fig. 7. Graph of values of the binomial action function $p = 1$.

One may, as it is so often done in this field of technological and physiological parallels, argue that in a physiological nerve-net, descending and bifurcating axons from cells in a certain layer L_s may proceed in a random-walk fashion, connecting themselves to cells in a next lower layer L_{s+1} according to a normal distribution function

$$F_+(d) = a_1 e^{-(d/x_1)^2} \tag{2}$$

with F_+ indicating excitation and d, representing horizontal distance x_1 the variance of the distribution, and a_1 an arbitrary constant. Since a similar distribution can be assumed for inhibition (indices "-" and "2"), we obtain for the action function of this particular kind of random connectivity:

$$F = F_+ - F_- = a_1 e^{-(d/x_1)^2} - a_2 e^{-(d/x_2)^2} \tag{3}$$

With such an action function we can now easily determine the stimulus strength coming from an infinitesimal region dV^n at point p in layer L_s to a particular point q in layer L_{s+1}. We have in general:

$$d\sigma_{L_{s+1}}(q) = \sigma_{L_s}(p) F(d_{p,q}) dV^n \tag{4}$$

If the arithmetic operation performed by point q on all incoming stimuli $d\sigma(q)$ is merely summation, we have

$$\rho(q) = \int_{}^{\infty} d\sigma(q) = \underbrace{\int_{}^{\infty} \int_{}^{\infty} \int_{}^{\infty} \int_{}^{\infty} \cdots \int_{}^{\infty}}_{n} \sigma(p) F(d) dV^n \tag{5}$$

If, again for illustrative purposes, we restrict ourselves to only one dimension ($n = 1$), utilize the particular action function as suggested in equation (3), and demand that for a uniform stimulus $\sigma = \sigma_0 =$ constant, no response should occur:

$$P_{L_{S+1}} = \sigma_0 \int_{-\infty}^{+\infty} \left[a_1 e^{-(d/x_1)^2} - a_2 e^{-(d/x_1)^2} \right] d\,(d) = 0 \qquad (6)$$

we find a relation between $a_1 a_2$ and $x_1 x_2$:

$$a_1 x_1 - a_2 x_2 = 0 \qquad (7)$$

It is easy to show that for the n-dimensional case this condition reads:

$$a_1 x_1^n = a_2 x_2^n \qquad (7')$$

The condition of zero response for uniform stimulus as expressed in equation (6) may, at first glance, look somewhat arbitrary. However, you may recall that our original scheme of Fig. 3 exhibited this important property, which biologically may be justified by the insignificance of uniformity. It is the perturbation of uniformity which is to be detected.

Observing the restriction as put forth in equation (7), we may now compare our action function defined in equation (3) with the action function in the discrete case of Fig. 3. In Fig. 8 this com-

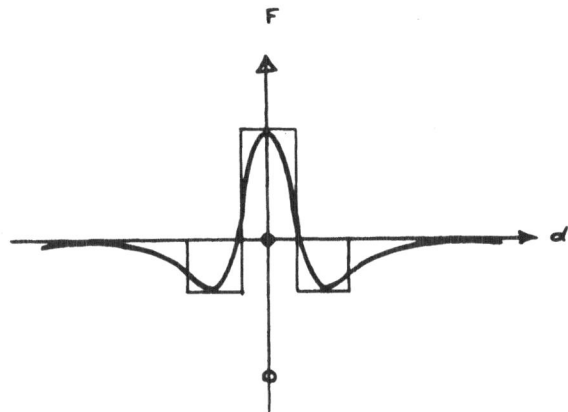

Fig. 8. Comparison of values of the binomial action function $p = 1$ with a continuous action function obtained by superposition of a Gaussian facilitatory and inhibitory distribution.

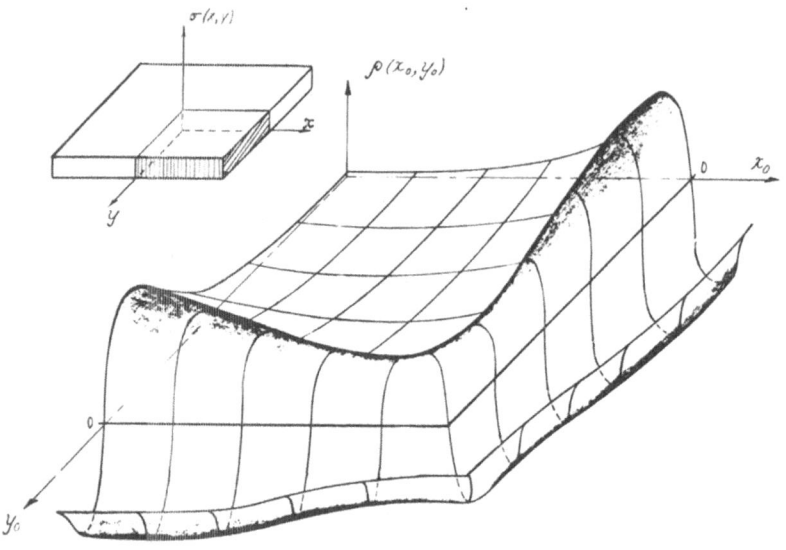

Fig. 9. Response distribution elicited by a uniform stimulus confined to a square. Contour detection is the consequence of a continuous action function obtained by superposition of a Gaussian facilitatory and inhibitory distribution.

parison is made and we find indeed a smooth approximation to the original step function (-1), (+2), (-1). This encourages us to test whether the continuous action function would also perform the extraction of an edge, as it was the case with the discrete example. In Fig. 9* we have calculated the response density function $\rho(x_o, y_o)$ in a two-dimensional layer x_o, y_o as a result of a uniform stimulus in form of a square in a two-dimensional layer x, y. A two-dimensional Gaussian distribution is assumed and condition (7') is observed. The result clearly shows that this action function performs as well a contour extraction as does its discrete counterpart and thus may well be used for the detection and localization of contrasts in the visual field of an artificial or, perhaps, a physiological retina.

*The cumbersome calculation, as well as the drawings of Figs. 9 and 11, was done by Alfred Inselberg.

However, before this jump from an apparently artificial action function to a concrete physiological case can be made, additional justifications have to be brought into play. One may concede that the original assumption under which this action function was derived, the random-walk growth of axons of cells in one layer toward the cells in the adjacent layer, had the ring of plausibility. However, the condition for zero response at uniform stimulus, as expressed in equation (7), seems to represent organizational difficulties which can hardly be explained by postulating "genetic programing." It is hard to believe that, in spite of the permissible random-walk growth of the axons, cells in the first layer keep track of how many end-bulbs of their axons attached themselves to perikarya of the cells in the second layer, thus providing facilitation, and of how many axons terminated in the dendritic region of second-layer cells, thus providing inhibition. However, there is a simple way out of this dilemma, if only a single additional feature is added to the biological system. The only trick that is necessary to produce an ideal contour extractor by random-walk growth is to provide a mechanism which stimulates growth of axons as well as dendrites in the interface between the two layers as long as the response net is active. This stimulation will increase the density of dendrites, and descending axons will terminate with increasing probability within dendritic ramifications. This will go on until the response layer is completely inhibited, at which instant condition (7') is fulfilled, the

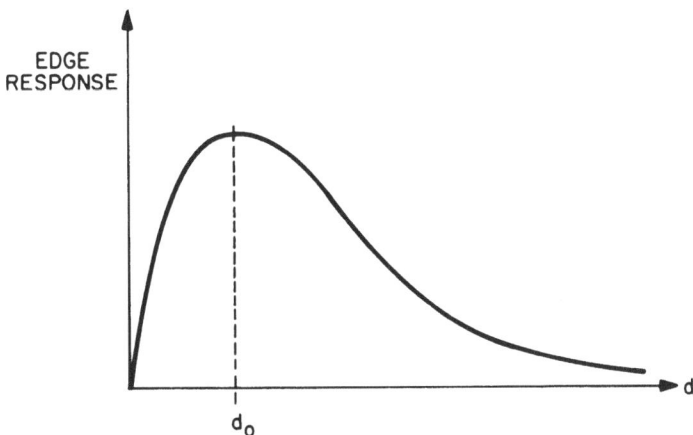

Fig. 10. Maximum of edge response as a function of diameter of a uniform circular stimulus distribution.

growth stimulus ceases, and the perfect contour detector is established.

I must leave it to the neurophysiologists to give their verdict
to the plausibility of this mechanism. However, before they give
their final judgment, let me briefly report another feature of the two-
dimensional Gaussian action function. If a uniform stimulus with
circular boundaries is given to the sensory layer L_1, the amplitude
of the edge response in layer L_2 will depend upon the diameter of
the circle. This relationship is sketched in Fig. 10, and one notices
that for a particular size d_0 of the image, the response is maximum.

Just to satisfy my curiosity I have calculated this critical diameter for the frog. If facilitation variance is three rods across
(hexagonal arrangement of retinal elements) and inhibitory variance
about six, maximum response is expected for an object the size of
a fly sitting about two feet away from the frog.

I am perfectly aware of the fact that analogy of function may
not mean analogy of structure. But I thought that these coinci-
dences may suggest looking further into possible similarities.

As I will show later, the extraction of a contour of an image of
an object is a very useful operation. Permit me, therefore, to spend
a few more minutes on a more general approach to this problem. I
may add that I owe the following ideas on contour extraction to
Lars Löfgren [8], who is presently on a visit to our laboratory in
Illinois.

Let the image of an object be projected on a photosensitive
layer L_j. The response distribution ρ_{L_j} of this layer stimulates a
second layer L_i. We want the response ρ_{L_i} from this second layer
to be zero at points which correspond to the interior and exterior of
the object. At points corresponding to the contour of the object we
want a nonzero response.

Now, what distinguishes the points along a contour from interior
and exterior points? Outside the contour ρ_{L_j} is (precisely) zone, and
inside $\rho_{L_j} = 0$. Hence, passing the contour, there will be a discontinuity, if not in ρ_{L_j} itself, at least in some higher order derivatives
of ρ_{L_j} in the normal direction of the contour. Hence a reasonable
contour indication is the νth derivative in the normal direction:

$$\frac{d^\nu}{dx_n^\nu} \rho_{L_j} \qquad\qquad (8)$$

The higher we make ν, the better will be the contour extraction. We can actually allow variations of ρ_{L_j} inside the contour which correspond to a polynomial of degree ν-1 and still be sure of a zero indication inside (and outside) the contour region.

In the one-dimensional, discrete case, $\rho_{L_j}(p) = \sigma_i$ is the stimulus at point $p = i$ ($i = \ldots, -1, 0, 1, 2, \ldots$). The νth derivative of the stimulus function is approximated with a finite difference polynomial:

$$\frac{d^\nu \rho_{L_j}(p)}{dp^\nu} \approx \sum_{\mu=-s'}^{s''} a_\mu D^\mu \sigma_i = P_W \sigma_i \qquad (9)$$

where D^μ is a displacement operation $D^\mu \sigma_i = \sigma_{i+\mu}$ and a_μ are the coefficients. The following condition holds for s' and s'': ·

$$s' + s'' + 1 = W \geq \nu \qquad (10)$$

An ideal contour extracting network would hence be represented by

$$\rho_i = \kappa P_W \sigma_i \qquad (11)$$

where κ is a constant.

However, it is reasonable not only to deal with ideal connections which correspond to the polynomial P_W but to consider a Gaussian distribution of connectivities corresponding to each ideal correctivity as represented by $P_{,W}$. The choice of a Gaussian distribution is, in the biological case, motivated by a not ideal growth of the connectivities between the layers L_j and L_i.

The choice of a Gaussian connectivity distribution requires that equation (11) should be replaced by

$$\rho_i = \kappa \sum_{n=-\infty}^{\infty} \sum_{\mu=-s'}^{s''} a_\mu D^\mu \sigma_{i-n} \cdot e^{-(n/x_1)^2} = \kappa \sum_{n=-\infty}^{\infty} P_W \sigma_{i-n} e^{-(n/x_1)^2} \qquad (12)$$

Here D^μ and P_W operate only with respect to the index i.

Let us from here go over to the continuous case. Equation (12) corresponds to

$$\rho(x_0) = \kappa \int_{-\infty}^{\infty} \left[\frac{d^\nu}{dx_0^\nu} \, \sigma(x_0 - x)\right] e^{-(x/x_1)^2} dx$$

$$= \kappa \int_{-\infty}^{\infty} \left[\frac{d^\mu}{dx_0} \, \sigma(x)\right] e^{-[(x-x_0)/x_1]^2} dx \tag{13}$$

$$= (-1)^\nu \kappa \int_{-\infty}^{\infty} \sigma(x) \cdot \frac{d^\nu}{dx^\nu} \, e^{-[(x-x_0)/x_1]^2} dx$$

One may note that the last expression of equation (13) is of the same form as our earlier equation (3). In general, equation (13) will give a better approximation to an ideal contour extraction the larger ν, and the smaller the variance x_1.

For the sake of generality, let me quickly conclude the discussion on contour extraction with the two-dimensional case. Let us start directly from the discrete case with a Gaussian distribution of connectivities instead of an ideal connectivity between the layers L_j and $L_{j'}$. The equivalent to equation (12) is

$$\rho_{ij} = \kappa \sum_{n=-\infty}^{\infty} \sum_{m=-\infty}^{\infty} \sum_{\mu_1} \sum_{\mu_2} a_{\mu_1\mu_2} D^{\mu_1\mu_2} \sigma_{i-n,\, j-m} \cdot e^{-\left[(n^2 + m^2)/x_1^2\right]}$$

$$\tag{14}$$

In the continuous case, equation (14) goes over into

$$\rho(x_0, y_0) = \kappa \int_{-\infty}^{\infty} \int_{-\infty}^{\infty} \left[\sum_{s+t=\nu} \frac{\partial^s}{\partial x^s} \frac{\partial^t}{\partial y^t} \sigma(x,y)\right] e^{-\left[(x-x_0)^2 + (y-y_0)^2\right]/x_1^2} \, dxdy$$

$$\tag{15}$$

Let us specifically consider the derivative:

$$\sum \frac{\partial^s}{\partial x^s} \frac{\partial^t}{\partial x^t} \, \sigma(x,y) = \left(\frac{\partial^2}{\partial x^2} + \frac{\partial^2}{\partial y^2}\right) \sigma(x,y) = \Delta \, \sigma(x,y) \tag{16}$$

Here we can apply Green's theorem:

$$\iint_R (\phi \Delta \psi - \psi \Delta \phi) \, dxdy = \int_\Gamma \left(\phi \frac{\partial \psi}{\partial n} - \psi \frac{\partial \phi}{\partial n}\right) ds \tag{17}$$

with

$$\phi = \sigma(x, y)$$

$$\psi = e^{-\left[(x-x_0)^2 + (y-y_0)^2\right]/x_1^2}$$

which gives the following equivalent to equation (15):

$$\rho(x_0, y_0) = \kappa \int_{-\infty}^{\infty} \int_{-\infty}^{\infty} \sigma(x, y) \cdot \Delta\, e^{-[(x-x_0)^2 - (y-y_0)^2]/x_1^2}\, dx dy \tag{18}$$

which is of the desired form, equation (15). The action function

$$K(x, y, x_0, y_0) = \Delta\, e^{-[(x-x_0)^2 + (y-y_0)^2]/x_1^2} \tag{19}$$

can be approximated by

$$K^*(x, y, x_0, y_0) = a_1\, e^{-(x-x_0)^2 + (y-y_0)^2]/x_1^2} - a_2\, e^{-[(x-x_0)^2 + (y-y_0)^2]/x_2^2} \tag{20}$$

with the conditions

$$a_1 - a_2 = 1 \qquad a_1 x_1^2 - a_2 x_2^2 = 0 \tag{21}$$

which means that the function

$$\rho^*(x_0, y_0) = \kappa \int_{-\infty}^{\infty} \int_{-\infty}^{\infty} \sigma(x, y)\, K^*(x, y, x_0, y_0)\, dx dy \tag{22}$$

also acts as an approximative contour detector and this the better, the smaller the values of x_1 and x_2. It was precisely this function that was used in my earlier example with the illuminated square (Fig. 9). We used the following values:

Length of edge of square: $D = 20$

Variances: $x_1 = 1$; $x_2 = 2$

Facilitation and inhibition amplitudes: $a_1 = 2$; $a_2 = 1$

As seen in Fig. 9, the contour extraction for this approximation is quite good. However, a much more drastic contour indicator is obtained utilizing an action function as indicated in equation (19). Figure 11 gives the response function in the second layer for the same square as above, with variance of the distribution function $x_1 = 1$.

I have suggested earlier in my discussion that the operation of extracting the contour of an image of an object can be used for further operations. I shall forego a treatment of the analysis of contours in general and shall restrict myself to a special case which may amuse you.

Assume that I have now three layers L_i, L_j, L_k, where the first layer L_i receives the image of an object and passes this information on to the next layer L_j by an action function which extracts the contour of this image. I shall call this layer the "contour layer." All points p in this contour layer I propose to connect with an action function $K(p, q)$, to be specified later, with all points q in our third layer L_k.

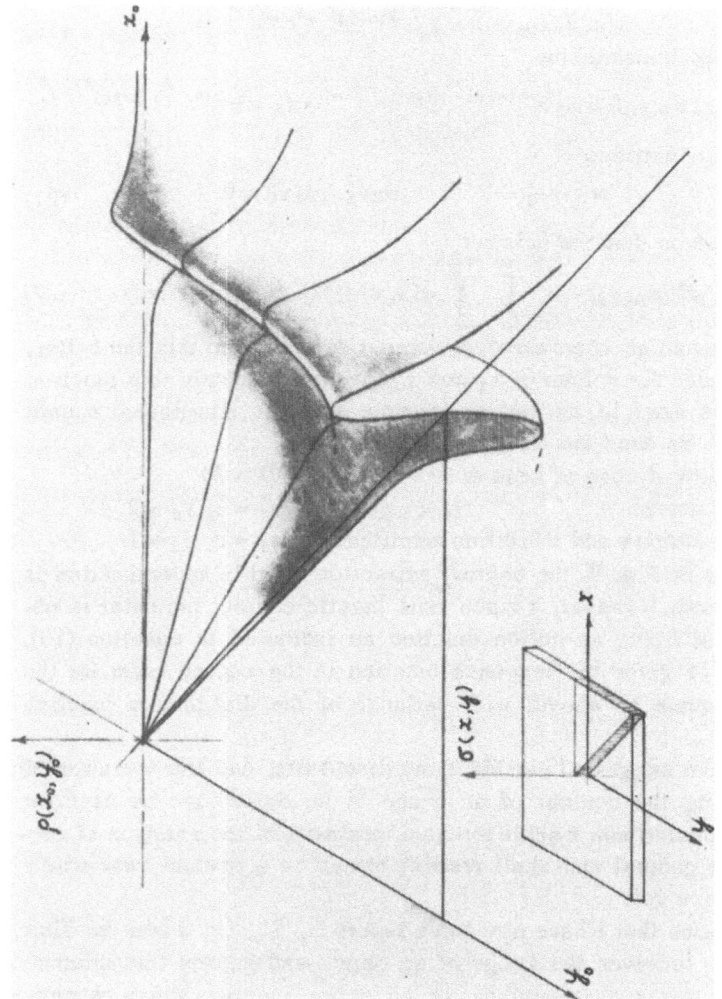

Fig. 11. Response distribution elicited by a uniform stimulus confined to a square contour detection is the consequence of a continuous action function representing the second derivation of a Gaussian distribution.

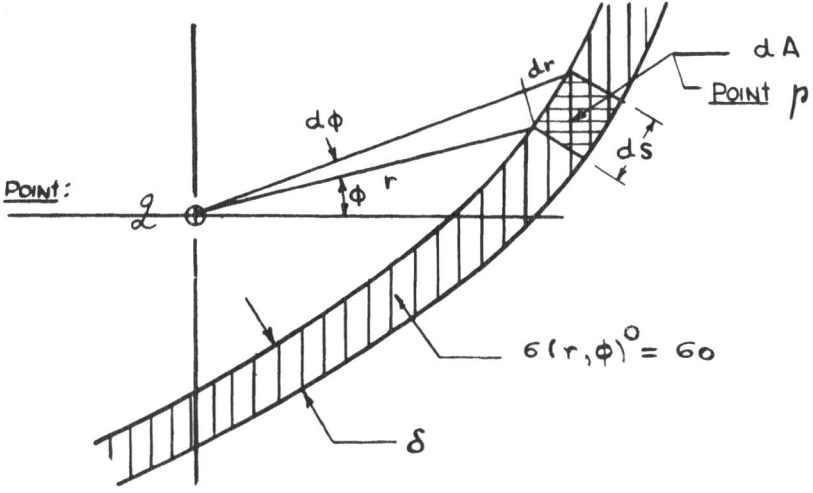

Fig. 12. Representation of a "line stimulus" of width δ in polar coordinates.

Before going into further detail, let me first simplify the procedures by approximating the response activity in the contour layer L_j by a uniformly excited strip of thickness δ (see Fig. 12). Utilizing polar coordinates, with the point (q) acted upon as origin, the differential element of length is

$$(ds)^2 = (dr)^2 + r^2 (d\phi)^2 \tag{23}$$

and, thus, the differential element of area

$$dA = \delta ds = \delta dr \sqrt{1 + \left(\frac{rd\phi}{dr}\right)^2} \tag{24}$$

Having decided that only along the contour Γ a uniform excitation of magnitude σ_0 should prevail, and anywhere else $\sigma_0 = 0$, we are now in a position to define the total action of all excited elements in layer L_j on point q in layer L_k. We have

$$\rho(q) = \int_\Gamma K(p, q)\, \sigma(p)\, dA \tag{25}$$

Hence with equation (24) we get

$$\rho(q) = \sigma_0 \delta \int_\Gamma K(p, q) \sqrt{1 + \left(\frac{rd\phi}{dr}\right)^2}\, dr \tag{26}$$

In order to solve in a specific case the above integral, two functions have to be specified:

(1) The equation of the contour in polar coordinates has to be stated:

$$\phi = \phi(r) \tag{27}$$

(2) A particular choice of the action function has to be made:

$$K(p,q) = K(r,\phi) \tag{28}$$

I propose to use an action function with a somewhat peculiar aniso-tropic property:

$$K(r,\phi) = e^{-(r/r_1)^2} \cos(2\phi) \tag{29}$$

In other words, facilitation and inhibition at any point in the detec-tor field will have different values depending in which direction one looks with respect to an arbitrary 0-direction. In this 0-direction east-west, all is facilitation. At 45° no action takes place (cos 90° = 0), while straight north-south all is inhibition. The excitation decays with a Gaussian. Let us now investigate what happens to a point in layer L_k if the contour layer L_j is active along a straight line. In other words, the stimulus function for L_k is

$$\phi = \text{arc } \cos(r_0/r) + a \tag{30}$$

where a represents the angle between the straight line and the arbi-trary 0-direction, and r_0 gives the perpendicular distance from point q to the line. The response function in layer L_k is now determined. Substituting equations (29) and (30) into equation (25) and carrying out the integration between the limits $-\infty$ and $+\infty$, one obtains after some arithmetic [9]:

$$\rho(q) = C(r_0) \cdot \cos(2a) \tag{31}$$

where

$$C(r_0) = \sqrt{\pi}\,\sigma_0\delta\left[r_1 e^{-r_0} - 4\sqrt{\frac{\pi}{r_0}}\,e^{r_0} \cdot \text{erf}(\sqrt{r_0})\right] \tag{32}$$

and

$$\text{erf}(x) = \frac{2}{\sqrt{\pi}} \int_x^\infty e^{-t^2}\,dt$$

The response in layer L_k to a straight line in layer L_j or to a straight edge in layer L_j preserves the directionality of the original stimulus, as seen by the factor cos $(2a)$ in equation (31).

Suppose now that one connects the activity in layer L_j according to our action function equation (29) to three layers L_{k1}, L_{k2}, L_{k3}, whose 0-directions are 60° inclined to each other. The corresponding points q_1, q_2, q_3 in these three layers will respond with response functions:

$$\rho_1(q_1) = C \cos 2a$$

$$\rho_2(q_2) = C \cos 2(60°\text{-}a) = C \left[-\frac{1}{2} \cos 2a + \frac{3}{2} \sin 2a\right] \qquad (33)$$

$$\rho_3(q_3) = C \cos 2(120°\text{-}a) = C \left[-\frac{1}{2} \cos 2a - \frac{3}{2} \sin 2a\right]$$

If we let these three activities converge on a fourth layer L_s, which simply adds at point q^* the stimuli coming from the three corresponding points q_1, q_2, q_3 of the three layers L_{k1}, L_{k2}, L_{k3}, its response function is

$$\rho_s(q^*) = \rho_1 + \rho_2 + \rho_3 = 0 \qquad (34)$$

In other words, this final layer L_s will show no activity, if straight edges are presented to sensory layer L_i, independent of their direaction and independent of the amount of illumination. However, curvatures will elicit immediate responses. Thus, if this layer is an inhibition layer to another network, the cessation of inhibition will cause activity, and the system will scream loud, if a straight edge is present in the visual field. Hence the whole system of seven layers will act as a "straight-line detector."

   Although this system seems to be quite complex for such a simple task as the detection of a straight line, its technology is not too difficult at all, owing to the identity of most of the components involved. These are the blessings of parallel computation. Physiologically, however, I have my doubts whether Lettvin's frogs recognize straight edges acording to this scheme.

   In all the previous cases I have talked as if it would always be possible to distinguish between stimulating and stimulated regions, or, in other words, as if it would be possible to separate an acting and receiving region, where the amount of action of the one region upon the other one is defined by an "action function." In many cases this distinction may be impossible to make and for generality, one has to consider the possibility of every element in a particular region being able to interact with any other element in this region, including self-interaction. I shall now briefly discuss this case,

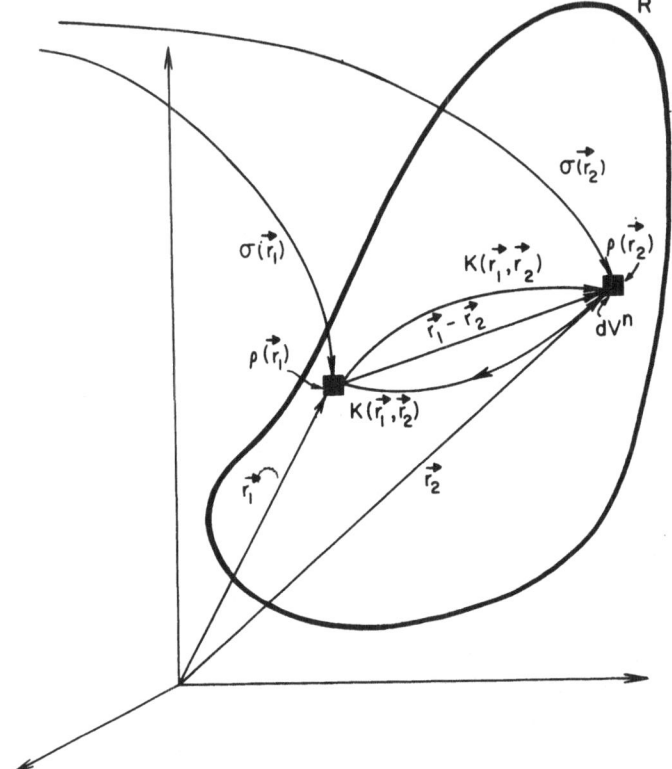

Fig. 13. Interaction of two points in an n-dimensional continuum.

restricting myself for the moment to linear interaction, but returning later to the interaction case by presenting a few nonlinear examples.

I shall first tackle the general situation of linear interaction, where the region of activity is excited by a stimulus distribution σ, and where each point in this region interacts with any other point, as indicated in Fig. 13 for two arbitrary points r_1 and r_2.

I wish to calculate at point r_2 in an n-dimensional manifold the response activity $\rho(r_2)$ which is composed of the stimulus strength $\sigma(r_2)$ at this point and of the sum of the elementary contributions of the response activity $\rho(r_1)\,dV^n$ in all other volume elements of this n-dimensional region. Observing Fig. 13 we obtain for the desired response activity at r_2

$$\rho(r_2) = \kappa\,\sigma(r_2) + \gamma \int_R K(r_1 r_2)\,\rho(r_1)\,dV^n \qquad (35)$$

where $K(r_1, r_2)$ will be appropriately termed the "interaction function" between points r_1 and r_2. This function is analogous to the action function in my earlier discussion and defines the amount of activity transferred from one point to another. The quantities κ and γ are constants.

A brief inspection of equation (35) shows that it is impossible to solve this equation by merely carrying out the suggested integration, because the very variable for which we want to solve, namely ρ, is now part of the integrand. Expressions of this type are called integral equations and the one given in (34) belongs to the class of integral equations of the second kind. The function $K(r_1, r_2)$ is usually referred to as the "kernel," and methods of solution are known, if the kernel possess certain properties. A particularly "nice" property—that is, one which does not cause too much trouble in solving these equations—is that of symmetry. A kernel is said to be symmetrical if

$$K(r_1, r_2) = K(r_2, r_1) \qquad (36)$$

This means physically that point r_1 passes on to point r_2 the same fraction of its activity as point r_2 passes on to r_1. It is clear that an anisotropic kernel would not possess this friendly property and hence, the theory of anisotropic interaction presents some mathematical difficulties.

Since for a particular stimulus function σ the response function will be determined by the structure of the kernel K, the transform of

$$\rho = T\sigma \qquad (37)$$

is consequently a function of the structure of the interaction scheme

$$T = T(K) \qquad (38)$$

This equation represents in a nutshell the justification of the title of my paper, because the structure of the kernel K—or its circuitry when realized either in "hardware" or in "software"—provides the clue for the kind of abstraction, or "ideation," which this network is able to perform. In other words, the choice of the kernel K will define the property which is extracted by this interaction filter.

Without going too deeply into the theory of integral equations,

I may point out that under certain conditions of the structure of the kernel in combination with certain classes of stimulus functions, the interaction scheme can be transformed into an action scheme. Let me quickly demonstrate this idea in the finite, discrete case.

Assume n "boxes," $p_1, p_2, \ldots, p_i, \ldots, p_n$, each of which receives a stimulus σ_i, and is connected with every other box, receiving an amount a_{ji} from box p_j. The response of box p_i is thus:

$$\rho_i = a_{0i} \sigma_i + \sum_{j=1}^{n} a_{ji} \rho_j \qquad (39)$$

As brief inspection will show, this equation is the precise analog to our integral equation (35) in the continuous case, the a_{ji}'s replacing the interaction function $K(r_1, r_2)$, and the summation sign the integral sign.

Solving equation (39) for σ_i and introducing two column matrices $[\sigma]$ and $[\rho]$, we have

$$[\sigma] = M [\rho] \qquad (40)$$

where M is the quadratic matrix

$$M = \| m_{ij} \| \qquad (41)$$

with

$$m_{ij} = \begin{cases} -\dfrac{a_{ji}}{a_{0i}} & j \neq i \\[2em] \dfrac{1 - a_{ii}}{a_{0i}} & j = i \end{cases} \qquad (42)$$

Equation (40) can be solved for ρ by inverting the matrix M:

$$[\rho] = M^{-1} [\sigma] \qquad (43)$$

This is an expression for the simple fact that given n boxes p_i and their interaction matrix A

$$A = \| a_{ji} \| \qquad (44)$$

it is possible to design an action matrix $M^{-1} = \Phi(A)$, which is a function of the interaction matrix A, such that the action matrix will perform the same operation on the stimuli as did the interaction matrix. In other words, the action net M^{-1} is equivalent to the interaction net A. This transformation in indicated in Fig. 14. The original topology of the net of a single set of n interacting boxes p_i,

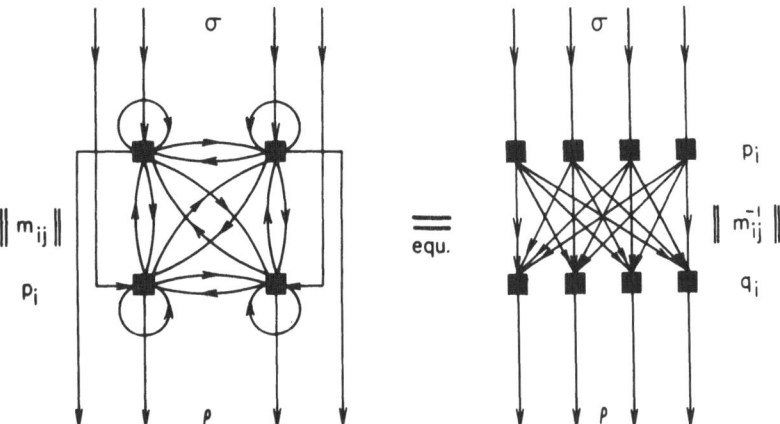

Fig. 14. Equivalence of an interaction net with an action net.

has been replaced by a net consisting of two sets, p, q, of n boxes each, p_i and q_i, where no interaction between elements of the sets takes place, but all elements of p act upon all elements of q.

However, this transformation is not always possible, because for the matrix M there exists an inverse M^{-1}, if and only if the determinant $|m_{ij}|$ does not vanish:

$$D = | \, m_{ij} \, | \neq 0 \qquad (45)$$

Of course, the same is true for the inverse case, namely that a certain action function $B = ||b_{ij}||$ cannot be replaced by interaction functions $A = ||a_{ji}||$, if the determinant $|b_{ij}|$ vanishes. It might be interesting to note that the action function adopted in the simple linear edge detector of Fig. 1, when connected to a ring with the matrix

$$
\begin{array}{ccccccccc}
2 & -1 & 0 & 0 & 0 & 0 & 0 & \ldots & -1 \\
-1 & 2 & -1 & 0 & 0 & 0 & 0 & \ldots & .. \\
0 & -1 & 2 & -1 & 0 & 0 & 0 & \ldots & .. \\
0 & 0 & -1 & 2 & -1 & 0 & 0 & \ldots & .. \\
0 & 0 & 0 & -1 & 2 & -1 & 0 & \ldots & .. \\
\vdots & \vdots & \vdots & \vdots & \vdots & \vdots & \vdots & \ldots & .. \\
\vdots & \vdots & \vdots & \vdots & 0 & 0 & -1 & 2 & -1 \\
-1 & \vdots & \vdots & \vdots & 0 & 0 & 0 & -1 & 2 \\
\end{array}
\qquad (46)
$$

cannot be replaced by an equivalent interaction net.

Similar restrictions in the conversion of interaction functions into action functions, as we have just encountered in the discrete case, hold also for the continuous case. However, a discussion of these restrictions would lead us too far into mathematical details which are not essential to my thesis.

Before concluding this brief exposé on linear interaction, let me only give you one example of a Gaussian inhibitory interaction function:

$$K = (r_1, r_2) = - \gamma \, e^{-p(r_1 - r_2)^2} \tag{47}$$

This is fortunately a typical "nice" kernel, because if the stimulus is a periodic function and obeys the n-dimensional wave equation

$$\Delta \sigma + k \sigma^2 = 0 \tag{48}$$

then the powerful Gauss transformation [10] can be utilized to produce immediately a solution for the integral equation (35). For n-dimensional continuum one obtains:

$$\rho(r_2) = \frac{\kappa}{1 + \gamma C} \cdot \sigma(r_2) \tag{49a}$$

with

$$C(n, k, p) = \left(\frac{\sqrt{\pi}}{p}\right)^n e^{-(k/2p)^2} \tag{49b}$$

As a physiological example I may suggest the mutually inhibiting action in the nerve net attached to the basilar membrane, which is suspected to have a "sharpening" effect with respect to localization of frequencies on the basilar membrane.

Suppose that the signal—in this case the displacement of the basilar membrane as a function of distance from its basal end—can be expressed in terms of a Fourier series $\sigma(a_l, b_l, \lambda)$, with coefficients a_l, b_l and the fundamental mode λ. Clearly, each term of this series satisfies the wave equation (48). Hence, the Gauss transform can be applied and the response function $\rho(a_l', b_l', \lambda)$ will be a Fourier series with the corresponding coefficients a_l' and b_l'. Utilizing equations (49a), and realizing that only lengthwise oscillations of the basilar membrane are to be considered ($n = 1$), we obtain the relationship between the coefficients of the response function to those of the stimulus function:

$$\frac{a_l'}{a_l} = \frac{b_l'}{b_l} = \mu_l = \frac{\kappa}{1 + (\gamma/p) \, e^{-(2 \sqrt{\pi} \, l/\lambda p)^2}}$$

Since always $\mu_{i+1} > \mu_i$, the higher modes are enhanced and it is clear that a mutual inhibition function with Gaussian distribution produces indeed a sharpening of the original stimulus.

After these examples of linear action and interaction functions, I shall conclude my report on property extraction with two examples of nonlinear filters. Both of these filters are parallel computation networks which do the useful job of enumerating N, the number of disconnected objects whose images are projected on a two-dimensional "retina." No counting in the usual sense of a sequential operation takes place. These systems distinguish 15 from 7, for example, in one look as we would distinguish green and red in one glimpse: "15-ness" and "7-ness" are for these systems different properties as "green-ness" and "redness" are two different colors for us.

While the first of these two systems uses a topological property of connectedness which has been known since Euler, the latter one defines connectedness by recognition of "ON" states of immediate neighbor elements. The former system was suggested by Lars Löfgren [11], while the latter one has been built by Paul Weston [12] and has amused and puzzled not only many visitors to our laboratory but also stole the show at several technical meetings and exhibitions.

Let me first describe the principle of Löfgren's topological counting network.

Consider a two-dimensional layer of photosensitive elements as sketched in Fig. 15.

The elements are partitioned into three groups a_i^2, a_i^1, a_i^0 according to the figure. The cellular structure is divided into the topological cell pattern as indicated. The line segments have no physical significance. Each a_i^0 indicates a 0-cell, i.e., a vertex. A line segment connecting two adjacent 0-cells is a 1-cell with an a_i^0 as a representative. The face bounded by four adjacent 1-cells is a 2-cell with an a_i^2 as a representative.

When an image is projected onto the layer (L_j) some elements will be illuminated, i.e., give a quantized response, and the others will give no response. According to a well-known theorem in topology the number, N, of disconnected objects projected onto L_j will be:

$$N = \Sigma a_i^2 + \Sigma a_i^0 - \Sigma a_i^1 \qquad (50)$$

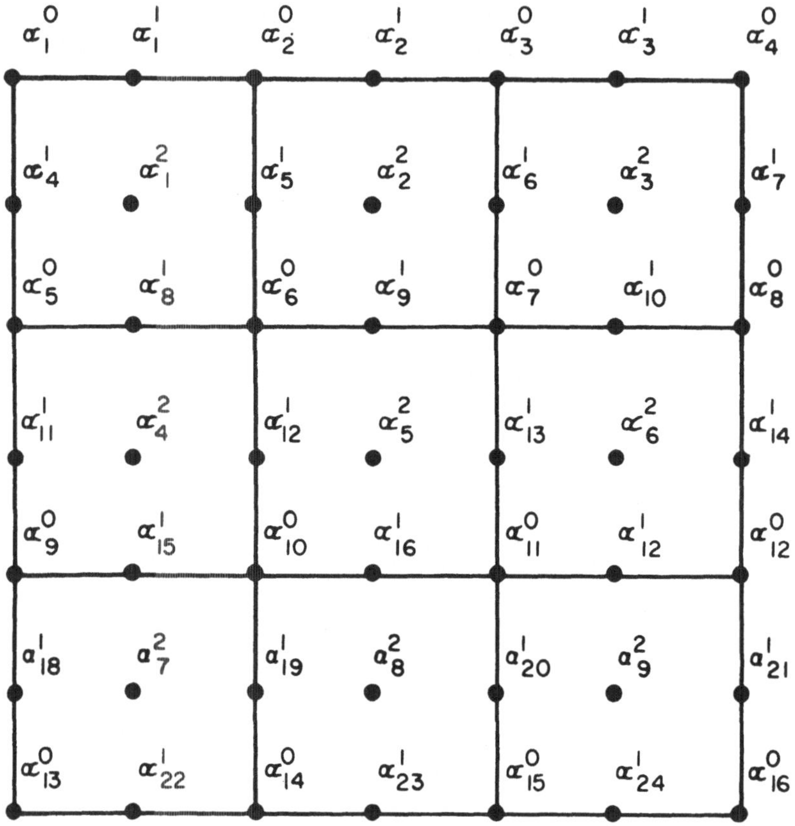

$$\alpha_1^0 \quad \alpha_1^1 \quad \alpha_2^0 \quad \alpha_2^1 \quad \alpha_3^0 \quad \alpha_3^1 \quad \alpha_4^0$$

$$\alpha_4^1 \quad \alpha_1^2 \quad \alpha_5^1 \quad \alpha_2^2 \quad \alpha_6^1 \quad \alpha_3^2 \quad \alpha_7^1$$

$$\alpha_5^0 \quad \alpha_8^1 \quad \alpha_6^0 \quad \alpha_9^1 \quad \alpha_7^0 \quad \alpha_{10}^1 \quad \alpha_8^0$$

$$\alpha_{11}^1 \quad \alpha_4^2 \quad \alpha_{12}^1 \quad \alpha_5^2 \quad \alpha_{13}^1 \quad \alpha_6^2 \quad \alpha_{14}^1$$

$$\alpha_9^0 \quad \alpha_{15}^1 \quad \alpha_{10}^0 \quad \alpha_{16}^1 \quad \alpha_{11}^0 \quad \alpha_{12}^1 \quad \alpha_{12}^0$$

$$a_{18}^1 \quad a_7^2 \quad a_{19}^1 \quad a_8^2 \quad a_{20}^1 \quad a_9^2 \quad a_{21}^1$$

$$\alpha_{13}^0 \quad \alpha_{22}^1 \quad \alpha_{14}^0 \quad \alpha_{23}^1 \quad \alpha_{15}^0 \quad \alpha_{24}^1 \quad \alpha_{16}^0$$

Fig. 15. Topological cell pattern with sensors for corners (a^0), edges (a^1), and loops (a^2).

where the summations are to be taken over the fully illuminated ν-cells ($\nu = 0, 1, 2$). This provided that the 2-cells form a fundamental set. This is in our structure always the case if each object projected onto L_j has only one boundary.

We will now formulate connections between the elements in layer L_j and the elements of layer L_i which map (1-1) each (topological) cell of L_j onto a point element R_k^ν in L_i.

$$a_k^\nu \Longleftrightarrow R_k^\nu$$

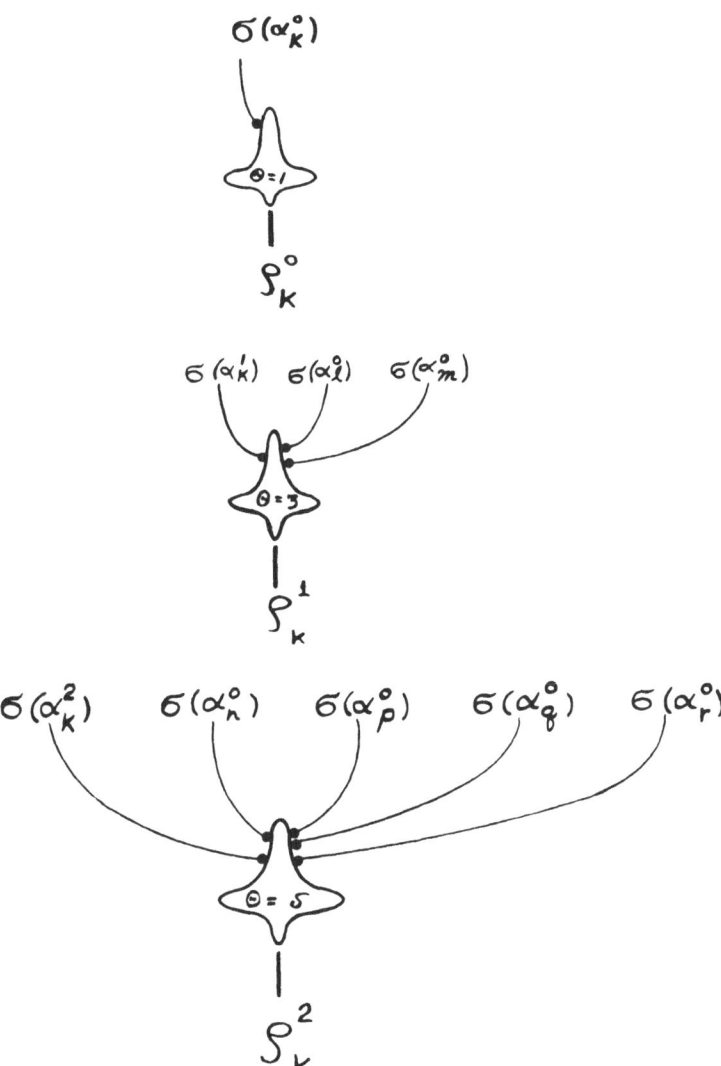

Fig. 16. Three different kinds of elements in a second layer responding to the activity of the sensors in the first layer of Löfgren's topological counting network.

The response R_k^ν from each point R_k^ν in L_l will be:

$$\rho_k^0 = \sigma(a_k^0)$$

$$\rho_k^1 = \sigma(a_k^1) \cdot \sigma(a^0) \cdot \sigma(a_m^0) \tag{51}$$

$$\rho_k^2 = \sigma(a_k^2) \cdot \sigma(a_n^0) \cdot \sigma(a_p^0) \cdot \sigma(a_q^0) \cdot \sigma(a_r^0)$$

The meaning of the index notations is as follows. $\rho_k^0 = 1$ (R_k^0 gives a response) only if $\sigma(a_k^0) = 1$ (the element a_k^0 of layer L_i is illuminated). R_k^1 gives response only if the element a_k^1 and its two adjacent a_k^0-elements are illuminated. R_k^2 gives response only if the element a_k^2 and its four adjacent a^0-elements are illuminated. This specifies the connections between the layers L_j and L_l and the operation of the elements in L_l.

With this mapping, the relation (50) between the number of disconnected objects, N, and the topological cells of L_j will correspond to the following relation between N and the responses ρ_k^ν of the elements in layer L_l:

$$N = \Sigma \rho_k^2 + \Sigma \rho_k^0 - \Sigma \rho_k^1 \tag{52}$$

The summation (52) can be formed in a third layer containing the elements e_l.

In Fig. 16 we have illustrated the three different kinds of elements of layer L_l responding to the elements of layer L_j (Fig. 15) according to equation (52). Figure 17 illustrates the elements of the final layer L_k. The responses of these elements give in binary form the desired number N. All elements are illustrated in terms of McCulloch neurons.

Notice that the thresholds θ_ν of the neurons in the final layer L_k depend on the responses of other neurons in the same layer according to:

$$\theta_\nu = M \left[\sum_{\mu=1}^{\nu-1} \frac{\rho_\mu}{2^\mu} + \frac{1}{2^\nu} \right] \tag{53}$$

where M stands for the range of N. This means that the activity of this third layer is of the interaction type. The response ρ_ν is the νth binary digit of the number of disconnected objects, N.

Before I describe Weston's counting network, the "Numa-Rete," let me point out two more features of Löfgren's three-layer system.

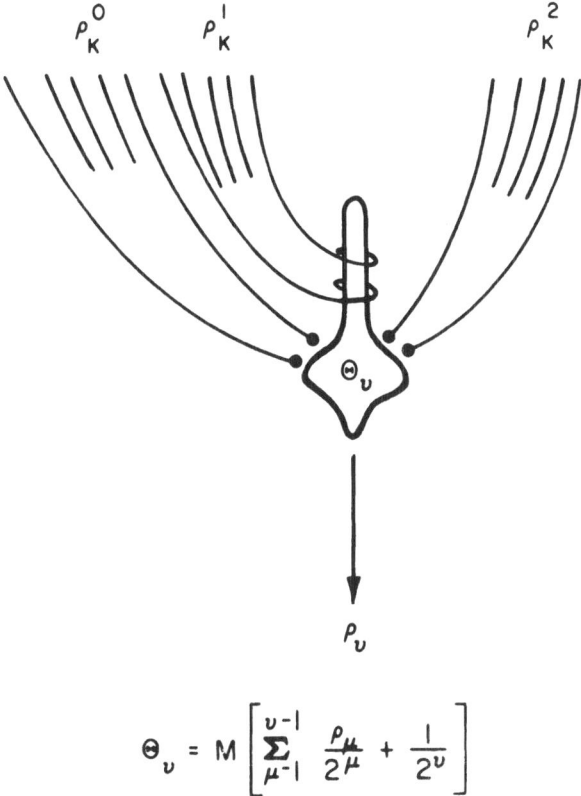

$$\Theta_v = M \left[\sum_{\mu=1}^{v-1} \frac{\rho_\mu}{2^\mu} + \frac{1}{2^v} \right]$$

Fig. 17. "End-neuron" in Löfgren's topological counting network.

First, the working principle of this system doesn't require a decomposition of the sensory layer into squares as suggested in Fig. 15. We could have worked with any other decomposition into topological v-cells, as, for instance, with triangles. Second, images with higher topological connectedness, as for example rings or pretzels, would give a response per image of magnitude (2-C), where C is the connectivity number. Thus, a ring would give no response (C = 2) and a pretzel (C = 3) would give a response of negative unity. However, these objects can easily be detected by combining Löfgren's system with the counting network I am going to describe now. This counts every object as "one," independent of its topological connectedness.

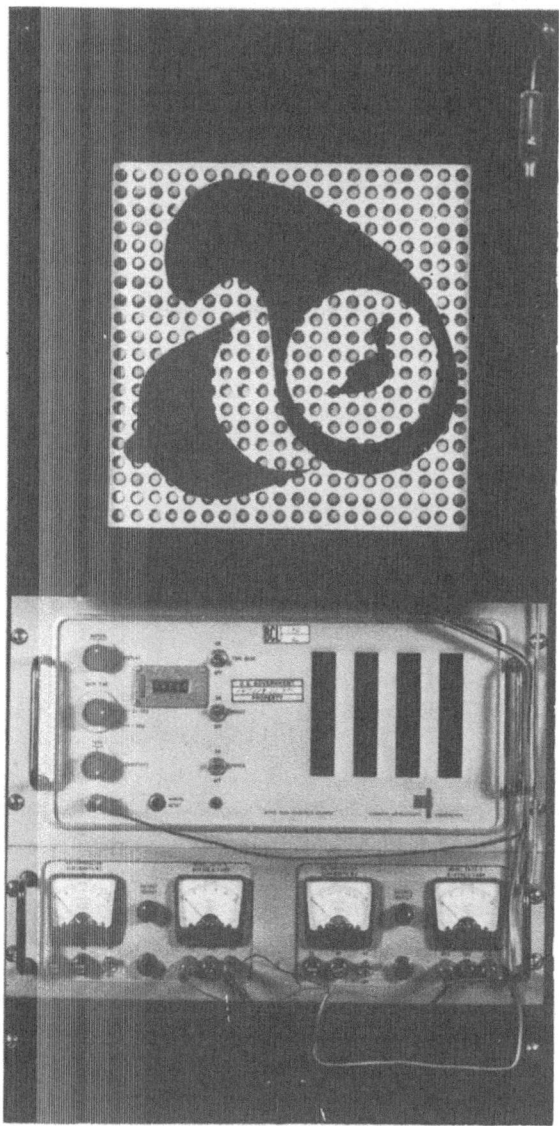

Fig. 18. The Numa-Rete in the process of counting the
number of oddly shaped objects. Power supply and decimal
counter are seen below.

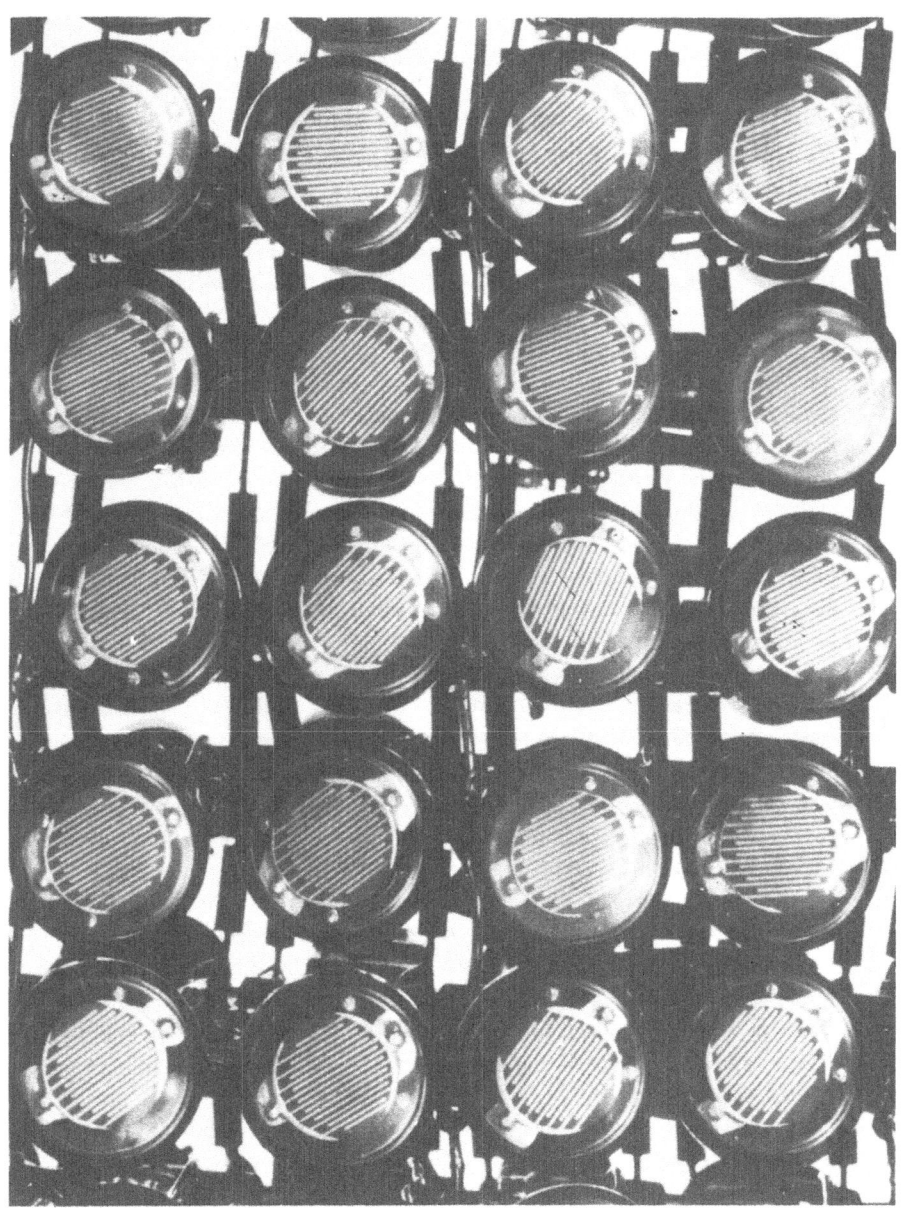

Fig. 19. Small section of the quadratic array of photocells in the Numa-Rete.

The instrument, which is a system of transistorized printed circuits, is shown in Fig. 18. Since this network is a "retina" which sees the number of objects, we dubbed it the "Numa-Rete."

Structurally, the network is a rectangular array of 20 × 20 photocells (Fig. 19) connected point by point to an identical array of bistable elements, or flip-flops. The flip-flops are connected bilaterally along rows and columns of the array such that when one is in its "ON" state it will force those directionally connected to it to go on, provided these are connected to photocells in shadow. Lighted photocells prevent the associated flip-flops from going "ON."

Operation begins with all flip-flops in the "OFF" state. Several distinct shadows of objects of any shape whatever—subject only to resolution limitations—are allowed to fall on the retina and a flip-flop connected to a photocell under one particular shadow is turned on. All other units under the shadow will go "ON" while the remainder of the network is unchanged. A scanning program, which sequentially turns "ON" all elements which are "OFF" and not inhibited by a photocell signal, will thus reveal all of the objects in turn. Appropriate output signals are obtained by observing changes in state of the over-all network, there being one of these for each separate object during each scanning program.

These changes are observed one after the other by a simple sequential counter which finally gives the total number of disconnected objects in the visual field of the Numa-Rete. Although speed was of no concern in constructing this instrument—it was built solely for demonstration purposes—the Numa-Rete can count up to 10,000 objects per second.

Simple extensions of the principles of this device could yield size and position information for each object as well.

With this practical application of some of the principles I have been talking about I shall conclude my discussion of the various ways in which "properties" can be extracted from a set of stimuli which represent some of the intrinsic order of the environment from which they originated.

I hope that the thoughts I was permitted to present may serve as clues to the basic idea that in order for us to be aware of the magnificent order of our universe, part of this order must be inherent in us.

REFERENCES

1. J. Y. Lettvin, H. R. Maturana, W. S. McCulloch, and W. Pitts, "What the Frog's Eye Tells the Frog's Brain," Proc. IRE, Vol. 47, pp. 1940-1951 (1959).

2. H. K. Hartline, "The Response of Single Optic Nerve Fibres of the Vertebrate Eye to Illumination of the Retina," Am. J. of Physiol., Vol. 121, pp. 400-415 (1938).

3. H. K. Hartline, "Receptor Mechanisms and the Integration of Sensory Information in the Eye," in "Biophysical Science," edited by J. L. Oncley, John Wiley & Sons, New York, 1959, pp. 515-523.

4. S. W. Kuffler, "Discharge Patterns and Functional Organization of Mammalian Retina," J. Neurophysiol., Vol. 16, pp. 37-68 (1953).

5. H. Von Foerster, "On Self-Organizing Systems and their Environments," in "Self-Organizing Systems," edited by M. C. Yovits and S. Cameron, Pergamon Press, London, 1960, pp. 31-50.

6. H. Von Foerster, "Some Remarks on the Design of Biological Computers," in "Second International Congress on Cybernetics," Namur, 1958. Association Internationale de Cybernétizue, Namur, 240-255 (1960).

7. G. Pask, "The Growth Process Inside the Cybernetic Machine" in "Second International Congress on Cybernetics, Namur, 1958," Association Internationale de Cybernétizue, Namur, 1960, pp. 765-794.

8. A. Inselberg, L. Löfgren, and H. Von Foerster, "Property Detector Nets and Fields," in "Some Principles of Preorganization in Self-Organizing Systems," Tech. Rept. 2, Contr. Nonr 1834(21), Electrical Engineering Research Laboratory, Engineering Experiment Station, University of Illinois, Urbana, Ill., 1960, pp. 21-30.

9. See Reference [8], pp. 30-37.

10. W. Magnus and F. Oberhettinger, "Special Functions of Mathematical Physics," Chelsea Publishing Co., New York, 1949, pp. 138-139.

11. See Reference [8], pp. 37-41.

12. P. Weston, "Some Notes on the Synthesis of Property Filters," in "Some Principles of Preorganization in Self-Organizing Systems," Tech. Rept. 2, Contr. Nonr 1834(21), Electrical Engineering Research Laboratory, Engineering Experiment Station, University of Illinois, Urbana, Ill., 1960, pp. 61-69.

CHAPTER V

THEORETICAL MODELS
OF SPACE PERCEPTION*

DONALD M. MacKAY

1. INTRODUCTION

1.1. How can we characterize perceptual activity from the standpoint of information theory? There are obviously several lines of approach. First, *functionally*, we may consider perception as the organism's answer to the challenge of *redundancy* in the flux of environmental events to which an adaptive response is required— or rather, redundancy in the sequence of adaptive responses required [1-4]. Perception is concerned with the statistically stable or quasi-stable features of the environment. Percepts are essentially *regularities* or compounds of regularities persistent or recurrent over a significant interval of space and/or time, and hence capable of becoming reflected in the adaptive organizing system.

1.2. But not every method of profiting from redundancy would satisfy us as a model of perceptual activity in animals, still less in the human organism. We have therefore a second approach to make to this problem, that from the *structural* side. We may expect perceptual activity to be characterized structurally, and distinguished from other activity in the receptor/effector system, by certain topological features of the information-flow pattern within the organism. Not every stimulus received by the retina, for example, is represented in what is perceived at any one time. Perception is selective; and whatever activity in the information-flow system of an organism mediates perception, it must possess a corresponding independence and selectivity of function.

*Revised version of a paper read at the Cambridge Conference on Thinking, Sept. 1955, under the title, "Some Perceptual Problems in Terms of Information Flow."

Our second line of approach is therefore to consider perception as a characteristic activity within the information-flow structure of the organism. Various information-flow structures which might satisfy the first functional requirements may then be tested against what is known of psychophysiology, with a view to narrowing down the field. We may, for example, search for features that are common to all known perceptual activity, and absent in activity (even of receptor organs) that has no known perceptual correlate. We can then turn to the possible information-flow structures and ask which of these show a correspondingly fundamental distinction between perceptual and other activity.

1.3. There is a third line of approach which must of necessity be more tentative and cautious, but which I think supplies an essential check on any hypothesis that survives the first two. I mean the testing of the would-be model in the critical light of our subjective experience of perception. Subjective impressions we all know to be potentially misleading. I think it perfectly fair nonetheless that if something purports to be a model of my own information-flow system, I should be able to ask what goes on in the model when I experience various subjective sensations, and that I should be guided at least negatively in my evaluation of the model by the way in which it stands up to such a test. In these brief notes I do not intend to discuss perception in detail under the foregoing heads. I have mentioned them only to indicate that all three lines of approach have contributed to the suggestions which follow, and may properly be used in testing their further implications.

I propose to focus discussion around one central aspect of the problem of perception—that of the stability of the perceived world—or, if you like, the perception of *change in space*. This will lead us in passing to consider voluntary activity on the one hand, and perceptual anomalies and disorder on the other. Throughout we shall have as a background to the discussion the approach outlined in earlier papers [1,2,5,6] but familiarity with these papers will not be essential in following the present argument.

2. A FAMILIAR EXAMPLE

2.1. Let us begin with a familiar example of the problem of stability. When I move my line of gaze voluntarily from left to right, the visual field does not appear to move, although the visual image moves across my retina. When, however, I move the line of gaze through the same angle by pressing on the corner of the open eyelid, so gently as to rule out any possibility of mechanical distortion of the eyeball, I perceive violent movement of the visual field from right to left.

2.2. The "explanation" usually offered for this effect is that the innervation of oculomotor muscles provides "compensation" which is absent when rotation of the eyeball is due to other causes. This is rather vague, and suffices only to raise further questions. *How* does innervation of eye muscles result in such accurate compensation for the retinal image displacement? Is it done by precomputation on the basis of the outgoing oculomotor stimuli (the "outflow" theory)? If so it relies with remarkable success on the transfer characteristics (the input-output relations) of the oculomotor system. Is it done by postcomputation on the basis of proprioceptive stimuli from the oculomotor muscles (the "inflow" theory)? This is perhaps one way in which a designer of automata would solve the problem. It exchanges uncertainty as to the transfer characteristics of the oculomotor system, for uncertainty as to those of the proprioceptors, which might well be more stable—if in fact there were proprioceptors of adequate accuracy in the right places and in adequate numbers. But are there? In the goat, Whitteridge [7] has found some, and in man they have been reported, but with little evidence of anatomical connections, and still less of accuracy, of the sort required by a "compensation" theory. Clearly this would be a shaky hypothesis on which to base a general theory of the observed stability of the visual world—though I confess that for a time I could think of no better, and the notion has recently been canvassed afresh [8].

2.3. But in fact there is another possibility, which takes us a stage further back. We have so far been considering the voluntary eye movement itself as a *fait accompli*: something that has happened for reasons of its own, with certain unfortunate consequences for the retinal image which we must now annul as best we can. Suppose, however, that we ask how—in what circumstances and in what way—the voluntary movement itself comes about. When do I move my eye voluntarily?—When I want to look elsewhere. How do I judge the movement is satisfactory?—*By the change which has taken place in the retinal image.*

Here surely is the key to our problem. The change in the retinal image under voluntary movement is not merely a *consequence* of the movement: it is its *goal*. The stability of the visual field under voluntary movement is not a *deduction* from cues, but a *presupposition* or *null hypothesis* on which the voluntary movement is based. Such at least is the view which I want to put forward now and to explore a little further. We might express it, at this level, as suggesting that in voluntary eye movement the retina is *steered* over the visual image; i.e., that there is a close analogy between the use of oculomotor muscles to enable the optical projection of the retina to crawl or hop over the visual field, and the use of leg and arm muscles to enable the body to crawl or hop over the locomotor (tactile) field. In each case the activity results in changes in sensory input; but if a man crawls hand-over-hand through a familiar room in the dark, it never occurs to us to suggest that the succession of tactile motion-signals he receives must be internally "compensated" by "inflow" or "outflow" signals from his locomotor system. Of course not. It is by these motion-signals (*inter alia*) that he is steering. Were they to *disappear*, he would have the impression that his world was unstable—had ceased to be a stable framework within which to navigate.

Similarly with oculomotion, I suggest that we have just as little reason to invoke a "compensatory" mechanism to explain the stability of the perceived world. The oculomotor system pushes the retinal image behind it, so to speak, as a man walking over a field pushes the ground behind him. A voluntary movement is not complete until the retinal image has changed in the required way to its new goal-state. The visual field seems to move only when the current state of the retinal image differs sufficiently from the current goal-state. This implies that in some special cases a sensation of field movement may be expected even with a stationary retinal image: namely, in cases where the image displacement that is the goal of a voluntary eye movement is prevented by some external means. (This does not, however, furnish a specific test of the hypothesis, since the same could hold for the two first considered.)

3. THE ALTERNATIVE FLOW SYSTEMS

3.1. Let us now discuss the three hypotheses more generally in terms of the information-flow systems concerned. The problem is

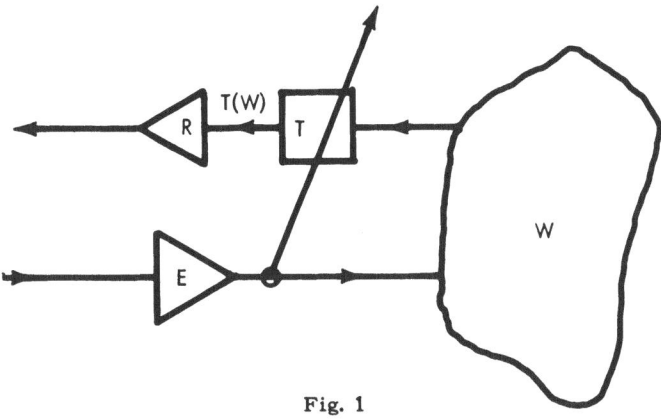

Fig. 1

posed in Fig. 1. The receptor system R of an organism receives signals in various modalities from the world of activity W. The signals from W undergo various transformations T as a result of the activity of the organism's effector system E. For example, E may rotate the eyeball and so displace the visual image of W on the retina; or it may move the whole organism in the world and so produce relative motion among portions of the visual image, changes in binocular disparities, and the like. E may also act mechanically on objects in the world W, but the changes so brought about in the signals from W are not included among the transformations T. The latter represent changes only in the characteristics of the *information channel* from W to R, brought about by voluntary activity, and not changes in W itself, even though such changes may be necessary accompaniments of the changes in the information channel.

Thus if I walk toward a radio set, the attenuation of the acoustic channel between it and my ears is reduced. Such a change is included in the transformation T. If at the same time (as is quite conceivable) the movement of my body upsets the radio and, let us say, reduces its acoustic output, this change is not included in the transformation T. The reduction in output is a genuine change in state of the world, and not merely a transformation of the channel by which the world is observed.

To sum up, then, the organs of the receptor system R receive an input $T(W)$ which embodies a representation of the world of activity W. This representation is liable to be transformed in a variety of ways (represented by different forms of the operator T), depend-

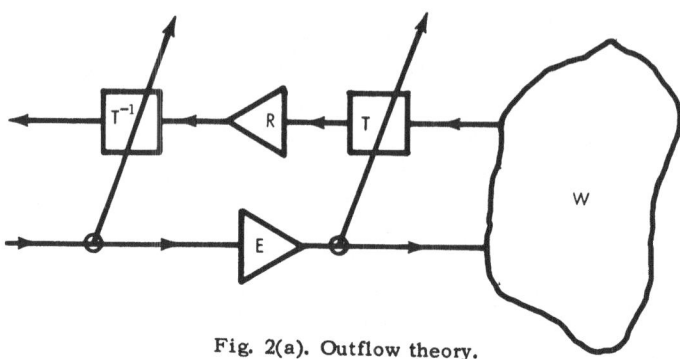

Fig. 2(a). Outflow theory.

ing on the activity of the effector system E. The result is an out-put from R which varies with the activity of E even when the world W is stationary. The problem is to devise a satisfactory informa-tion-flow model in which transformations resulting from voluntary effector action do not give rise to the spurious perception of change in the world W.

3.2. The two possibilities considered and rejected at the be-ginning of this section are illustrated in Figs. 2(a) and 2(b). In both, the output from R is passed through a compensating system adjusted to perform the transformation *inverse* to T—to cancel the effect of T. Following the usual convention we may call this trans-formation T^{-1}. The compensating transformation is selected in Fig. 2(a) according to signals from the input to the effector system. This arrangement clearly relies on the stability of E's transfer charac-teristic. In Fig. 2(b) compensation is controlled according to sig-

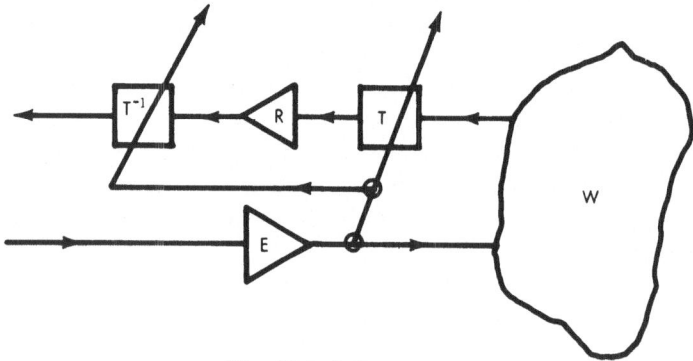

Fig. 2(b). Inflow theory.

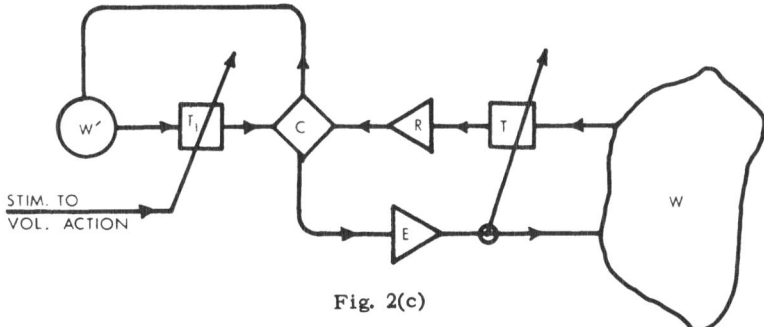

Fig. 2(c)

nals from the output of E—in practice generated by proprioceptive organs whose stability must again be relied upon. (This is the usual way of stabilizing a radar picture on board ship against the movement of the ship's head.)

In both of these theories the stimulus to effector action is taken for granted and its origin is not considered. The problem is regarded as one of stabilizing the received input against transformations produced by all effector activity, however stimulated.

3.3. Figures 2(c) and 2(d) show two possible alternatives to these hypotheses, along the lines of our present approach. In both, the stimulus to *effector* action comes by way of a discriminator of mismatch or "comparator" C, whose function is to drive the effector system until the received signals $T(W)$ match an internally prescribed standard. In Fig. 2(c), a stable internal representation of the world W undergoes a transformation T_1 before comparison with the output of R. If the internal representation of W is correct, the comparator C will drive E until T matches T_1. Voluntary activity, on this model, is initiated by *altering the internal transformation,* T_1.

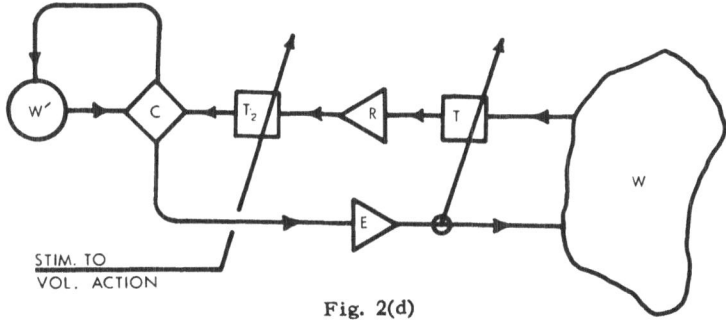

Fig. 2(d)

In Fig. 2(d), it is the output of R that undergoes a transformation T_2 before comparison with the stable internal representation of W. Here C will drive E until T matches the *inverse* of T_2, if the internal representation of W is correct. Voluntary activity is again initiated by *altering the internal transformation, T_2*.

In both of these cases the stimulus to the effector system arises from mismatch between the goal-state prescribed by the internal transformation (T_1 or T_2) and the actual state of the transformed recepta $T(W)$. Thus the change in the transformation T which results from voluntary activity is a change *toward* equilibrium (the new equilibrium prescribed by the change in T_1 or T_2) and not a *disturbance* of equilibrium. If we make the reasonable assumption that perception of change is aroused only by *disturbances* of equilibrium, we shall not in these circumstances expect any world-change to be perceived.

4. THE SIMPLIFIED FLOW MODEL

4.1. When we come to consider practical details, Fig. 2(c) and 2(d) are not as greatly different as they might seem at first sight. In practice the transformations T_1 might well be achieved by adjustment of the operating conditions of the comparator C, which will of course be an exceedingly complex network. If T_1 and T_2 are incorporated into C we arrive at a single flow system as in Fig. 3, where the stimulus to voluntary action is effectively a change in criterion of mismatch in the comparator C.

4.2. We may now consider briefly how this system would respond to other than voluntarily induced changes in signals from the world. In the first place, an alteration imposed on T at point (b) in Fig. 3 (for example, a forced rotation of the eyeball) will give rise to an immediate mismatch between the inputs to the comparator, which its output cannot remove if (b) is firmly held. The only way of removing mismatch is to alter the internal representation of W or of course to change the goal-setting of C. Both of these, as we shall see, may be considered *acts of perception*, on the present model.

4.3. A change actually taking place in the world W [point (c)] cannot in general be matched by alterations of T or C and demands, as it should, a change in the internal representation of W before balance can be restored.*

---

*In some well-known cases, however ("illusions"), it can be satisfied by more than one change in W', or by *noncorresponding* changes.

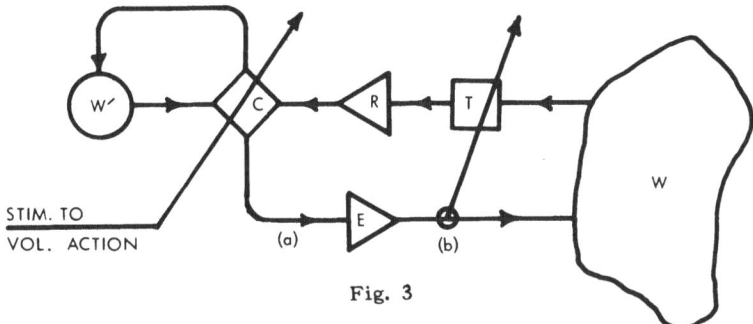

Fig. 3

4.4. Artificial stimulation of the effector system [point (a)] will generally give rise to similar perceptual effects to those of the imposed alteration at point (b), considered above. The chief difference will be in the proprioceptive signals generated, which will have opposite sense in the two cases. (The proprioceptive system is not shown in Fig. 3.)

4.5. Paralysis of the effector system will give rise to uncorrectable mismatch signals whenever voluntary movement is attempted, so that the world-representation will be displaced in the direction of the attempted movement.

4.6. These examples are far from exhaustive, but they may indicate the kind of test to which this flow model is open.

5. THE INTERNAL REPRESENTATION OF THE WORLD

5.1. So far, apart from our brief indication that a genuinely changing world could be matched only by a change in the internal representation of it, we have been assuming a stationary world of activity. We have in fact been tackling the problem of the *nonperception* of *apparent* change. This brings us to the point at which we link up with the earlier papers [1, 2, 3, 4, 6] and go on to discuss more briefly the perception of genuine change in W. Along our present line, this amounts to discussing possible ways in which the internal representation W' may be kept modified to match the changes in W.

5.2. It will be remembered [2] that the system is presumed to be continually guiding itself toward the achievement of a hierarchy of goals, the avoidance of undesirable limits, and the establishment of desirable relationships, by the continual selection of appropriate effector activity. The goal we have so far considered is that of maintaining a match between the internal world-representation W' and the world W. If the changes in W showed absolutely no redundancy (in the information theorist's sense) in their demands on the internal representation, there would of course be no scope for conceptualization or perception in terms of invariants. The system embodying the internal representation could only be a completely flexible "imitator" devoid of any stable structure. The appropriate representation to match the input from receptors could be selected under the guidance of the mismatch signal from C, by an internal department or "bureau of internal affairs" of the effector system, E_i (Fig. 4). (The "bureau of external affairs" is now represented by E_e.) The informational requirements of E_i for adaptive success have been discussed elsewhere [1]. Suffice it to say that with no redundancy, if C does not supply information in enough detail, the deficit can be made good only by successive approximation in W', and then only if the features to be perceived in W are changing sufficiently slowly.

5.3. If, however, the changes in W show redundancy (statistical regularity) in their demands on W', the information required from C may be much reduced, in two ways.

(a) In the first place, sequences of changes in W' which are frequently called for may be generated as "wholes" by suitable internal "organizing subroutines," instead of having to be guided in detail by C. These subroutines may be partly inbuilt, partly developed as the result of experience [1,2].

(b) In the second place, the received signals, suitably filtered, together with proprioceptive and other internal data, may be used as cues for the selection of the appropriate subroutines.

5.4. We thus find a place for two kinds of process by which invariant features of the field of activity may find internal representation. In earlier papers [1, 3, 4] I have drawn a sharp contrast between representations using (a) an outwardly directed, internal matching-response to the input and (b) an inwardly directed filtrate of the input. Here we see how the two, nevertheless, may function in combination to make efficient perception possible. The second kind, according to this model, may serve to adjust the relative probabilities of different modes of activity of the first kind. But, as earlier, I would tentatively associate perceptual activity only with (a) the outwardly directed internal response, and not with (b) the incoming signals from the filter.

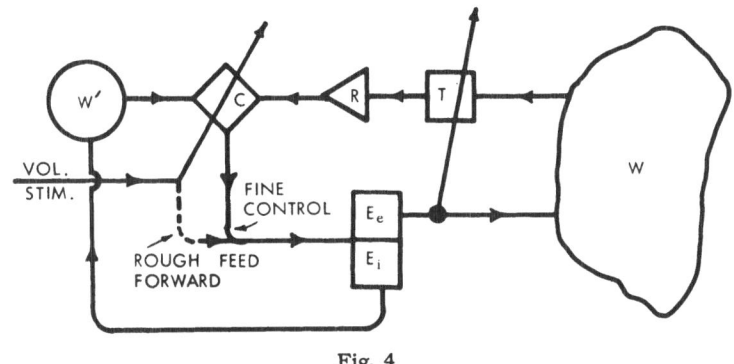

Fig. 4

6. PERCEPTION AND ACTION

6.1. The biggest difficulty in theoretical model making such as this is to perceive and profit from the simplifications which are possible in design, owing to the interdependence of the various functional demands made on the information-flow system. Our thinking, in other words, has constantly to be disciplined and pruned by an apprehension of the organism in its environment as a functioning whole. The sheer difficulty of bearing in mind all, or even enough, of the consequent easements of design criteria, is responsible in practice for many a false start. The designer of information-flow systems has certain well-established techniques for transducing, classifying, and employing information. It is natural for him to begin model building by combining his standard techniques in physiologically conceivable ways, and only afterwards asking what simplifications may be allowed (or demanded) in the special case of the living organism. But by then it may be too late. We have met one case in point at the beginning of this paper. We now proceed to a second illustration.

6.2. The primary function of perception is to prepare the organism for action appropriately adjusted to the state of affairs perceived.

The designer of automata might first naturally argue as follows.

"(1) The picture of the world presented by the receptors (of all modalities) to the organism will depend on the whereabouts of the organism in its world, and on the relative positions, orientations, etc., of the stable or quasi-stable objects which may move about in the world. We must therefore begin by incorporating a system to transform each particular picture into a representation in terms of invariant features or "universals" plus their accidental properties (position, brightness, loudness, or the like).

"(2) We must next arrange that this representation of the received information modifies and keeps up-to-date an internally stored representation of the total world of activity of the organism. [Whether this abstracting system generates its output as a passive filtrate of the input or an active matching-response to it (5.4) does not at this point make any difference.] This must be coupled to a control system in which the conditional probabilities of effector action in different circumstances are adjusted. With the help of logical computing networks, we can ensure that the implications of each item of abstracted information are reflected in the conditional probabilities of action in all possible circumstances (the *conditional probability matrix* or C.P.M.)."

The total system resulting from this approach is outlined in Fig. 5. A is the abstracting system which breaks down the information from the receptor system R into terms of universals and their particular qualifying properties, and supplies it to the stored representation P of the world W. S is the control system that receives the data from P and sets the conditional controls (configuration of thresholds) of the effector system E in such a way as to further the goals of the organism.

6.3. But let us see what happens when we begin to prune. Dominant in the stored picture P of the world, kept up-to-date by A, there is the representation of the organism itself in its world. (Dr. von Foerster has pointed out that the devotees of this model stand in danger of a logically infinite regress, having to represent a picture within a picture within a picture...indefinitely.) Every movement of the organism, whether voluntary or otherwise, must be reflected in changes of the stored picture of the organism-plus-world, producing corresponding changes in the C.P.M. for effector action—the "total state of readiness." At the same time, such movements must have demanded corresponding changes in whatever rules of transformation are used within A to compensate for the effects of the movement on the received signals. The same is true for any other changes in the field. If they are to be categorized, and to have appropriate effects on action and readiness for action, they must induce corresponding changes within A, P, and S. If a cup of tea is is placed in front of me, for example, (a) I perceive not a series of

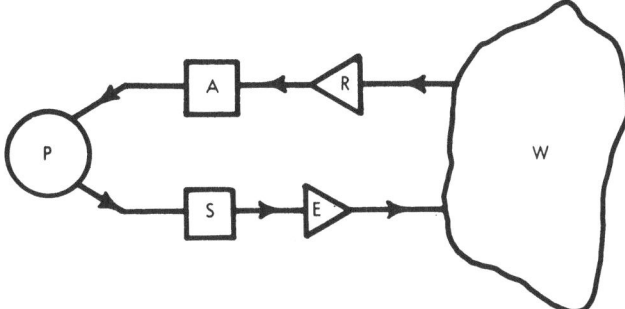

Fig. 5. A popular but highly inefficient model of information processing in the organism.

cups,* but a single cup in motion, coming to rest at a certain position; (b) from now on I know it is there; (c) my motor system is adjusted so that I am not only ready to pick it up, but also (I hope)
to avoid knocking it over in any other movements I make. On the
naive model of Fig. 5, (a), (b), and (c) entail separate but correlated
changes in A, P, and S. Again, if I turn my chair through a right
angle, further triply correlated changes of another sort are necessary in A, P, and S.

Now what are changed in A and S are essentially the *rules of
transformation* by which on the one hand (in A) a particular picture
is transformed to a description in standard categories or "universals," and by which on the other hand (in S) a desired pattern of
action described in standard categories is transformed into a particular sequence of effector activity.

At once we ask ourselves: Does the system ever in practice
have to alter one set of rules without the other? If not, then it may
be unjustifiably complicated. We have allowed it to develop as if a
master controller were sitting at P, receiving predigested information about the world from A, and issuing orders couched in general
terms, which have to be transformed by S into particular instructions. This has led us at first to install two separate transformation systems, A and S. But if A and S are always linked, as in practice they would seem to be, then we naturally ask whether one unit
could not be used for both purposes. Can we not consider a model
in which the incoming data from receptors and the outgoing instruc-

*It may be noted, however, that with some types of brain lesion the patient
complains of just such a "palinopsia" [9,10].

tions to effectors pass in opposite directions through the same
transforming network, thereby ensuring that perception and readiness for action are automatically matched?

6.4. As a simple illustration of this principle, we could imagine
a lamp signaler on board ship, sending and receiving messages to
and from an aircraft through a mirror system. If the ship changes
course, the received image will normally change its position, and
the transmitted beam will likewise move off target. But if the mirror
system is automatically adjusted to compensate for the movement,
then both the received and transmitted beams can remain on target;
and as the aircraft moves, the operator on board ship need allow
only for its own movement. The transformation performed on the
received signal is inverse to that performed on the transmitted one.

The illustration brings out a further point. The setting of the
mirror system at any one time forms a *representation* of the relative
bearing of the aircraft and ship. It represents one relevant structural feature of the field of activity. If the mirror system were in
two parts, one compensating for ship movement, the other for aircraft movement relative to the earth's surface, then they would
represent two corresponding structural features, and so on.

6.5. We are thus led to a final suggestion. Could not the total
structure of the transforming network which combines the functions
of *A* and *S* serve also as the internal *representation* of the whole
world of activity? This would in Fig. 5 dispense with *P*, in which
the changes were always correlated with those in *A* and were thus
informationally redundant. It would also obviate any danger of a
logical regress, since in this form self-representation would be implicit instead of explicit.

This suggestion is feasible only if we can contrive the necessary transforming network to combine the functions of *A* and *S*. The
difficulty is that not all transformations of signals in a network can
be inverted simply by passing the signals backward through the
same network. It is true that size dilatation, rotation, and the like
are readily reversible in some kinds of network; but not all even of
these are physiologically realistic.

I have not attempted to devise networks which might be used
reversibly in this way, for there is a simpler solution open to us. In
6.2 we agreed that *A* might function either (a) by filtering the input
through suitable networks to produce invariant outputs, or (b) by
generating invariant internal matching-responses to the recepta. In

case (a), the transformation produced by *A* has to be effected on *inwardly* directed signals. In case (b), however, the signals to be transformed are *outwardly* directed matching-responses.

If then we choose (b) as our basic perceptual model, we dispose of any necessity to postulate a reversible network, or to realize the inverse to all likely transformations. The transformations required in both *A* and *S* will then be essentially the same, and will each be effected on *outwardly* directed responses. In the jargon of control theory, the inverse of the transformation in *S* will be realized in *A* by using the same network in a feedback loop.

6.6. So, finally, we abandon the initial approach of Fig. 5, which has served us well enough, albeit treacherously, as preliminary scaffolding. Instead we arrive at Fig. 6, which I think shows promise of providing a firmer skeleton. It is essentially the system described in references 1 and 2; but we have arrived at it from a different direction. In the earlier papers the emphasis was on the exploitation of redundancy. In our present approach we have been concerned with the transformations of activity patterns needed to match a particular kind of redundancy—that which is related to movements of the organism and of entities in its world of activity.

In Fig. 6 the core of the organism is a hierarchically organized active system *O* of organizers, whose statistical pattern of interconnections implicitly depicts the organism's world of activity, as so far discovered by it. The main lines of organization may be supposed to be genetically determined; the details will be "self-organized" [2]. These organizers form an "internal department" of the effector system (the "bureau of internal affairs"), framing internal

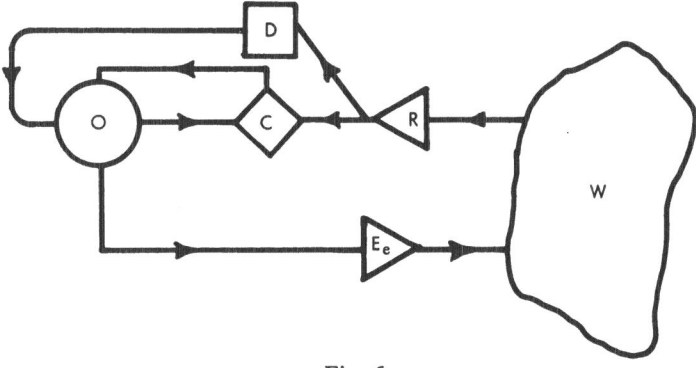

Fig. 6

Fig. 7

representations of percepts by generating matching-responses under
the guidance of the comparator C, and at the same time organizing
appropriate external effector activity by E_e (the "bureau of external
affairs"), in W. The relative probabilities of different trial activities in O are weighted by the detector system D, which filters from
the recepta such clues as they provide to the choice of an appropriate organizing routine to match a given sensory input.* The structures of Fig. 3 are included within O in Fig. 6. Dr. Beurle has made
the attractive suggestion that our sense of the familiarity of well-
known objects may derive from the output of the comparator, C.

7. SOME ILLUSTRATIVE ILLUSIONS

Two striking illusions discovered in the course of experiments
in this field [12] may help to bring out in conclusion the main point
of this paper.

7.1. If a pattern such as Fig. 7 is viewed with one eye covered,
and its image slightly displaced to and fro on the retina by the

*An important example of such a detector system would appear to exist in
the eye of the frog [11].

gentlest of pressure on the corner of the open eyelid, a striking distortion of the field is seen. Rays lying in the direction of image displacement appear to move to and fro, fanwise, at right angles to the direction of motion, as if on an expanding and contracting surface. When, however, a marker such as a black thread is laid across one side of the pattern, perpendicular to the direction of image displacement, the "rubbery" expansion in its neighborhood is inhibited, though it continues on the opposite side of the center, where there is no marker.

The moral would seem to be that the changes in W' (which constitute perception) are the most informationally parsimonious that will match the incoming stimuli: in other words, that perception is organized on the principle of a grudgingly modified null hypothesis. Since only the motion-component normal to a smooth contour generates a signal, this is all that is perceived and the metric of space as perceived is warped accordingly. With a marker to give a second contour at right angles, full motion must be represented in W' and space is no longer perceived as warped.

7.2. If a self-luminous object such as the glowing cathode of a tube is viewed monocularly in a room lit by intermittent flashes at perhaps 5 to 10 per second, and the eyelid similarly pressed in and out, the sensitivity to displacement of the image of the room is dramatically less than that for the self-luminous cathode, which can be seen to move bodily out of and into its glass envelope while the latter appears to remain at rest [12]. Displacement of the image in a mirror has a similar effect. Once again the illusion presses home the moral that what is perceived, however conceptually improbable, is the most informationally economical transformation of W' that will match the input. In a stroboscopic image the absence of *velocity* can apparently reduce the information content of the mismatch signal (due to image displacement) below the threshold for the comparator C, so that for small displacements (easily seen in a self-luminous image), no motion is perceived.

7.3. To these illustrations may be added a host of others, some of which were referred to in our discussion. Thus with distorting spectacles [13, 14] the "renormalization" of the world is greatly hampered unless the subject can move freely in it, and is accelerated in those regions with which he interacts. Dr. Beurle has remarked on the sensation of "swimming uphill" in a pool on a rolling ocean liner. A striking kinesthetic parallel can be noticed when

driving a car if the accelerator is depressed when the engine is un-
expectedly inoperative (as when running out of fuel): one has a
strong momentary sense of being "thrust back." Examples like these
bring out the force of the "null hypothesis" principle on which perception is organized.

7.4. This leads us back to our original problem, the question of
why the world does not seem to move with voluntary eye rotation.

Our solution, it will be remembered, has been to regard the image
displacement in that case as a change *toward* (maintaining) equilibrium: a matching-response to a change in the goal-setting of the
oculomotor-retinal system. The point that remains to be made is
that the threshold for mismatch detection in such goal pursuit can
(and should from an informational standpoint) be much higher during
eye movement than during steady fixation. It should in fact vary
directly with the precision of the effector action giving rise to the
image displacement. To return our earlier analogy, if a man can
jump with an accuracy of ±1 ft, he cannot justifiably infer that he
is on an unstable platform unless the position of the configuration
around him when he lands differs by more than 1 ft from that which
he intended. Yet once he has landed, he could detect a movement
of a fraction of an inch. Similarly, in a saccadic eye movement it
would be absurd (and quite unnecessary) to postulate that the goal
is prespecified and pursued with an accuracy comparable with the
resolution of the stationary eye. In such a case the target might
simply be "get the image over this way until it roughly meets such-
and-such a criterion"; and provided that the criterion was not trans-
gressed *significantly* (in the informational sense), no question of
instability in the visual world could be raised by such image
changes as take place. One way of putting it is that these changes
have no selective information content, since they are 100% redundant.

7.5. The nearest relative to the present theory in neurological
literature is, I think, von Holst's postulate of a "reafference principle" [15], devised originally to explain the optically guided pursuit
of prey in animals. As I was unaware of this work when the present paper was first drafted (in 1955), the relation of the two approaches may bear some comment. As shown by Fig. 8, taken from
a more recent paper [16], he regards voluntary eye movement as entailing the matching of the optical motion-signals ("*reafferenz*")
against an "*efferenzkopie*" derived from the innervation of the ocu-

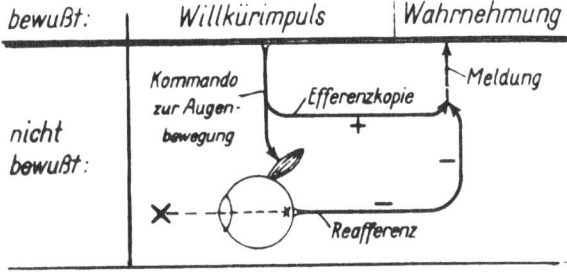

Fig. 8

lomotor system, the difference between the two giving rise to perception of motion. Thus (if I understand von Holst correctly), the normal image displacement is a change *toward* equilibrium, as in our model; yet curiously enough the flow map of Fig. 8 is almost exactly that of Fig. 2(a), with the inverse transformation T^{-1} simply a subtraction of the "efference copy" of motion desired, from the motion of the retinal image. The stimulus to the oculomotor muscles is represented as a "command from a higher center" [16], and the "efference copy" is precomputed from it, as in Fig. 2(a); whereas in our present model we have found it desirable to make the comparator system itself at least partly responsible for driving the muscle, and the voluntary "command from a higher center" would function by changing the *criterion of equilibrium* of the comparator, *together with its threshold for discrimination of mismatch*. Without these provisions it is difficult to see how the theory represented by Fig. 8—despite its important insight into the status of receptor signals resulting from voluntary movement—can escape the stock objections to a "compensatory" version of Fig. 2(a).

8. CONCLUSIONS

8.1. The main argument of this paper is that the problem of the perceptual stability of space has traditionally been wrongly posed. Instead of regarding *stability* as an achievement requiring continual and accurate informational justification, it is suggested that we should regard *perception of change* as the achievement requiring adequate information to justify it, with stability as the null hypothesis.

8.2. A model designed on these lines would maintain a stable internal representation of its world unless incoming signals differed *significantly* from the class of signals required on the null hypothesis; the threshold, and the criterion, of significant mismatch being determined by the nature of current activity.

8.3. On this model, the incoming signals resulting from voluntary activity in a stable world will be part of the *goal* of that activity, evoking no mismatch signals (and hence no spurious perception of instability) so long as the activity organized on the null hypothesis is successful within the limits of accuracy of the effectors concerned. Only if the incoming signals *fail* to register the required changes will the null hypothesis be disconfirmed, and change of the spatial frame perceived. This will occur either if genuine change takes place in the world or if the effector chain is hindered sufficiently from its normal function.

8.4. In keeping with this view, the stimulus to voluntary activity will be a change in the criterion (including normally the threshold) of mismatch between the incoming signals and the current goal-state, rather than a direct signal to the effectors alone. The latter will receive at least some of their controlling signals from the comparator system that evaluates mismatch, driving them to reduce the mismatch.

8.5. Since voluntary movement requires exactly correlated transformations in (a) the internal representation of the organism in its world, (b) its repertoire of adaptive acts and readiness-to-act in the world, and (c) its criteria of mismatch for the signals received from the world, it seems natural to postulate that all three transformations are mediated in the same network: that the motion of the organism in the world is implicitly represented by the transformations which it demands.

8.6. By the same token, genuine motion of the environment will be represented by corresponding changes in the network that organizes behavior to match it, including its visual and other correlates. The activity of keeping this network up-to-date is then the correlate of perception.

8.7. Although perception is thus regarded as an outwardly directed "matching-response," it may be greatly facilitated and accelerated by incoming "filtrates" of statistically significant features in receptor signals, serving to narrow the range of possible matching-responses. Geometrical and other illusions can be regarded as a result of the overbiasing of the criterion of mismatch by stimuli disproportionately rich in one such feature.

8.8. From a system-engineering standpoint the main difference between this type of model and those invoking "compensation" is in the standards of accuracy demanded in the various transducers, and in the use made of the "inflow" and "outflow" signals. It would seem therefore that the ultimate test of such a theory must be quantitative as well as topological.

REFERENCES

1. D. M. MacKay, "The Epistemological Problem for Automata," in "Automata Studies" (edited by C. E. Shannon and J. McCarthy) Princeton University Press, Princeton, 1955.

2. D. M. MacKay, "Towards an Information-Flow Model of Human Behavior," Brit. J. Psychol., Vol. 47, p. 30 (1956).

3. D. M. MacKay, "Mindlike Behaviour in Artefacts," Brit. J. Phil. Sci., Vol. 2, pp. 105-121 (1951).

4. D. M. MacKay, "Mentality in Machines," Proc. Arist. Soc. Suppt., Vol. XXVI, pp. 61-86 (1952).

5. D. M. MacKay, "On Comparing the Brain with Machines," Advancement of Science, Vol. 40, pp. 402-406 (1954).

6. D. M. MacKay, "The Stabilisation of Perception During Voluntary Activity," Proc. Fifteenth Intern. Congr. of Psychol., pp. 284-285 (1957).

7. S. Cooper, P. M. Daniel, and D. Whitteridge, "Afferent Impulses in the Oculomotor Nerve, from the Extrinsic Eye Muscles," J. Physiol., Vol. 113, pp. 463-474 (1951); see also S. Cooper and P. M. Daniel, Brain, Vol. 72, p. 1 (1949).

8. B. Kh. Gurevitch, "Possible Role of Higher Proprioceptive Centres in the Perception of Visual Space," Nature, Vol. 184, pp. 1219-1220 (1959).

9. M. Critchley, "Types of Visual Perseveration: 'Palinopsia' and 'Illusory Visual Spread'," Brain, Vol. 74, pp. 267-299 (1951).

10. H.-L. Teuber, W. S. Battersby, and M. B. Bender, "Visual Field Defects after Penetrating Missile Wounds of the Brain," Harvard University Press, Cambridge, Mass., 1960.

11. J. Y. Lettvin, H. R. Maturana, W. S. McCulloch, and W. H. Pitts, "What the Frog's Eye Tells the Frog's Brain," Proc. I.R.E., Vol. 47, pp. 1940-1951 (Nov. 1959).

12. D. M. MacKay, "Perceptual Instability of a Stroboscopically Lit Visual Field Containing Self-Luminous Objects," Nature, Vol. 181, pp. 507-508 (1958).

13. I. Kohler, "Über Aufbau und Wandlungen der Wahrnehmungswelt," Sitzber. Oesterr. Akad. Wiss., phil.-hist. Kl., Vol. 227, pp. 1-118 (1951).

14. I. Kohler, Die Pyramide, Vol. 3, Nos. 5-7 (1953).

15. E. von Holst and H. Mittelstaedt, "Das Reafferenzprinzip," Naturwiss, Vol. 37, p. 464 (1950).

16. E. von Holst, "Aktive Leistungen der Menschlichen Gesichtswahrnehmung," "Studium Generale," 10 Jahrg, Heft 4, 1957, p. 234.

17. D. M. MacKay, Mind, Vol. 69, pp. 31-40, 1960.

CHAPTER VI

LOGISTICON*

WARREN S. Mc CULLOCH[†]

SUMMARY

Any logical function of n arguments can be represented by a single Venn diagram, each of whose spaces contains a 0 or 1 in Boolean fashion. Using 1 for true and 0 for false they constitute the truth table of the function. The laws by which such functions operate upon each other will be simply stated, and the theory will be extended to cover probabilistic logic by the introduction of p's in the places normally restricted to 0 or 1, where $0 \leq p \leq 1$, thus producing a way of evaluating all such functions on simple digital calcula-

*In connection with his Summary the author wrote to us in a letter of April 20, 1960: "My title, however, is taken from the Pythagoreans, for I shall deal with the brain only as a device for handling arithmetic. Hence 'Logisticon,' and I will send you a copy of what I have proposed originally on this score to Colin Cherry." Because Dr. McCulloch's oral paper "Logisticon," summarized above, is so similar in its conclusions to what he presented at the Ninth Alfred Korzybski Memorial Lecture of March 12, 1960, the substance of that lecture—not heretofore released in book form— is now quoted *in extenso* with the kind permissions of both the author and the Institute of General Semantics, which had offset the lecture in Nos. 26/27 of its Bulletin under the title "What Is a Number, that a Man May Know It, and a Man that He May Know a Number?"—*Ed*.

†The work of the Research Laboratory of Electronics, of which the author is a staff member, is supported in part by the U.S. Army (Signal Corps), the U.S. Air Force (Office of Scientific Research, Air Research and Development Command), and the U.S. Navy (Office of Naval Research). The work of Dr. McCulloch's group also receives support from National Institutes of Health and Teagle Foundation, Incorporated.

tors. Every such Venn function can be realized by a formal neuron
at a fixed threshold which merely adds afferents. By changing the
threshold in unitary steps, any such neuron may be made to compute a dissimilar function for every step, thus producing $2^n + 1$
functions ranging from contradiction to tautology. It is necessary
and sufficient to assure excitation at the neuron, and inhibition of
two kinds, one of which raises the threshold of the neuron while
the other prevents an impulse over an afferent fiber from reaching
the neuron. The method of construction and minimization of the required constructions for such diagrams will be given.

Combinations of these diagrams will be used for the construction of infallible nets of fallible components for $n > 2$, and they
will be examined to show the limits of that infallibility under perturbation of threshold, amplitude of signals, synapsis, and even
scattered loss of neurons. We will show how nets can be constructed which are logically stable under common shift of threshold which
alters the function computed by every neuron but not the input-output function of the net. In passing, we will show the construction
of polyphecks, that is, all of those Venn functions which, when
given n arguments, can produce all functions.

Finally, we will examine the flexibility of minimal nets, consisting of $n + 1$ neurons with n inputs for $n = 2$ and $n = 3$, and show
that the former can compute 15 out of the 16 logical functions, and
the latter 253 out of 256.

THE LOGIC OF RELATIONS

The logic of relations and the logic of propositions really began
in the latter part of the last century with Charles Peirce as their
great pioneer. As with most pioneers, many of the trails he blazed
were not followed for a score of years. For example, he discovered
the amphecks—that is, ⌐not both ... and ...⌐ and ⌐neither ... nor⌐,
which Sheffer rediscovered and which are called by his name for
them, "stroke functions." It was Peirce who broke the ice with his
logic of relatives, from which spring the pitiful beginnings of our
logic of relations of two and more than two arguments. So completely
had the traditional Aristotelian logic been lost that Peirce remarks
that when he wrote the *Century Dictionary* he was so confused concerning abduction, or Apagoge, and induction that he wrote nonsense. Thus Aristotelian logic, like the skeleton of Tom Paine, was
lost to us from the world it had engendered. Peirce had to go back

to Duns Scotus to start again the realistic logic of science. Pragmatism took hold, despite its misinterpretation by William James. The world was ripe for it. Frege, Peano, Whitehead, Russell, and Wittgenstein, followed by a host of lesser lights, but sparked by many a strange character like Schroeder, Sheffer, Gödel, and company, gave us a working logic of propositions.

By the time I had sunk my teeth into these questions, the Polish school was well on its way to glory. In 1923 I gave up the attempt to write a logic of transitive verbs and began to see what I could do with the logic of propositions. My object, as a psychologist, was to invent a kind of least psychic event, or "psychon," that would have the following properties. First, it was to be so simple an event that it either happened or else it did not happen. Second, it was to happen only if its bound cause had happened—shades of Duns Scotus!— that is, it was to imply its temporal antecedent. Third, it was to propose this to subsequent psychons. Fourth, these were to be compounded to produce the equivalents of more complicated propositions concerning their antecedents. In 1929 it dawned on me that these events might be regarded as the all-or-none impulses of neurons, combined by convergence upon the next neuron to yield complexes of propositional events.

A NEURON CALCULUS

During the nineteen-thirties, under influences first from F. H. Pike, C. H. Prescott, and Eilhard von Domarus, and later from Northrop, Dusser de Barenne, and a host of my friends in neurophysiology, I began to try to formulate a proper calculus for these events by subscripting symbols for propositions in some sort of calculus of propositions (connected by implications) with the time of occurrence of the impulse in each neuron.

Neurophysiology moved ahead and, when I went to Chicago I met Walter Pitts, then in his teens, who promptly set me right in matters of theory. It is to him that I am principally indebted for all subsequent success. He remains my best adviser and sharpest critic. This will never be published until it has passed through his hands. In 1943, he and I wrote a paper entitled "A Logical Calculus of the Ideas Immanent in Nervous Activity." Thanks to Rashevsky's defense of logical and mathematical ideas in biology, it was published in his journal where, so far as biology is concerned it might have remained unknown; but John von Neumann picked it up and

used it in teaching the theory of computing machines. I will summarize briefly its logical importance.

Turing had produced a deductive machine that could compute
any computable number, although it had only a finite number of parts
which could be in only a finite number of states and although it
could only move a finite number of steps forward or backward, look
at one spot on its tape at a time and make, or erase, 1 or else 0.
What Pitts and I had shown was that neurons that could be excited
or inhibited, given a proper net, could extract any configuration of
signals in its input. Because the form of the entire argument was
strictly logical, and because Gödel had arithmetized logic, we had
proved, in substance, the equivalence of all general Turing machines—man-made or begotten.

But we had done more than this, thanks to Pitts' modulo mathematics; in looking into circuits composed of closed paths of neurons
wherein signals could reverberate we had set up a theory of memory—
to which every other form of memory is but a surrogate requiring
reactivation of a trace. Now a memory is a temporal invariant. Given
an event at one time, and its regeneration at later dates, one knows
that there was an event that was of the given kind. The logician
says "there was some x such that x was a ψ. In the symbols of the
Principia Mathematica, $(\exists x)(\psi x)$. Given this and negation, for which
inhibition suffices, we can have $\tilde{}(\exists x)(\tilde{}\psi x)$, or, if you will, (x)
(ψx). Hence we have the lower predicate calculus with equality,
which has recently been proved to be a sufficient logical framework
for all of mathematics.* Our next joint paper showed that the ψ's
were not restricted to temporal invariants but, by reflexes and other
devices, could be extended to any universal, and its recognition,
by nets of neurons. That was published in Rashevsky's journal in
1947. It is entitled "How We Know Universals."

Our idea is basically simple and completely general, because
any object, or universal, is an invariant under some groups of transformations and, consequently, the net need only compute a sufficient number of averages a_i, each an Nth of the sum for all trans-
forms T belonging to the group G, of the value assigned by the
corresponding functional f_i, to every transform T, as a figure of
excitation ϕ in the space and time of some mosaic of neurons. That
is,

$$a_i = \frac{1}{N} \sum_{\substack{\text{all} \\ T \epsilon G}} f_i[T\phi]$$

*The "all" is questionable here, as arithmetic is uncompletable, and
mathematics in general has no decision process.—Ed.

About this time Pitts had begun to look into the problem of randomly connected nets. And, I assure you, what we proposed were constructions that were proof against minor perturbations of stimuli, thresholds, and connections. Others have published, chiefly by his inspiration, much of less moment on this score, but because we could not make the necessary measurements he has let it lie fallow. Once only did he present it—at an early and unpublished conference on cybernetics, sponsored by the Josiah Macy, Jr., Foundation in 1952. That was enough to start John von Neumann on a new tack. He published it under the title, "Toward a Probabilistic Logic." By this he did not mean a logic in which only the arguments were probable, but a logic in which the function itself was only probable. He had decided for obvious reasons to embody his logic in a net of formal neurons that sometimes misbehaved, and to construct of them a device that was as reliable as was required in modern digital computers. Unfortunately, he made three assumptions, any one of which was sufficient to have precluded a reasonable solution. He was unhappy about it because it required neurons far more reliable than he could expect in human brains. The piquant assumptions were: first, that failures were absolute—not depending upon the strength of signals or on the thresholds of neurons. Second, that his computing neurons had but two inputs apiece. Third, that each computed the same single Sheffer stroke function.

VON NEUMANN'S PROBLEM

Let me take up these constraints one at a time, beginning with the first, namely, when failures are absolute. Working with me, Leo Verbeek of the Netherlands has shown that the probability of failure of a neural net can be made as low as the error probability of one neuron (the output neuron) and that this can be reduced by a multiplicity of output neurons in parallel. Second, I have proved that nets of neurons with two inputs to each neuron, when failures depend upon perturbations of threshold, stimulus strength, or connections, cannot compute without error any significant function except tautology and contradiction. And last, but not least, by insisting on using but a single function, von Neumann had thrown away the great logical redundancy of the system with which he might have bought reliability. With neurons of two inputs each, this amounts to 16^2; with three inputs each, to 256^3, etc.—being of the form $\left(2^{2^\delta}\right)^\delta$, where δ is the number of inputs per neuron.*

*Notationally ambiguous, since $(2^2)^3 \neq 2^{(2^3)}$. What is needed is $(2^{(2^\delta)})^\delta$.—Ed.

There were two other problems that distressed von Neumann. He knew that caffeine and alçohol changed the threshold of all neurons in the same direction so much that every neuron computed some wrong function of its input. Yet one had essentially the same output for the same input. The classic example is the respiratory mechanism, for respiration is preserved under surgical anaesthesia where thresholds of all neurons are sky-high. Of course, no net of neurons can work when the output neuron's threshold is so high that it cannot be excited or so low that it fires continuously. The first is coma, and the second, convulsion; but between these limits our circuits do work. These circuits he called circuits logically stable under common shift of thresholds. They can be made of formal neurons even with only two inputs, to work over a single step of threshold, using only excitation and inhibition on the output cell; but this is only a fraction of the range. Associated, unobstrusively, with the problem is this fact: of the 16 possible logical functions of neurons with two inputs, two functions cannot be calculated by any one neuron. They are the exclusion "or," "A or else B," and "both or else neither"—the "if and only if" of logic.

Both limitations point to a third possibility in the interactions of neurons and both are easily explained if impulses from one source can gate those from another so as to prevent their reaching the output neuron. Two physiological data pointed to the same possibility. The first was described earliest by Matthews, and later by Renshaw. It is the inhibition of a reflex by afferent impulses over an adjacent dorsal root. The second is the direct inhibition described by David Lloyd, wherein there is no time for intervening neurons to get into the sequence of events. We have located this interaction of afferents, measured its strength, and know that strychnine has its convulsive effects by preventing it. This is good physiology, as well as logically desirable.

My collaborator, Manuel Blum of Venezuela, now has a nice proof that excitation and inhibition of the cell plus inhibitory interaction of afferents are necessary and sufficient for constructing neurons that will compute their logical functions in any required sequence as the threshold falls or rises. With them it is always possible to construct nets that are logically stable all the way from coma to convulsion under common shift of threshold.

The last of von Neumann's problems was proposed to the American Psychiatry Association in March 1955. It is this. The eye is only two logical functions deep. Granted that it has controlling signals from the brain to tell it what it has to compute, what sort of elements are neurons that it can compute so many different functions in a depth of two neurons (that is, in the bipolars and the ganglion cells)? Certainly, said he, neurons are much cleverer than flip-flops or the Eccles-Jordan components of our digital computers. The answer to this is that real neurons fill the bill. With formal neurons of 2 inputs each and controlling signals to the first rank only, the output can be made to be any one of 15 of the possible 16 logical functions. Eugene Prange, of the Air Force Cambridge Research Center, has just shown that with neurons of 3 inputs each and controlling signals to all 4 neurons, the net can be made to compute 253 out of 256 possible functions. Many of our friends are building artificial neurons for use in industry and in research, thus exposing to experiment many unsuspected properties of their relations in the time domain. There is now a whole tribe of men working on artificial intelligence—on machines that induce, or learn, and machines that abduce, or make hypotheses. In England alone, there are Ross Ashby, MacKay, Gabor, Andrews, Uttley, Graham Russell, Beurle, and several others—of whom I could not fail to mention Gordon Pask and Stafford Beer. In France, the work centers around Schützenberger. The Americans are too numerous to name.

I may say that there is a whole computing machinery group, followers of Turing, who build the great deductive machines. There is Angyon, the cyberneticist of Hungary, now of California, who had reduced Pavlovian conditioning to a four-bit problem, embodied in his artificial tortoise. Selfridge, of the Lincoln Laboratory, M.I.T.— with his Pandemonium and his Sloppy—is building abductive machinery. Each is but one example of many. We know how to instrument these solutions and to build them in hardware when we will.

THE PROBLEM OF INSIGHT

But the problem of insight, or intuition, or invention—call it what you will—we do not understand, although many of us are having a go at it. I will not here name names, for most of us will fail miserably and be happily forgotten. Tarski thinks that what we lack is a fertile calculus of relations of more than two relata. I am inclined to agree with him, and if I were now the age I was in 1917, that is the problem I would tackle.

That process of insight by which a child learns at least one logical particle, neither or not both, when it is given only ostensively—
and one must be so learned—is still a little beyond us. It may perhaps have to wait for a potent logic of triadic relations, but I now
doubt it. This is what we feared lay at the core of the theoretical
difficulty in mechanical translation, but last summer Victor Yngve,
of the Research Laboratory of Electronics, M.I.T., showed that a
small finite machine with a small temporary memory could read and
parse English from left to right. In other languages the direction
may be reversed, and there may be minor problems that depend on
the parenthetical structure of the tongue. But unless the parenthetical structures are, as in mathematics, complicated repeatedly at
both ends, the machine can handle even sentences that are infinite,
like "This is the house that Jack built." So I'm hopeful that with
the help of Chaos similar simple machines may account for insight
or intuition—which is more than I proposed to include in this text.

BEYOND VENN DIAGRAMS

I shall now take some minutes to make perfectly clear that non-
Aristotelian logic invented by von Neumann and brought to fruition
by me and my coadjutors.

My success arose from the necessity of teaching logic to neu-
rologists, psychiatrists, and psychologists. In his letter to a German princess, Euler used circles on the paper to convey inclusions
and intersections of classes. This works for three classes. Venn,
concerned with four or five, invented his famous diagrams in which
closed curves must each bisect all of the areas produced by previous closed curves (see Fig. 1). This goes well, even for five, by

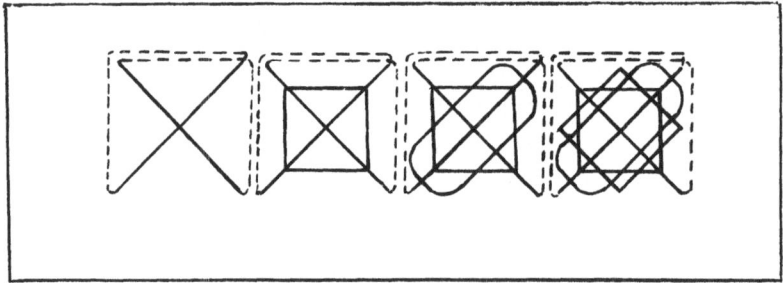

Fig. 1

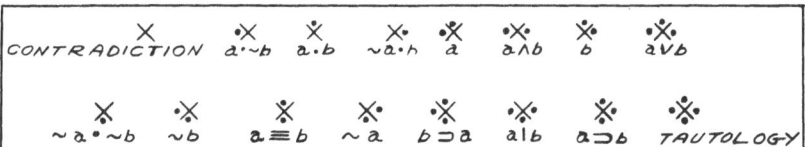

Fig. 2

Venn's trick; six is tough; seven, well-nigh unintelligible, even when one finds out how to do it. Oliver Selfridge and Marvin Minsky (also of Lincoln Laboratory), at my behest, invented a method of construction that can be continued to infinity and remain transparent at a glance. So they formed a simple set of icons wherewith to inspect their contents to the limit of our finite intuitions. The calculus of relations degenerates into the calculus of classes if one is only interested in the one relation of inclusion in classes. This, in turn, degenerates into the calculus of propositions if one is only interested in the class of true, or else false, propositions, or statements in the realistic case. Now this calculus can always be reduced to the relations of propositions by pairs. Thanks to Wittgenstein we habitually handled these relations as truth tables to compute their logical values (see Fig. 2). These tables, if places are defined, can be reduced to jots for true and blanks for false. Thus every logical particle, represented by its truth table, can be made to appear as jots and blanks in two intersecting circles. The common area jotted means both; a jot in the left alone means the left argument alone is true; in the right, the right argument alone is true; and below, neither is true. Expediency simplifies two circles to a mere chi or X (see Fig. 3). Each of the logical relations of two arguments, and there are 16 of them, can then be represented by jots above, below, to right, and to left, beginning with no jots and then with one, two, and three, to end with four. These symbols, which I call Venn functions, can then be used

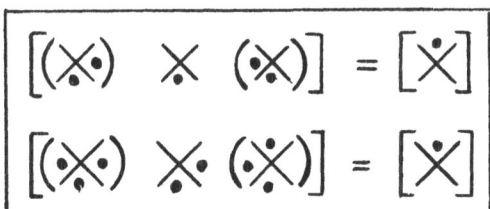

Fig. 3

to operate upon each other, exactly as the truth tables do, for
they picture these tables. A twelve-year-old boy who is bright
learns the laws in a few minutes, and his friends start playing
jots and X's. A psychiatrist learns them in a few days, but only
if he has to pay twenty-five dollars per hour for this psychother-
apy. Next, since here we are generating probabilistic logic—
not the logic of probabilities—we must infect these functions with
the probability of a jot instead of a certain jot or a certain blank.
b/e symbolize this by placing 1 for certain jots, 0 for certain blanks,
and p for the probability of a jot in that place. These probabilistic
Venn functions operate upon each other as those with jots and
blanks, for true and false, utilizing products; instead of only 1×1
$= 1$ and $1 \times 0 = 0$ and $0 \times 0 = 0$ we get 1, p, p^2, p^3, 0, etc., and
compute the truth tables of our complex propositions. This gives us
a truly probabilistic logic, for it is the function, not merely the argument, that is infected by chance and is merely probable. This is
the tool with which I attacked the problem von Neumann had set us.

A tool is a handy thing—and each has its special purpose. All-
purpose tools are generally like an icebox with which to drive nails—
hopelessly inefficient. But the discovery of a good tool often leads
to the invention of others, provided we have insight into the operations to be performed. We have. Logicians may only be interested
in tautology—an X with 4 jots—and contradiction—an X with none.
But these are tautologically true or false. Realistic logic is interested in significant propositions—that is, in those that are true, or
false, according to whether what they assert is, or is not, the case.
Nothing but tautology and contradiction can be computed certainly
with any p's in every Venn function, so long as one makes them of
two and only two arguments. This restriction disappears as soon
as one considers Venn functions of more than two arguments in complex propositions.

When we have functions of three arguments, Euler's three circles replace the two of conventional logic; but the rules of operations with jots and blanks—or with 1, p, 0—carry over directly, and
we have a thoroughly probabilistic logic of three arguments. Then
Venn and Minsky-Selfridge diagrams enable us to extend these
rules to 4, 5, 6, 7, etc. to infinitely many arguments. The rules of
calculation remain unaltered, and the whole can be programed simply into any digital computer. There is nothing in all of this to prevent us from extending the formulations to include multiple-truth-
valued logics.

CHAPTER VII

THE LOGIC OF BIOSIMULATION
CHARLES ARTHUR MUSES

> "The beginnings of things are therefore to be
> looked into, that amendment may be made of
> that which is amiss, for one error there will
> hazard the loss of labour in all that is built
> upon it."
> —John Sparrow's Preface to Boehme's
> *Mysterium Magnum*, London, 1656

0.0. THE RAISON D'ETRE OF THE SUBJECT MATTER

0.1. Delimiting the key word of our title, we can more specifically confine ourselves and speak of the logic of anthroposimulation, the most advanced type of biosimulation possible, since man is the highest known living form. Actually, the Locarno Conference of 1960 is interesting from the viewpoint of the history of science because it was the first symposium ever held on the general problem of what might be termed "robotics" or the electromechanical (subsuming "chemico-" under "microelectro-") simulation of man by man.

0.2. The field, though new, is a very natural one, for the behavioral evolution of mankind has since the mid-nineteenth century veered markedly and ever more self-reinforcingly toward man as *homo faber* de luxe, the super-tool maker, the *ne plus ultra* machine maker. Tubal Cain, the ancient artisan of Genesis, has had an overriding historical success. So has his ancestor, since humanity has overwhelmingly voted for Cain's as against the Abel-Seth lineage. Cain and not simply Tubal Cain—for man has learned how to kill his brother in ever increasing numbers as his tool-making powers have evolved to more puissant levels.

A tool is quite detached, and the same knife that gives life in the hands of the surgeon may unjustly take it in the hands of the murderer. Only the value system ultimately gives meaning to the tool. Here is one of those crucial beginnings.

0.3. The apotheosis of man's technical accomplishments, which had already challenged the humanities in the nineteenth century and in the twentieth overthrew them, would be a replication of his own powers in a machine to the greatest degree possible. This would constitute the highest, the most advanced tool possible. Foreboding to some or not, this is the aim and pinnacle foreshadowed ever since man's hand chipped the first flint. We shall explore in this paper the extent of that "greatest degree."

Logically inevitable since paleolithic times, man's destiny-involved aim has finally come upon him in the second half of our century like the sudden blossoming of an Aristotelian entelechia—the final cause and dominating peak of human constructive activity: the man-made replication of man as far as possible.

0.4. What has become historically evident as man's dominating aim is thus the replication of himself by himself by technological means. The form of this dominating aim becomes hence a super-machine, self-operating, self-instructing, and man-controlled, though this latter process may be reduced to a minimum in the sense of metalinguistic program information initially imparted or in-built.

Although the technical form of man's fundmental historical aim is a machine, the psychological and human content of that aim is *control*, mastery, the ability to impose his whims at will upon as much of the rest of the natural universe as possible.

0.5. Partially self-operating machines, even to the point of supplying their own fuel needs, are now feasible realities. The machine has evolved through the stages of first mere adjuncts to the artisan's hand; then through hand-driven devices which progressively became less and less humanly operated. Machine exploration of the environment in search for the ingredients out of which to synthesize fuel or even parts for itself is a not too difficult step ahead. We have already reached the point of being able to build brain-like machines that can direct the activities of other machines which are muscle- and organ-like. Yet these directing machines are only very distantly brain-like, for they must still have their instructions* pre-

---

*Including even most general rules and, of course, the very construction of the device; for construction is a form of instruction.

conceived, predigested, and fed to them by human beings. This is why the electronic "brains" are not brains, all the confusing anthropomorphisms of the prevalent loose but convenient terminology notwithstanding.

We have advanced but very little distance and comparatively very slowly into the area of the truly brain-like machine, the machine able to instruct itself by testing out and reacting to its own environment and able also to learn to talk about that environment. Such a machine finally would have to be able not simply to learn how to survive in a given environment or game, but also to formulate linguistically what it had done, as well as its current plans of future action. It would have to be able to talk about its environment in some manner communicable to other similar machines and to humans, and not merely to servomechanisms. It would also have to be able to function in semi- or nonprotected environments, i.e., in games where its opponents received no handicaps.

0.6. Now I am going to explore the question, How far are all these goals and intentions logically justifiable? Or, what, if any, are the inherent limitations of these aims within the context of their own defined means, i.e., electromechanical components in the broad sense already defined in 0.1? This discussion will take us principally on excursions into logic, mathematics and abstract linguistics.

1.0. THE APPROACHES TO THE PROBLEM

1.1. We may make a spectrum of the types of human knowledge as follows: (A) Philosophy (including logic and aesthetics), (B) Mathematics, (C) Physics, (D) Chemistry, (E) Biology, (F) Psychology (including sociology, ethnology, anthropology and the behaviorial sciences in general), and (G) Eventology (a term coined for want of one word to express the *theory* of history, including the history of all the other fields listed).

All these fields can be applied as well as theoretic, and may be single or combined into a compound field. Applied aesthetics would comprise, among other things, dancing, painting, and the composition and performance of music; applied chemistry would involve chemical engineering; applied history and psychology appear in politics and law. What we have on prior occasions termed chronotopology would combine theoretic and applied phases of categories (G), (A), (B), and (C). Medicine and biosimulation are applied fields combining in the second instance, (A), (B), (C), (F), and also (D) and (E). The further distinction within the applied fields, particularly in applied aesthetics, of "composing" versus "performing," can also differentiate valid emphases, connoted, for instance, in the designation "research physician" as distinct from "practising physician."

Literature searching, abstracting, and information retrieval have as their central problem that of an accurate indexing system. Both classification and cross-indexing (which is more sophisticated form appears as coordinate indexing in an agreed-upon meaning space) possess serious shortcomings in solving that problem. But the same problem of proper and adequate categorization is central to the quest in biosimulation for a language of power—a linguistic substrate so fundamental, fluid, and accurate that commands and reactions (including verbal reactions such as descriptions) could be formulated in it that would lead to intelligent behavior on the part of machine or human hearers and speakers of such a language.

The indexing problem concerns itself, in the context of biosimulation, with the nouns of the language of power: the categories that structure observable existence. We suggest a typological indexing system as sketched above, with at least the vertical levels mentioned, which run through the horizontal typological spectrum: namely, *theoretic* and *applied*, the latter further subdividing into *composing* and *performing*.

1.2. But all the categories of knowledge are unified in the world, which of itself makes no distinction between sociology and physics, emphasizing no particular context of interpretation. The fields of knowledge become separate only on analytical reflection and in precise imagination. Nature is not nicely divided into biology, mathematics, chemistry, and so forth. Yet language by its very nature must so divide. Division arises with communication.

Now the smallest single unit that contains all the categories, as nature or the world contains them, is *man*. More accurately, two human beings; for only then is response to an equal, and hence a full or unitary psychology, possible. Actually, four human beings in the form of two pairs is the operationally irreducible minimum, as then responses of each sex to a member of its own *and* of the opposite sex become possible, providing in miniature one of the two basic contexts of possibility in human relationships. The second context is age. If we combine with the four units we already have the three fundamental subdivisions of age—younger, same age, and older—we then arrive at 12 as the primary sociological group.

Such a group would thus comprise our basic two pairs in the three age-types and so be a paradigm of all interhuman relationships. The relation of human beings to what in comparison is sexless and ageless (mostly called God or the Divine, and lately in totalitarian regimes, "The State") provides a 13th and central, although abstract, component for the 12-fold group minimally necessary for *society*. Thus 12 is the sociological unit, 2 (the conversational minimum) is the psychological unit, and 1 is the biological unit in general, becoming 2 for sexed species' survival.

1.3. Just as all the categories of knowledge merge implicitly in the human being, just so *a fortiori* must all scientific disciplines, which are after all but the systematic reflection of these categories, merge in anthroposimulation in its completest sense; that is, a necessary condition for man's artificial replication of himself is clearly the convergence of all the scientific disciplines, principally philosophy (as logic and epistomology), mathematics, physics, biology, and psychology. It is these fields that must intimately interact in any attempt to solve the problem and answer the riddles posed by anthroposimulation.

But in such an attempt the convergence of the categories we have just mentioned must be explicit and not merely implicit. Let us try to gain a graphical idea of how this may be accomplished. We perform an inversion transformation on the development of all knowledge throughout the categories, the human being as the originating and implicit center for all this knowledge being the basic fact of the entire process. If we perform such an inversion on the endless radii of the endlessly subdivided directions of knowing, we obtain a new center combining all fields explicitly, whereas they were all combined implicitly in the first center which was the constitution of the human investigator. The shape of the mapping is, of course, a circle of infinite radius and in general a corresponding hypersphere of whatever dimensionality is given to knowledge. Our previous typology (1.1) employs a seven-dimensional manifold for the mapping of knowledge, which is symbolically attractive—in addition to its nonarbitrary conformity to the facts themselves—since the n-hypersphere attains maximum spread or "surface" only in the seventh dimension, that maximum being $(16/15)\pi^3$ for a 7-D hypersphere of unit radius.

In employing this working typology one must bear in mind two indispensable facts. The first is, that by "knowledge" in this context we mean understanding and not simply description or a memorized catalogue of empirical observations without explanation of why they are as they are, or how they came to be as they are. The second fact is that the ordinal number of each of the categories we already listed possesses significance. Their sequence is one of decreasing knowledge in the sense just specified: we have more explicit conclusions in logic and mathematics than in physics; more in physics than in chemistry; more in chemistry than biology, etc. We have least scientific knowledge of history, knowing very little indeed about the patterns of movement of events, either human or natural. There is a profound connection between this decreasing sequence and the very constitution of man's ability to know. It is such connections that provide keys to unlock the biosimulation problem.

1.4. The subject of inversion mapping leads us quite naturally to the concept of entropy, which can be considered as a logarithmic inversion-mapping $[\log (1/p)]^*$ of the probability of deviation from a statistical norm. In other words, entropy increase is concomitant with non-deviation. Information in the Shannon sense, on the other hand, results from a logarithmic inversion-mapping of a measure of the probability of conformity to a statistical norm. Thus entropy measures conformity or expectedness; and information, unexpectedness, which is at the heart of the meaning of "news." The fact that the concepts of deviation and conformity have heretofore not been explicitly mathematically connected with those of information and entropy, accounts for much of the lack of sharp and clear thinking on these concepts in their modern form, despite the amount that has been written on them.

1.50. The nature of both information and entropy may conveniently be considered in the context of a logarithmic inversion-mapping of a probability: the logarithm of the reciprocal of a probability. Great semantic confusion has arisen in the literature, however, because the probability in each case happens to be the contrary of the other probability; so that though the formulas looked alike, the semantic referents were mutually contradictory. We can, however, write unambiguous formulas in a manner that follows.

*Or $(E)p = 1$, where (E) is $\exp E$, E being the entropy, and p is the probability mentioned. (See 1.50.)

Since 1956 the writer has been developing a generalization of the notion of entropy, to be released for publication, along with other material, in due course.* Suffice it here to state that entropy, H, in its most general form, turns out to refer to an average interval or mean period, P, measured in time or some time analogue, between perturbations in the system whose entropy is sought. Generalized Shannon information, S, becomes then related to the frequency of perturbation, f, defined in terms of the limit of the ratio of the number of observations evidencing perturbations, to the total number of observations.

Specifically (f being measured as stated),

$$f = P^{-1} = \text{antilog}_2 (-H)$$

whence

$$H = - \log_2 f$$

the base 2 being convenient because it can so easily handle switching circuits and by reason of its deep involvement with the theory of combinations, since $\log_2\left(\sum_{r=0}^{n} {}_nC_r\right) = n$ for integral n.

The probability of any particular moment of observation *not* showing a perturbation is thus $[1-\text{antilog}_2 (-H)]$, which defines p_c, the probability of conformity. We can now, in the spirit of Gibbs, write for the generalized Shannon information $S = -\log p_c$, noting that $p_d = f$ where p_d is the probability of deviation or perturbation, whence by substitution

$$p_d^{\frac{S}{H}} + p_d - 1 = 0$$

Recalling that $p_d = 2^{-H}$ we have $2^{-S} + 2^{-H} = 1$ as the fundamental condition of invariance in the theory of generalized entropy.

The fact that H and S combine in any case to yield an invariant is noteworthy. This invariance, however, is not absolutely fundamental,[†] for it holds only for a closed system, logical or physical.

---

* "Alphabets of Reality" (2 vols.), now in preparation.

† This fact constitutes a restriction on Dr. MacKay's conclusion in [16]. MacKay's notice of the confusion between thermodynamic and informational ideas was interesting to the writer, coming to his attention after the present paper was completed; for it demonstrated that without a generalized concept of entropy, any categorical distinction between thermodynamic and informational contexts (such as MacKay attempts) tends to produce as much or more confusion as the confusion it essays to correct.

Note that if we defined S as $(-\log_2 P)$ we would then simply have a more arbitrary result from the viewpoint of statistical mechanics. The equation of invariance then becomes $1 - 2^S = 1 - f$ or $H + S = 0$, the usual popular assumption. However, this invariant is not nearly so much in accord with the facts as is $2^{-H} + 2^{-S} = 1$; for in the latter, when H is infinite, S is zero as it then should be. Hence $S = -\log_2(1-2^{-H})$, as already derived, is preferable. An interesting parameter arises on setting $S = \log_2 \csc^2\theta$, $H = \log_2 \sec\theta$, wherein θ has a time-like character.

1.51. In any given physical instance, both H and S can be derived from the probability of deviation from or conformity to a statistical norm. That is, the first probability p_d is a mean probability of scatter; the second, p_c, a mean probability of cluster within the given distribution representing the system. Since p_d and p_c have an inverse relationship, if either is 1(0), the other is 0(1). Total conformity is a zero scatter, the values of all data falling within a certain range of each other, thus determining the norm. Total scatter, the values of no data being within a certain determined distance of each other, is zero clustering.

In terms of a Gaussian distribution, which has a central region of conformity (definable most simply as composed of all the ordinates between the two points of inflection) and a pair of regions of deviation on either side, p_d and p_c become accordingly measured. In a secant-curve type of distribution, where there is one central region of deviation surrounded by a pair of regions of polar conformity, p_c and p_d are accordingly different. Such a type of distribution, for instance, would characterize iron particles in a magnetic field. In any case, p_d — and hence p_c— is empirically calculable in any situation by direct observation, if explicit calculations of the distribution mapping of the situation or system are not available.

1.52. The units of H and S are now unified and made mutually intelligible by the considerations of the foregoing paragraph, in which the primal invariant is explicitly derived from operational definitions. There has been much confusion connected with the statement "information is negative entropy"—for in Gibbs's formulation thermodynamic entropy too was the negative logarithm of a probability, and Shannon's later work resulted in the same functional form for the quantity he thereby defined as information. The fundamental difference between Gibbs's entropy and Shannon's information lies in the *period-frequency relation* between the two concepts, and they are clarified as well as unified only by that relation. The heart of our generalization of entropy consists in pointing out the fact that the nature of entropy is that of a mean period between perturbations. The nature of Shannon information is that of a perturbation frequency. This conception, as we have seen, includes both thermodynamics and communication theory as aspects of itself, along with other disciplines.

Thus by these unified definitions, whose unity is made possible through the basic and very general concept of entropy as an average period between perturbations in a system,* we can speak easily and accurately of the entropy of an author's style, of an esthetic design, or of society under a given political system. Also biological entropy becomes quantitatively discussible. One approach would be to determine the maximum interval between heart-beats just able to sustain animal life at a given metabolic rate. This interval, that rate being a minimum, as in hibernation, would then measure the upper allowable limit of biological entropy for the given species.

1.53. In a different field, that of political theory, the number of perturbations or disagreements permitted by a government would provide an inverse measure of the entropy of society under that government. It is readily seen that the ideal of the totalitarian and "welfare" state of paternalistic socialism is that H should approach infinity, whereupon by 1.50, $S = 0$: that is a condition of no disagreements whatsoever with the ruling clique (who in political fact are "The State") on the part of the rank and file.

On the other hand, democracies also, but to a lesser extent, develop pro-entropically to form steering committees, lobbying groups, or other forms of more or less concealed power groups, each of which (run by cliques) carries also on a smaller scale totalitarian aims and methods in itself, and all of which disagree with one another except for the temporary combinations formed for transient expediency to thwart another power group or a combine of them. Here, though entropy is maximized regionally, it is still kept down

---

*A necessary qualification, since perturbations irrelevant to the system are not referred to Shannon information but to noise. However, all noise conveys some Shannon information if the system context is accordingly widened. The two kinds of perturbations have a flexible boundary, to be redefined in each instance according to the scope or context of the system being considered. What was once just the noise of static has become radio astronomy, for example.

with respect to the whole society by the continual mutual perturbations of the different groups. Thus the conformism of the mass-
state (a society consisting of large numbers of confused and propa-
gandized individuals easily commanded by a single dominant power
clique) is, in the generalized theory of entropy, isomorphic to a very
slow heart-beat, approaching death, the death of maximal positive
entropy. For although ideally $S = 0$ only if H is infinite, in the
nonlinear context of bio-entropy, life is generally stifled and ceases at some critical value long before S is reduced to zero, just as
in physical observation oscillation damped by friction will not continue to decrease indefinitely but will suddenly stop when the amplitude energy is reduced to the point where it cannot cope with the
coefficient of friction. Hence there is a final sharp cut-off.

Yet—now turning to the game theory of political survival—the
totalitarian State, being less constrained in its external strategy
by internal disagreements (the fact that the internal conformity is
gained via brutality and consequent apathy in critical areas matters
here not a whit), tends in situations of conflict and war to have a
winning advantage over more democratic systems, which are ex-
ternally more constrained by their allowed internal perturbations as
well as by their value systems being opposed to the brute material
utilitarianism of the termite totalitarians.* The same situation
arises between two opponents, one more unscrupulous than the
other. We can state as a theorem of strategy that, other things being equal, the more unscrupulous will win because his strategy is
less constrained. Without the advent of a highly improbable perturbation from the unknown, it is not the meek but the most unscrupulous who will inherit the earth. This is a purely objective

---

*The image is not simply formal, but exact. Termites, the result of some
200×10^6 years of communism—older even than the bees and the ants—
eat each other's excrement until it is inedible further even by them, and
then—use it for wall mortar! In the final obscene triumph of utilitarianism, communism ends in coprophagy.

Here is the inglorious end, as proved by guaranteed survival practices
over hundreds of thousands of milennia, of the Totalitarian State's
promises. The end, ironically enough, results in the degeneration of
individuality even in the power clique that first made those promises in
order to subjugate the masses it hypocritically and ruthlessly pretended
to be rescuing from the terrible responsibility of standing on their own
two feet and helping each other as need be and as men, from the varied
richness of their own individualities, now long since brain-washed away.

corollary of our theorem of strategy, just given. Of course there is another possibility: the earth, in that case, may be destroyed or rendered unlivable for man before it could be so claimed. The possible third alternative is given in the preceding footnote.

1.54. It is apparent that the generalized notion of entropy is part of the theory of all changes whatsoever, and hence fundamental to what we in 1958 termed chronotopology, the study of the structure of time. Moreover, generalized entropy is vital to what we may call meta-level cybernetics (the principles of control over the science of control itself), since control is now seen necessarily to involve the increase of entropy; while, conversely, the increase of perturbations would decrease control.

One of the inherent limitations of biosimulation is now evident. A perfectly controllable simulation could not be a perfect simulation because the basic negatively entropic characteristics of living things could not be constructible in the automaton.* On the other hand, a perfect simulation by the same token would be uncontrollable to an inescapable extent.

1.55. We must also remind ourselves while on this subject that "information" in the Shannon sense is not meaning but "statistical news," as it were. Thus, nonsense words relative to, say, English, contain *more* Shannon information than a lexicographical message, for the simple reason that the nonsense message is, English-wise, more statistically unexpected, and hence in this sense more "newsy" or "informational," though by no means more informative. These limitations on the use of the brilliant Shannon definition of information may be disregarded only at one's peril.

1.6. The reason for the importance in biosimulation of Shannon information, involving $-H$ as it does, is simply the fact of the central importance of communication as a means of organizing interactions and of coordinating action programs. Communication always has as its aim the reducing of information of this kind. The more informed an entity is, the less it can be surprised.

Thus to decrease Shannon information in a system is to control the system, and hence to make it meaningful to the controller because unpredictability for him is eliminated. Where information-reduction is impossible, so is control, and thus also the conveyance

---

*This fact will also emerge in the discussion of supra-Turing machines in section 3 of this paper.

of our meaning (via instructions or commands) into the "system" which in the context of the problem of this Symposium is a humanoid or man-like machine operating in a given environment. Without a flow of communication from the environment feeding back through the machine to keep Shannon information a minimum according to in-built instructions, the humanoid could not operate.

Further probing into this question of information-reduction or control leads us to a crucial point, now considered.

1.7. A major conclusion emerging from the foregoing discussion is that the logic of machine construction and that of scientific discovery are fundamentally denials of each other. This is a basic metalogical theorem in the logic of biosimulation. The theorem is important principally in the psychological-sociological context, and provides the means of reaching an advanced level of insight leading to self-development on the part of the human operator, should he so desire. Let us look now at the practical denouement of the theorem.

The scientific discoverer seeks to expose himself to more and more unexpectedness in order to be able to deepen his hypotheses and theories accordingly. He seeks thus to introduce more and more Shannon information into the system of observer-nature. The system designer or the cyberneticist, on the other hand, seeks to eliminate as much as possible all Shannon information from the system of machine-plus-environment, where the "machine" may be man-like or even contain human components. The apotheosis of such a development would finally have to seek to eliminate the distinctly human character of the human components, for along with unexpectedness dies individuality, and Hitler's "Gleichschaltung" or psychological leveling is achieved. Eliminated too, in such a development—a process which modern states seem to find more and more convenient as the population grows—would be, by the inherent metalogic of the situation, the very type of scientific-discoverer intellect which gave birth in the first place to the possibility of the machine. Fanatical cybernetics can thus end in failure.

It is important to note here on purely logical grounds that the continued application of the machine-idea to human groups will work against the logic of scientific discovery in terms of the metalogical theorem above stated, eventually resulting in the degeneration of that activity and in the death of the goose that laid the golden egg. The fact that such a degeneration is called "efficiency" as a thinly veiled form for "control" will matter very little in the final result.

If this theorem of the opposing logical demands of cybernetic control and scientific discovery in the societal context is disregarded, the price of invalidity in this case is nothing less than the progressive loss of the ability to create and of the creative imagination of man.

1.8. The nature of randomness, chance, nonsense, and probability involves concepts at the heart of the theory of entropy and information, and hence, as we have seen, of biosimulation. These will bear some discussing within the logical context that the theme of the present paper sets. Our ideas may perhaps best be fixed by considering first the nature of probability.

2.0. PROBABILITY, RANDOMNESS, AND NONSENSE

2.10. When it is said that an event, E, considered as one possibility in given situation, has an occurence probability—or simply a probability of, say, 0.333..., it is meant that if the occurrence situation be indefinitely repeated the proportion of the number of times that E occurred to the number of times that E did not occur would approach 1:3 as a limit.

The distinction between "indefinitely repeated" and merely "indefinitely prolonged" is crucial: probability theory has meaning only within the context of a situation which in some way is cyclic or repeatable. Without such a periodic context the concept of a *trial* is meaningless.* Thus, p_g being the probability of an event g and G_t being the number of observed occurrences of g in t trials, while $\bar{G}_t$ is the number of non-occurrences of g in t trials, we have

$$p_g = \lim_{t \to \infty} \frac{G_t}{t} = kn^{-1} \quad \text{and} \quad p_{\bar{g}} = \lim_{t \to \infty} \frac{\bar{G}_t}{t} = (n - k)n^{-1}$$

$p_{\bar{g}}$ being the probability of non-occurrence, where n is the total number of possibilities in that context of the situation which is being observed, such that k of them include g and hence $(n - k)$ of them exclude g's occurrence.

2.11. It is also essential to the concept of probability that the conditions in the situation which ensure the possibility of repetition or recurrence either remain constant or change predictably as a

---

*In fact, the applicability of scientific method itself is directly dependent on repetitive or cyclic elements in the environment's structure and/or development.

function of time. It is equally essential to the concept of probability that the initiating forces which precipitate each repetition or trial do not remain either constant or predictable, but vary stochastically over at least a range sufficient to ensure the occurrence of the same total of events which include the event whose probability is sought. (If these forces were predictable no question of probability could of course arise, since the situation then would be wholly determined.)

2.12. As an ideal experiment and example let us consider a numbered wheel like a roulette wheel except that no ball is used as an indicator, but rather an arrow pointing toward the center of the wheel from a little distance beyond its rim. The coefficient of axial friction of the wheel is a constant, or it may even be expressible as a definite function of the initial angular velocity and the time. If the wheel is spun, say, clockwise and stops so that the arrow points exactly to the line between two numbered sectors, then the convention is adopted that the result is taken to be the number just about to be indicated. One may talk meaningfully about the probability of a given number being indicated on such a wheel just so long as the initial force setting the wheel in motion is unpredictable on any given occasion or if the number of divisions on the wheel, furnishing the total number of possible indications, does not unpredictably change. If this number predictably changed, then one could still speak meaningfully of probability which would, however, no longer be expressible as a limit ratio but as a limit function.

It is easily seen that the unpredictability of the initial and subsequent perturbing forces is just as essential as the predictability of the cyclic conditions in defining and validating the concept of probability. In most cases where the application of the probability concept is valid, this latter predictability is usually present in elementary form as constancy or virtual constancy within the pragmatically allowable limitations of experiment.

Several things are already clear from the discussion. It is obvious in examples such as the wheel just mentioned that if we knew the initiating and perturbing forces there would be no probability at all involved. In such cases the notion of probability hence assumes a purely subjective character and corresponds to the amount of Shannon information, or unexpectedness, that there is for us in such a situation because of our incomplete knowledge of it. For an observer with complete knowledge of such a situation there would be no question of the notion of probability arising. At the other extreme, purely statistical probability arises where both n and k in the equations of 2.10 are not known, but only G_t.

2.13. It is now also clear that probability and statistical prediction are two variations of the *same* concept. This was already evident in part from the fact that a probability concretely arises as a limiting ratio between the number of occurrences of two types of events as the number of trials increases indefinitely. Such probabilities are calculated from a definite knowledge of the structure of the situation in the sense of the conditions in that situation which control and shape the possible outcomes of some definite repeatable manipulation termed a trial. Statistical predictions are, however, calculated without knowledge of the controlling conditions, but only of the types of events which those conditions produced. Thus statistical probability and probability *per se*, which is calculated *before* the fact, are differentiated essentially only by the observer's degree of knowledge of the situation.

2.14. Even in probability in its most knowledgeable and pure form there is an absolutely necessary statistical factor: for, as we have seen, the variation of at least the initiating forces (whose effects may in turn be varied by subsequent perturbing forces impinging on the trial before its outcome, such as air movement and pressure modifying the twisting trajectory of a tossed coin) must have some sort of statistical distribution in the sense of being explicitly unpredictable. Indeed, if the entire notion of probability, including statistical inference, is to be something more than simply a reflection and a mapping of subjective ignorance, then there must be an element of absolute unpredictability in the variation of the trial-controlling forces. The condition of "absolutely unpredictable" is essential, for if the variation were only relatively unpredictable in our present state of knowledge, the prediction might always be refined until it would become evident to all that the prior "unpredictability" had been merely a subjective matter.

2.15. Hence, if the notion of probability has any objective as well as a merely subjective meaning, absolute unpredictability must be present in the situation. It is worth noting what this in turn implies. Absolute unpredictability would be nothing less than the observable behavior of a free will somewhere along the line. This logical step is further clarified by keeping in mind that absolute unpredictability means also that the unpredictability would remain despite any lack of limitation on the means of observation. With any such limitation the predictability would only be relative again, this time not directly to the knowledge of the situation but rather to the means of gaining such knowledge, that is, to the means of observation.

In the light of the present discussion it can be seen that practically all usage of the notions of probability and statistical inference refers to subjective ignorance. The only case where it would not, would be those situations where free will was critically present so as to affect the outcomes of the trials. Probability (other than 0, impossibility; or 1, certainty) as objective reality is logically inextricable from the objective reality of a free will in operation.

2.16. There is only one further point to be made here; namely, the simple fact of the objective nonexistence and consequent inapplicability of the commonly used and received expressions "equally probable," "equiprobability," "equally likely," *et al.*

Even in the very simplified example of the wheel mentioned above, it is clear that the wheel always must be spun with its numbered sectors in some definite configuration with respect to the deciding arrow. With any given set of initiating and perturbing forces it is also clear that no two numbers have the same chance of being chosen. In fact, it is not difficult to calculate, from any such initial configuration, the numbers which and only which might be chosen by the arrow, given a small enough range of unpredictability in the forces such that less than one complete turn of the wheel could eventuate from that unpredictability, or a range such that only some fractional number of turns of the wheel is involved. If the angular difference between the final position of the wheel caused by the maximum possible forces and that caused by the minimum possible forces were equal to an exact number of turns, then only would we have a situation of equiprobability, and only even then if the unpredictability were such that it was absolutely evenly distributed throughout the range of its possible results. Only in this extremely special type of stochastic function could nothing whatsoever be said of a particular number except that as the number of trials was indefinitely prolonged, its appearance in front of the arrow would tend to eventuate in $(1/n)$th of all the trials performed, where n is the number of divisions on the wheel. If, however, the unpredictability of the forces were not associated with an exact number of turns, then certain numbered divisions would at once be favored, given any initial position of the wheel at rest with respect to the arrow. It is clear that equiprobability is an extremely rare situation.

2.17. The theory of partitions can also be used in demonstrating the extreme unlikelihood of "equally likely." When we study the possibilities of partitioning a given number of units, we are at once struck with the fact that the particular partition comprised of equal portions is not the most probable. Indeed, the frequency of recurrence of such partitions decreases in an exponential function as the number of units to be partitioned increases. Thus, while the probability of equipartitions resulting from partitioning five units is approximately 0.286, the probability of equipartitioning seven units falls to about 0.133, or less than half. The rate of fall would be even faster had we not included in each instance the anomalous partition, composed of only one group, as an equipartition. The use of the theory of partitions is particularly appropriate in probability theory because the partitions of a number represent the various ways an addition may be performed to produce the same number. Similarly, all the probabilities of the various outcomes of a given situation must sum up to 1 or certainty.

There is a useful isomorphism between the various kinds of partitioning of numbers and the various outcome structures, based on probability magnitudes, in a given situation; as well as between the theory of partitions of numbers and the partitioning or parceling of energy in situations where the distribution of energy among a number of otherwise similar units, such as molecules, is being considered. Thus, for instance, there would be possible 15 different energy distributions in a group of 7 particles, the partition 3-2-1-1, for example, denoting that distribution involving 4 different energy levels, 3 of the particles being on one level, 2 sharing another level, and the third and fourth levels being each occupied by 1 particle. The 15 possible energy distributions in this case arise immediately from the fact that 7 can be partitioned in a maximum of only 15 ways. The theory of partitions, though it has heretofore not been used much, if at all, in problems of probability and energy distribution, can shed powerful light on those subjects. Similar invalidities in the naiveté of assuming "equal likelihood" attend the indiscriminate use of a heuristic concept of "equipartition of energy" among particles for which the greatest probability for any energy state is in fact attached to those states characterized by an *unequal* partitioning of energy among the particles.

2.2. The terms "random" and "randomness" are surrounded by much the same semantic traps and confusions as the term "probability," and must be very clearly analyzed.* In the theory of feedback control systems, when the controlled variable becomes uncontrollable by the reference or command variable, it is often abused in the literature and called "random" or senseless, in much the same way as a driver might abuse his donkey if it didn't go where he wanted it to go. But from the donkey's point of view there is nothing random in the response at all: the grass is just good at that part of the road. Actually, the only logical meaning of "random" in a scientific context is "irrelevant." A random response thus becomes simply a response irrelevant to what we are considering should be its controlling cause, and without sense within the limitations we have set for the sensible.

2.21. These considerations confront us again directly with the logical demands of scientific discovery *versus* machine design, which we saw before in 1.7. Let us imagine that a scientist performs an experiment with a certain set of ideas and hypotheses in mind. But something interferes with his predicted effect each time he performs the experiment—some apparently "random" phenomenon. After rechecking his apparatus to weed out possible instrumental defect or failure as the source of the interference, his results continue to be perturbed and differ from his predictions of what they should be and of the outcome of what to him should be a controlled situation. Incidentally, the situation so far is the typical setting for a new scientific discovery.

But our "scientist" now simply calls the disturbing effect "random" and reduces his apparatus and his ideas until he can perform an experiment that omits the disturbing effect. He makes nature or the environment conform to his hypothesis by the simple expedient of reducing his outlook.

In the research laboratory we would call such a man the perfect non-scientist, i.e., the one having no scruples or perhaps even cognizance about employing Procrustean distortions in attempting to coerce the environment to conform to his partial notions of what it should be. Yet in the logic of machine design and systems control such a practice is perfectly legitimate and even necessary.

*As an example of the confusion turned full circle, the term "random" has even been misdefined as "equiprobable" or "equally likely," confusing "random" with an erroneous notion of probability to begin with! (See 2.16.)

Here we *must* try to eliminate from the machine's or system's behavior all "instability," which is to say all nonconformity with our commands, instructions, or desires. In systems control and machine design you must use the opposite logic to that which you would use in seeking to make a new scientific discovery.

2.22. It is now evident that the rules for successful sociopolitical organization, whether in a secular or ecclesiastical framework, are much more similar to the rules of systems control and machine design than to the *modus operandi* and outlook of the scientific discoverer, or the creative individual in general. The first type of logic seeks and must seek to eliminate nuances and individual differences because they are uncontrollable or deemed irrelevant to the aims of control; the second type of logic and outlook must equally seek to pay attention to all such differences because of their significance in the context of understanding and experiencing reality. The latter seeks to make effective what the former seeks to make ineffective.

2.23. The misuse besetting the first type of logic is not that a control or forcing set of values must be adopted in the theory of automation. But the danger is that such a value system, by dint of constant use, shall gradually habituate its users to itself and pervade their entire behavior, becoming their dominant logic in all situations, even those where only the second type of logic and outlook is valid. This type of validity is particularly characteristic of human beings when their distinctive humanity is being considered. Thus all theories of society based on maximizing communications, in order to reduce Shannon information in the service of eventual conformity to some kind of centralized monolithic "planning," are foredoomed to failure by the inherent inadequacies of their logic.

Now we are appropriately ready to consider the meaning of "nonsense," having just witnessed that the ungoverned use of cybernetic logic can provide such an excellent example of it.

2.3. We must be careful to distinguish between the "nonsensical" and the "irrelevant," and avoid erroneously using the former in a pejorative sense to denote the latter. Randomness is quite properly irrelevance, but irrelevance is not nonsense, which is a much stronger term involving either (a) impossibility, or (b) contradiction, or both. Something irrelevant may become relevant when a wider circle of relatedness or a deeper criterion of consideration, involving a new dimension of inclusiveness, is introduced. There is no such thing as absolute randomness or irrelevance. See in this connection, in the Appendix on the axiom of choice, the portion discussing random point sets in n dimensions.

But to be absolute nonsense is to be inherently not amenable to any criterion but that of nonsense itself, which is not a criterion of inclusion but of exclusion from all categories of logical inclusion. As distinct from absolute irrelevance, absolute nonsense, as we shall presently see, may be possible. Relative nonsense or non-sense restricted to a certain universe or universes of discourse, certainly is possible. For something may be perfectly possible under one set of conditions while utterly impossible under a more re-stricted set of conditions. Another aspect of nonsense, self-con-tradiction, is simply the expression of a certain type of impossi-bility. Thus, "the brown horse is green" becomes possible and non-self-contradictory in the context of "is" meaning "is paint-ed." "The wind is blowing west and east over this hill" is self-consistent if "is blowing" means "is blowing on two different at-mospheric levels."

2.31. Much nonsense or paradox is due simply to ambiguous or omitted modifiers of meaning which are essential to self-consis-tency. "I was lying then" poses no problem; but the truth value of "I am lying now" has bothered logicians ever since ancient Greece, one of the latest unsuccessful attempts to grapple with it being found on pp. 19-21 of a useful article on automata in the January 1961 issue of *Behavioral Science*. However, the second statement is no more essentially difficult of truth analysis than the first. We must simply recall that this use of the present tense must refer to another content, to another sentence. Thus, "I am lying" means "I am lying if or when I say so and so." To take the grammatically complete sentence "I am lying" as semantically complete is the en-tire source of the fallacy and the confusion in such problems. In general it has not been seen that grammatical completeness is by no means a sufficient condition for semantic completeness. Now matters are clear. If "so and so" is false, then "I am lying" is true; and if "so and so" is true, "I am lying" is false. But grammatically complete sentences cannot be truth-evaluated without knowing their omitted portions. Thus much of what on a more superficial view ap-pears to be nonsensical becomes sense on a hard second look. Such statements may be called pseudo-nonsense. Most paradoxes are.

2.32. Sentences can refer both to their grammatical or physical structure and to their semantic content without any necessity for paradox arising if we keep in mind that they can do the latter only if they are semantically as well as grammatically complete. Since having been subjected to the now happily waning influence of logical positivism or dogmaticism, we have been far too psychologically enmeshed in the glorification of syntax and grammar at the expense of the basis of the premises on which the truth (as distinct from the mere validity) of all conclusions must rest, that basis being semantic or pertaining to meaning in the sense of a verifiable correspondence with experience.

Validity is a necessary but not at all sufficient condition for truth, which involves always the fact that the language used must be an experientially verifiable mapping of an experience already made. The confusion of validity with truth and of grammatical with semantic completeness has been fertile of misunderstanding in this domain. These matters are important for biosimulation, for we must know how to code instructions to an automaton unambiguously and without involving commands impossible to perform under the conditions of performance laid down in the metalogic of the system. We later will consider the theory of instruction, which is important enough to deserve a section to itself.

2.33. A second (for the first, see 2.31) famous but quite different example of nonsense, which even the fine thinker F. P. Ramsey did not penetrate because for the traces he followed he did not have the tools, is the old but still undigested chestnut of the *Principia Mathematica*: the "paradox" of the "class of all classes." Here the difficulty arises from another fertile source of logical error: using the same word in the same phrase or sentence, once in a lexicographically correct sense and then in a totally or partially erroneous sense which does not belong to it. Mostly this is done unconsciously because the user himself did not perceive the illicit semantic shift. "A class" of objects means a selection of p properties (where $p \geq 1$), these p then being used to gather together as a "class" all the objects possessing (as qualities, rather than characteristics of position in some space) that property or group of properties denoted here by p.

Now the extent P of all *possible* properties is provably infinite, because the number of possible mapping rules is at least as infinite as function space; and conformity to a function (e.g., the function "greater in a specified degree than 17") is a property. This being so, it is at once seen that no class or selection can exhaust P. "The class of all classes" is a nonsense phrase in an absolute sense (see 2.3), for the first use of the word "class" is not lexicographical, because something absolutely rather than merely relatively all-inclusive is no longer a class or selection.*

3.0. THE MAJOR PROBLEMS AND INHERENT LIMITATIONS IN ANTHROPOSIMULATION

Some indicated directions toward solutions of the first, and some adaptations to the second, will be sought.

3.1. If we want to replicate a human we must at least be able to replicate what human thinking can do. Hence demonstrations of the human mind's capabilities can serve as practical targets for biosimulatory research. More important to the theme of this paper, such demonstrations can also throw light on the subject of whatever inherent limitations may exist in the nature of the anthroposimulation problem. Sources for the derivation of minimal conditions of automaton capacity are also thus revealed. We shall now discuss some such demonstrations which appear notably useful in the ways we have mentioned.

3.2. *Question to the reader*: If an evil and very wily jinn offered you your choice of existing henceforth in any dimension through, say, the tenth, with the one condition that you would be forever confined to the topological possibilities of the dimension you chose, which would you pick? Perhaps the seventh, which maximizes the "surface" or $(n - 1)$-dimensional content of a hyper-

---

*"The class of all classes" is an example of absolute nonsense; more absolute than even Lewis Carroll's hypothetical pigs with wings, for it is not inconceivable that morphogenetic forces could have produced a porcine form possessed of appendages for flight, just as they did for that rodent with wings, the bat. It is difficult to match the depth of nonsense of a "class of all classes" by any of the actually far less nonsensical "nonsense rhymes" of Carroll.

It is interesting to note that Russell in other instances shows a recurrent contempt for lexicography, which discipline, however, must remain the basis of honest and meaningful communication. We cannot use a word in an admitted lexicographical sense and then proceed to use the same word in an unallowable way which does violence to the first sense. This feint becomes even more indictable when, as with Bertrand Russel, it is employed without either warning or admission.

sphere, or the fifth, which maximizes its "volume"—or the fourth, which contains the greatest numbers of kinds of regular hyperpolyhedrons of any other dimension. All these would seem to offer possibilities, and yet they would all land the chooser in an eternal dungeon as the everlasting slave of the wicked jinn.

The only correct answer, as in the old fairy tales, seems the most humble, the dull lead concealing the real gold. A wise man, forced to choose, would say "I choose, O Jinn, the zeroth dimendimension, the point." At this the demon would vanish into an angry grease spot in his defeat. For any point, as we shall immediately see, can be shown to be developable into an n-dimensional space ($0 < n \leq \infty$) of either finite or infinite extent, a point thus being able to contain a mapping of all Hilbert space.

3.3. The fact that an infinity of points can be mapped in one point is easily and first seen in the center of a circle, which maps every point on the circumference, or again, in a vertex point of an angle, which maps all the infinities of points of all the possible opposite sides that can be drawn to complete the triangle.

Now consider that any point may be regarded as a rolled-up line of finite length (not an infinite line, for that would coil up to yield a dimensionality of at least two). Hence any point, $0 = k/\infty$, can be topologically expanded by uncoiling into the line of finite length k. Now the infinity of points comprising k can also be uncoiled at right angles to the surface to produce a finite solid, and so on through the dimensions.

By a topologically double process we can do more. Imagine the infinity of points comprising k, now being uncoiled *along* the direction of the line, each uncoiling point pushing the rest of the line in that direction as they all uncoil. Now we have an *infinite* line generated from the original point. Continuing by uncoiling in this way we would have infinite space of any dimension. It is important to note that this line cannot in one step re-produce the point, but must first undergo a longitudinal coiling-up of all the unrolled points that compose k, thus producing the finite line k again. Now k in turn would have to roll up on itself in a second topological transformation, giving again the original point.

Shakespeare is thus literally vindicated of all poetic license when he exclaims through Hamlet: "Though bounded in a nutshell, I count myself the king of infinite space."

3.4. Obviously, on the strength of the demonstrations of 3.2 and 3.3 in the light of 3.1, our proposed humanoid would have to be able (that is, would have to be programed) to handle infinities and infinite sets as usable realities of its "thinking." We at once arrive at an inherent limitation on biosimulational goals, for by the very nature of the construction process—adding one part to another—a machine, however complex and subtle, could never be made, if an infinity of parts were necessary to its functioning, for the simple reason that it could never be finished in the first place, much less begin to operate.

Moreover, if the rules for handling infinite sets could be incorporated into the program of a finite humanoid, even then there would be the insurmountable barrier of how it could recognize the essential character of an infinite set, determining unambiguously that it *was* an infinite set. The fact of creative extrapolative thinking,* whereby not only previous results in a given context are extended, but whole contexts are leaped, appears to remain a distinctly human secret. That secret must remain in its ultimate reaches dark even to man himself, for the knower in us by definition cannot be known. Epistemology ends in a dark mirror. In analysis Socrates is overridden: we can *be* ourselves, but not explicitly know ourselves. The knower is always by the nature of things a meta-level above the known. Man cannot get behind himself, and to this extent cannot built himself.

3.5. There is another reason for the necessary stipulation of infinitization in the programing: a self-instructing machine, the complete humanoid, the full goal of biosimulation and cybernetics, must be self-determining or the goal is not achieved. Programing, as we have more and more learned since Goedel and Turing, must be in digital form to be adequate to the problem. But of all numbers only their upper limit, infinity, is self-determining. Whatever formal arithmetic operation is undergone by infinity by way of any other number, leaves infinity unchanged. It is ultrastable in Ashby's sense. Thus $\infty + k = \infty$, $\infty - k = \infty$, $\infty \div k = \infty$, and $\infty \times k = \infty$, where k is some finite perturbation operating on infinity. This is true of no finite number, even including zero as the lower limit of absolute value. One must hence analyze the nature of infinity to ascertain the boundaries of the biosimulation problem, a conclusion we have now reached for the second time and independently.

*Ordinary logic is interpolative and hence tautologous.

We have already (3.3) discussed something of the topology of the point, which we saw was far more complex than might be suspected. We have also alluded (3.1) to the simple fact that counting numbers is an endless process. Clear recognition of this fact, however, leads to far less trivial matters, and in particular to the conclusion of regarding infinity as a limit. Thus where n is the cardinal value of the kth ordinal number, counting by units in the most elementary fashion,

$$\lim_{k \to \infty} (n_k) = \infty \qquad \text{and} \qquad \lim_{k \to \infty} (n_k)^{-1} = 0$$

Thus, geometrically speaking, the limit of possibility in dividing a finite line segment into smaller and smaller portions is a point. Conversely, a figure of finite surface, say a square, can be considered as the area of an infinitely long line. This is most simply seen by extracting the infinitely long line from the square as one would extend a jointed measuring rod which had been folded up on itself in equal lengths. Obviously, only an infinite line could generate the square, for a finite line so folded up upon itself, however long, would result not in an area but simply in a line equal to the side of the square. Similarly, since a surface has no thickness, a finite strip would fold into a rectangle which, if the folding length were equal to the width of the strip, would be a square. But an infinite strip would thus generate a parallelepiped with a square base.

We therefore see that the minimal assumption required to define infinity with regard to real numbers is that infinity must refer to at least the $(n+1)$th dimension if the numbers represent magnitudes in the nth dimension. Similarly, under such circumstances, zero must represent at most the $(n - 1)$th dimension. Thus "zero volume" has a perfectly definable interpretation as either the finite surface S, the finite length L, or the point P. On the other hand, "infinite length" is definable minimally as a finite surface S, or generally as a finite content C in any dimension above the first. We have on previous occasions pointed out that complex numbers $Re^{\theta i}$, where $i^{-i} = e^{(4n+1)(\pi/2)}$, n being zero or integral, require three dimensions, and not simply two, for their adequate minimal representation. In the light of the present discussion, therefore, infinity in the context of complex numbers must refer to a finite content of at least a dimensionality of 4: twice the minimal dimensionality required to represent infinity for real numbers.

3.6. The essence of Turing's results [30, 31] consists in his showing that man could construct in machine form any finite number, where the size of the number represented the complexity or multiplicity of the machine's program. But typologically and essentially, there is no difference at all between any number, however great, and any other number with reference to infinity. Both 1 and 1 trillion become zero in that relation. Symbolically, $0 = k/\infty$, where k may assume any finite value. (If also $k = 0$, the zero defined by the previous equation is of higher order and we have $0/\infty = k'/\infty^2 = 0^2$; where $k = k'/\infty = 0$.)

Thus to construct a machine corresponding to infinity means to construct infinitely more than any ordinary or specialized Turing machine of finite order k. Now we shall seek a definition for the order of a Turing machine.

3.61. We might first try by the route of considering the quantity of information-communication characterizing a given Turing machine. In this context a reasonable measure might be the amount of information (defined in bits) absorbed by the processing center, plus the amount finally released, such a sum being reckoned per unit bittime of processing, or

$$\text{Performance} = \frac{b_a + b_r}{(bt)_p}$$

But such a merely quantity-base measure is crude here because it is inadequate for what we are seeking. (However, it does also inversely measure the complexity of a program: the greater the number of logical states in the program, the greater is $(bt)_p$ in proportion to $(b_a + b_r)$, which is as it should be; for all other things being equal, the greater the program complexity the less efficient the performance because the more time is wasted in the sense that the time is consumed more by the processing than it is freed for using the results.)

3.62. We do better in our quest of defining the order of a Turing machine by recalling that Turing's and Goedel's approaches deeply agree, and by seeking on that basis to arithmetize* the innate capability of a Turing machine.

---

*To arithmetize is, ultimately, to map on a linear continuum. This statement is now further explained. All of logic, as we pointed out in 1958, can be shown to be transformable into topology: to the connectivity of regions each of which we may call a given set of properties, $p \geq 1$. All logical relations may so be transformed into topological criteria, which in turn are grounded in the nature of the continuum. These matters will be more explicitly seen in the Appendix to this paper in the section on the axiom of choice.

Thus finally logic becomes a branch of topology; and, inversely, topology becomes a mapping of logic, which hence in its turn is able to be the *discussion* (that is, a linear permutational mapping of word symbols themselves compounded by permutation from a simpler set of symbols called an alphabet) of mathematical reality. Thus logic and mathematics, rather than either being primal to the other, are isomorphic.

Words and numbers (including syntax of words and operations on numbers) remain our two basic symbol systems which we must refer to and use in the precise expression of any act of thought. Both of these systems have as their fundamental characteristic the fact that they are linear and permutational. If we wish to express a thought, either audibly or visually, or by means of another sense such as touch—or even in the crude "words" of pantomimic gesture—we must use a linear permutation of symbols. This is true for the author trying to describe a scene, for the orator seeking to express his reactions to something, or for the deaf-and-dumb mute expressing thoughts by means of a system of touching in various orders different places on another's palm. It is also true of mathematics, whether in the domain of proofs or computations, that there is a system of experience involving linear permutations of symbols that is used.

Evidently, expression or recording, which is simply the fixing of expression in duration, is very deeply involved with the necessity of linear permutations, the linearity being ultimately imposed by the nature of occurrence. It is probably also imposed by the fact that our own natures are such that we can only with the greatest difficulty become aware of time in a more than one-dimensional fashion. The fact that we can even perceive our limitation in this respect, however, is sufficient for hope. For we could not see it unless we had in ourselves a more adequate perception of the nature of time than mere linear occurrence could afford.

The involvement of linearity in expression goes very deep, as even nature uses it in encoding our genetic traits in the long, helical chromosome molecules of our cell nuclei. In this connection the reader is referred to the Appendix to this paper, the section dealing with the DNA-protein code and the adequacy of linear permutations for the mapping of any configuration in a space of any dimensionality.

The English language is fortunate in having two words, "set" and "class," that refer to the isomorphic duality of topology-logic. The very etymology of the word "set" refers to position and placement, that is, to the topological aspect of the isomorphism; while "class" refers to quality and content, or to the logical aspect. Since the isomorphism is fundamental, it is useful and necessary not to use these two words interchangeably.

Although sets may be made to symbolize classes (the simplest example being Euler's circles), there is a certain reduction of naturalness of the symbol system, with a consequent increase of arbitrariness, if this is done. That is not to say, however, that doing it cannot be useful under certain circumstances; but we must nonetheless not lose sight of the limitations of what we are doing. For classes ultimately refer to content or nature, rather than to placement: to cardinal rather than ordinal numbers; while sets ultimately refer to placement and ordinality. The "ultimately" is specifically justified. The theorem (concluding the Appendix on the DNA-protein code) that linearity is adequate to reproduce and order a configuration of n elements in d dimensions, links sets with the ordinal numbers.

The interplay of these two fundamental categories of placement and content, ordinal and cardinal, is the basis of that stroke of probably ancient Pacific genius which eluded Sumero-Babylonia, Egypt, and Greece, and which gave us the first place-value number system, found originally only among the peoples of the Indian Peninsula and among the Mayan races, whose earliest colonies also bordered the Pacific Ocean, on the western coasts of Central America. The profound concept of an explicit, significant zero was, of course, part of this rich heritage since zero is the basis of any place-value number system.

Finally, then, we have the following:

A set is a group of elements all placed or *set* in a certain way so that they share one or more positional characteristics by reason of their placement or gross position.

A class is a group of objects *classified* or selected by their all sharing one or more characteristics which are independent of the objects' position or mutual configuration in some space, and which are independent of observing or viewing conditions except, obviously, when those conditions are themselves the class being considered; when, however, they must still be considered independently of any possibly superimposed second-order viewing conditions which in turn could distort them. Such characteristics in the domain of mathematical objects, for instance, could be intrinsic, non-projective size or shape.

The gamuts of relative or projective size and shape form sets rather than classes since they may be referred to and occasioned by viewing distance and viewpoint (viewing angle)—data of gross position.

Although transformations or encodings (the theory of transformations and the theory of codes are isomorphic) from sets into classes and classes into sets may be made by reason of the underlying isomorphism first noted in this discussion, what is still necessary is (1) always to know which is the reality and which is the imagined transformation of it in any given case, and (2) always to be aware, when one is using a map, code, or transformation, that one is doing so. *For isomorphism does not mean a relativity of reality.* One may, for instance, be perfectly entitled to map the elements of a given set as equilateral triangles, and all objects sharing another positional characteristic as squares. But that is a very different thing from saying that the objects in question *are* triangles and squares.

We can see then that an ordinary or specialized Turing machine can be represented by a number, k, connected in some specified manner with the complexity of its program, i.e., with the number of logical functions R and data types (independent variables) D which furnish by their combinations the number of internal states required by the program. Let us call such a machine T_k, where k is this number.

Considering the fact that all functions of two or more variables can be represented by a series of parametric equations relating the variables in pairs we have as a measure of k the expression $[R(D)!]/[(2)!(D-2)!]$ which reduces to $RD(D-1)/2$.* Furthermore, we see that

$$\lim_{k \to \infty} T_k = uT_n$$

In some situations sets may be fundamental reality-wise. Then any classes into which they are mapped are codes, with heuristic value. If, in a different situation, classes are the given realities, then the sets into which they may be encoded for purposes of consideration and understanding likewise must not be accorded the reality of the classes in this situation simply because the two are isomorphic.

Scientific method, indeed, can now be seen in its essence, which is to constantly deduce what is the intrinsic, and what the observational form and nature of a given phenomenon, and to carefully separate the two. That is why a dogmatic relativistic epistemology is actually anathema to science and defeats the scientific intention and the scientific quest and enterprise; for such dogmatism asserts that the observational form cannot be distinguished from the object, and thus that we cannot deduce what has given rise to our observations, whereas this sort of reconstructive deduction is the very essence of scientific method. Without it, science would degenerate into mere description, compounded with skeptical defeat. A very young child is a complete and natural convert to the relativistic epistemology, and is quite unable to distinguish between effects of viewpoint and intrinsic nature, regarding a circle seen in perspective as an ellipse, indistinguishable from an actual elliptical object of the same size. Much less would the baby—or the dogmatic relativist—be able to reconstruct the intrinsic object from the distortions or mappings of the sensory images to which it gives rise.

*It is an interesting sidelight that the sum of all integers from 1 through m is thus seen to be $_{(m+1)}C_2$ the combinations two at a time of $(m+1)$ things, which are of course the triangular numbers; and that in general $_nC_d$ furnishes the hypertetrahedral numbers in d dimensions.

where uT is a universal or general Turing machine, that is, one that can be made to simulate any given ordinary Turing machine T_k. Hence the above measure is not yet adequate to define a universal Turing machine since it would allow k to become infinite even though only R or only D did so. Yet a universal Turing machine must be able to imitate the program of any ordinary Turing machine with any number of logical relations or of data types in its program.

It is clear then that the infinity which k approaches to yield uT can be approached only if both R and D also approach infinity and not if only one does. The simplest function pattern expressing this requirement is that k should be measured by $RD/(R+D)$, which thus becomes a part of the theory of Turing machines. Here, unless *both* R and D are infinite, k is finite. Indeed, if we assumed that we could construct an ordinary Turing machine to handle an infinity of data types, then the above measure shows that its limitation, preventing it from being a universal Turing machine, would consist in the finite number of logical relations that it could handle, since under these conditions our measuring function would yield $k = R$. Since the function is symmetrical, the same results *mutatis mutandi* would obtain in the case of a Turing machine able to handle any logical relation but only a finite number of data types, thus yielding $k = D$. We may thus amplify our previous definition and write

$$\lim_{D,\ R \to \infty}(T) = uT_n$$

3.63. Turing, in calling the internal states of uT "states of mind," was plainly very close to the opinion that a universal Turing machine was the biosimulational goal. Let us, however, pursue the indicated development and specify the meaning of the number n above, where n refers to the order of uT in question. By what sort of metaspecifications is a universal Turing machine to imitate a T_k? This is the pertinent question behind the apparence of the new subscript n. Put another way, how does uT_n select among all the possible T_k? The specification of this "how" will also thereby specify that the uT we are considering is of the nth order; that is, n will be specified. And this "how" must be built into the uT. We can not talk logically or meaningfully about the properties of a machine if, as so many uncritical cyberneticists unfortunately persist in doing, we are including in those properties the presence of a hidden and unmentioned human operator who actually is running the machine by remote-control-in-time.

The last phrase is extremely vital to the subject because, though all of us are accustomed to the triviality of remote control through space (via wires or electromagnetic waves, for instance), we tend to forget the equal triviality of speaking of the "self-operation" of a machine remote-controlled not through space but through time,* by means of an ultimately humanly and previously designed program built into the machine's physical or operational structure. As we will again have occasion to mention in the portion of this paper devoted to the theory of instruction, a very basic form of instruction is *construction*. Programs may be constructed as well as encoded in the machine.

We have all seen dexterous street hawkers jerking "animated" cloth and metal rabbits by thin controlling threads invisible to the gullible crowd, staring in wonder at the portentous phenomenon of artificial animation. Let us not follow in the hawker's or stage illusionist's footsteps, deceiving ourselves in the bargain simply because we have complicated our spatio-temporal threads of control beyond our enfeebled powers of recognizability, drugged by our wishful thinking in terms of powers we would like to have but by no means yet possess.

The height of such misguided abuse of cybernetic thinking would finally amount to the open fanaticism (as has been done) of calling man inferior to his own constructions which are "free" of mind, which in turn is not "free" because it is "constrained" by its own intelligent memory! The sophistry of equating "free" with "free of" is apparent; a moron or a machine may indeed by *free of* intelligence, but an intelligent human being is *freer* than either of them. "*Free of*" simply means "without" and by no means "free." The constraints imposed by the knowledge of previous error and of how to avoid it *are* freedom in most tangible from. The word "constraint," as the word "free," has two very contary nuances, and the basic fallacy pointed out in 2.33 of using the same word in two quite different senses in the same passage so as to give the reader the impression that only one sense is being referred to, must be avoided like the moral and logical plague that it is.

Such a misuse of words, if allowed to invade our thinking, would finally transform scientific discussion into degenerate propaganda.

*For example, to say that a time bomb is "self-operating" simply because the human beings who built and set it are not there when it explodes, shows the sterility of ignoring remote control through time.

And twentieth-century life, surrounded by totalitarian dogmatism in one form or another, bears eloquent witness to the dangers and degradation which are the fruits of disregard of honest lexicography. A new Babel is arising, not out of the confusion of physical tongues but out of the confusion of meanings. If it is not protested and opposed by dedicated practice it will threaten the intellectual liberty and health of mankind.

3.64. So we see that to be free to choose among the T_k means exactly that there are specifiable grounds for the direction of the use of that freedom. Moreover, as before noted, this "how" must of necessity be built into the uT. The sole exception is when $n = 0$, uT_0 being simply a universal Turing machine without any power whatsoever to choose which program or programs it will simulate. In this case there must be the direct intervention of a human operator in deciding what T_k is to be simulated, or which in which order.

Where $n = 1$ the uT has the power of choosing various T_k in patterns stemming from a singly specifiable goal.* Where $n = 2$ the goal would be two-fold; and where $n = q$ the goal would contain q independent aims the union of which would constitute the goal. Thus for a universal Turing machine the complexity of goal structure† is analogous to the program complexity of an ordinary Turing machine. In the Appendix to this paper, in the section devoted to the axiom of choice, it will be evident that one can extend and further generalize the notion of a Turing machine; and that this generalization depends directly on the metadimensionality of meaning. There are only three higher-order generalizations or meta-levels of a Turing machine beyond uT, mention of which is made in the Appendix cited.

---

*It should be kept clearly in mind that though a machine can be said to have a goal it cannot have a purpose, for it simply imitates purposive behavior without the experience of the least trace of desire. All that machines can be made to do is more and more subtly, with increasing variety and finesse, to imitate animate behavior without experiencing or being able to experience that behavior in terms of emotion, desire, or feeling. Desire and emotion are not constructible. In the biosimulational context, only the imitation of behavior, and not the emotions behind it, is constructible. Thus robots cannot be said to be either ethical or unethical, no matter how complex their goal structures. Man cannot shift that responsibility to his creatures. That way madness lies.

†Measured as n in the uT_n of 3.62.

3.7. We have seen from paragraph 3.5 that infinity in relation to some finite T may be considered as denoting conjunctively (1) a higher dimension than that in which T exists; (2) the meaning of k in the sense of that which uses T and by which T is used as an element of an operation which stands in meta-relation to its elements, of which T is one*; (3) some finite, undetermined number in a higher dimension that that of T; and (4) something which T cannot render unstable.

Hence ultimately, "the meaning or significance of T," when T is a Turing machine of any constructible metalevel, becomes precisely the creator of the Turing machine, the human himself who uses it. Aside from him the machine has no meaning. Hence to construct infinity in the Turing-computability context means, among other things, to construct a device capable itself of constructing and using any such Turing machine or any general-purpose computer. We have reached von Neumann's problem. But there are still greater difficulties; for by the specifications (1) and (3) the construction of infinity would also include in its meaning finally something as much beyond devices or machines as a higher dimension is beyond the dimension below it, i.e., something with at least one more degree of freedom than a machine, however subtle. Hence the biosimulational goal is seen to envisage *not* a device, whatever else it may be, but something of a different order. That goal cannot be achieved simply in terms of a machine, however complex. The fond delusion of hoping that complex robots could "evolve" from more simply programed ones is thus seen for what it is: invalid. The possibilities must all be in the initial, finite program, and the "evolution" is tautologous. Non-trival evolution therefore depends on infinite possibilities in regions ultimately beyond any constructible meta-level, and hence only on something with at least one more degree of freedom than any constructible device, however subtle, as has before been shown.

3.8. We arrive at the same conclusions of 3.7 by considering the fact that infinity is by definition incompletable. Despite some erroneous usages observed in the literature, it is salutary to realize that "any number however great," E, is no more infinity than "any number however small," ϵ, is zero. In fact, as we saw in a somewhat different connection in 3.5, an entire dimension lies be-

---

*See the Appendix to this paper, the section on the axiom of choice.

tween E and ∞, or between ϵ and 0. Geometrically put, in any line segment of magnitude ϵ, however small, there is an infinity of points; and no line segment of magnitude E, however large, is infinite. The confusion between infinity and "a number increasing without limit" (as well as the like confusion between zero and "a number decreasing without limit") vitiates the bases of much of the "rigor" of even some twentieth-century proofs in analysis. Neither zero nor infinity are numbers, but refer instead to at least one dimension respectively below and above that in which the finite number system lies.

Thus a minimum of three dimensions is a necessary condition for a complete (self-contained) number system. This fact is independently corroborated by performing an accurate geometric analysis of the expression $e^{\theta i}$ where θ is real,* whereupon we obtain its minimal geometrical representation as a cone of unit slant height in three dimensions. Since any number can be represented as $Re^{\theta i}$ (R being the slant height) we have again the conclusion that the minimum number of dimensions of a complete number system is three.

3.90. A humanoid, in the full sense of the biosimulational goal, must hence be incompletable in its *possibilities* of performance, which imposes a far more stringent condition than simply the endless tape of any universal Turing machine. This criterion can be cybernetically proved, in addition to the demonstrations of 3.7 and 3.8, by considering that any completed machine could be rendered unstable and unreliable in the presence of some perturbation not contained in its necessarily finite vocabulary of response-formations. That is, any completable machine would reach a point where it could no longer minimize or even decrease Shannon information.

3.91. Whether man can construct a system incompletable in some sense weaker than the stringent one of 3.7 is answered in the affirmative by his construction of logic, which was shown by Goedel to be incompletable and hence undecidable, when it extended beyond the rather naive and reductive propositional logic of the *Principia Mathematica*, just as the entire set of natural numbers is so; and hence arithmetic is also incompletable.

Incidentally, considering (a) the one-to-one correspondence of the natural numbers with all propositions, and (b) their clear incompletability, is the swiftest means of arriving at Goedel's useful con-

*See [20], p. xlix passim.

clusion without the cumbersome methods stemming from a notation not completely appropriate to the problem. But probably if Goedel had said it more simply he would not have been so readily believed. Even so, it took about 20 years for his conclusions to be recognized, although they were long apparent in the simple fact that counting numbers is an endless process. So far removed from each other are the exigencies of truth on the one hand and human psychological needs on the other—needs which science futilely deceives itself do not affect it; although the same psychological forces that so violently and annually change the topological structure of ladies' hats dictate the far graver and less admitted fashions in the history of what is "acceptable" in scientific thinking.

3.92. Since the realization of a supra-Turing machine, $(\infty) T$, such as is discussed in 3.7, is the central problem of biosimulation, it will repay us to examine one further aspect of the nature of infinity, namely its relation to enumeration. It has been assumed since Cantor's time that there was such a thing as absolute nondenumerability and that this supposed fact was the basis for a higher order of infinity than the denumerable variety of, for instance, the set of algebraic numbers.

However, there is reason and evidence to conclude that there is no such thing as absolute nondenumerability, the apparent nondenumerability that exists merely reflecting our own ignorance of the nature of numbers and our lack of ingenuity of finding the basis for a serial order among the irrational numbers.

Thus the rational fractions are quite nondenumerable if taken in order of their magnitude. Under this criterion of sequence there is no "next" fraction. However, an absolute arrangement of all fractions in order of magnitude exists. For the rational fractions are denumerable if taken in order of magnitude of denominator, with magnitude of numerator as the sub-ordering rule, thus: 1/1, 1/2, 1/3, 2/3, 1/4, 2/4, 3/4, 1/5, 2/5, 3/5, 4/5, 1/6, etc. Thus denumerability simply means "possessing a rule of unique and exhaustive selection." The fractions are nondenumerable with respect to one criterion of selection (total magnitude) but are denumerable with respect to two submagnitudes (that of denominator and numerator taken seperately though in relation to each other). With the second criterion we can specify a "next" fraction, which on the basis of the total magnitude of a fraction is unspecifiable.

There is no reason to assume that we shall not find a constructive method of introducing a discrete type of serial order into the real numbers when we know enough about the order in the modes of structure of irrational and particularly transcendental numbers. We shall return to these problems presently, first considering some further aspects of denumerability.

For example, to define number as a class of all classes obtainable by one-to-one correspondence with itself is saying nothing more than that an integer is the sum of its units, something which had been, of course, known for centuries and which does not define number. Number will not be defined until we understand what is meant by a continuum, and its definition must embrace zero with its diaphanous clouds of infinitesimals and the infinites with their successive unscalable reaches. Number is not to be defined by Russellian word-play. Moreover, Russell is not even formally original in his definition. As a basis for cardinality, one-to-one correspondence was first put forth by Georg Cantor in the 1870's with some none too happy results, for Cantor's view of transfinite cardinality makes all denumerable infinities equal, which they are not. (See also 3.94.)

3.93. Infinity has never been clearly enough understood, nor has its reciprocal, zero. As already seen, these two mathematical concepts are not numbers, properly speaking, but rather designations for infinite classes (the orders of zero or infinity) of numbers, all characterized by the fact that they stand in relation to finite numbers as do limits to the terms of endless sequences.

It was stated in 1873 as a theorem by Cantor that the decimal forms between zero and one could not be ordered. Yet they can be uniquely ordered by the following rule: invert the decimals and use the integer so obtained as the ordinator.* Thus 0.0016 is the 6100th decimal; 0.14158 is the 85,141st; 0.1416 is the 6141st decimal, etc. Hence we can say, as shall soon be demonstrated by another method, that aleph-null = c, and there is no other transfinite number in the Cantorian sense. Yet even though the criterion of denumerability thus breaks down as a measure of cardinality in the infinite,

---

*The reader is referred to our abstract on the unique ordering of the decimal forms in the 1959 *Notices* of the American Mathematical Society. The fallacy in Cantor's proof is that what he terms an unspecifiable "number" is actually a function. The counter-example given in the text illustrates this logical lacuna explicitly.

we have a much more sensitive and accurate measure: that of ratio.

Dr. Warren McCulloch interestingly points out* that "there is one passage that I can only understand by supposing that he (i.e., Augustine) knew well why the existence of horn angles had compelled Euclid's shift to Eudoxus' definition of ratio... for things may be infinite with respect to one another and *thence have no ratio*" (italics ours). However, the indeterminate idea of infinity is what must be improved. First of all, it is necessary to see that two infinities may stand in ratio 0, 1, or infinity. Where a, b, c, d, r, and s are finite constants,

$$\lim_{x \to \infty} \frac{x^2 + ax + b}{x^2 + cx + d} = 1 \quad \text{and} \quad \lim_{n \to \infty} \frac{2^{n+r}}{3^{n+s}} = 0 \quad \text{while} \quad \lim_{n \to \infty} \frac{4^{n+r}}{3^{n+s}} = \infty$$

But two infinities may do more, and stand in the ratio of any finite number N. We have indeed been able to derive an expression for the square root of any number expressed as the limit ratio of two different power functions of the number as the highest exponent in both numerator and denominator approaches infinity. The formula is

$$x^{1/2} = \lim_{n \to \infty} \frac{\displaystyle\sum_{m=0, k=n}^{m=n, k=0} {}_{(2n+1)}C_{(2m+1)} \, x^k}{\displaystyle\sum_{m, k=n}^{m, k=0} {}_{(2n+1)}C_{(2m+1)} \, x^k}$$

Such limit ratios of two infinite functions provide a new calculus. The differential calculus is based on the finite limit ratio of two functions, each of which approaches zero, and may be symbolized as the operation evaluating $0/0$. The integral calculus may similarly be symbolized as the evaluation of $(0) \cdot (\infty)$. Finally, what we have just illustrated, and what we may call the *infinite calculus*, may be symbolized as the evaluation of ∞/∞. The mathematics of this calculus is still to be developed. Already, as we just saw, it has been able to provide the first explicit analytical expression for $x^{1/2}$ in terms of integral powers of x and integral coefficients.

3.94. By Cantor's definition of cardinality any two denumerable infinities are regarded as "equal" because such infinite sets may always be never-endingly paired off. But in Cantor's speculation it

*Page 3 of his lecture (the Ninth Alfred Korzybski Memorial Lecture) before the Institute of General Semantics, New York City, N. Y., March 12, 1960.

is forgotten that pairing off by units is a valid measure of comparative magnitude or cardinality only for *finite* sets. Two infinite denumerable sets A and B are inexhaustible by definition under the process of continuing to select a member not before selected. For if either could be thus exhausted it would and could not be an infinite set. New pairings of members from A and B may continue to be made indefinitely, simply by reason of the fact that it was given that both A and B were infinite sets with distinguishable members. Hence the unending ability to select and pair off members from such sets can give no inkling whatsoever of their comparative magnitude, much less provide a valid demonstration of their equality.

Indeed, the infinite set of all square integers is not only not equal to but is infinitely smaller than the infinite set of all integers, yet pairing them off endlessly can of course be done, for this is part of the definition or meaning of "an infinity of distinguishable members." We may arrive at the actual comparative magnitude of these two sets by considering that in the first x integers there are $f(x)$ squares, and $f(x) = [x^{1/2}]$, where the brackets indicate the nearest lower integer, taken to be the square root itself if x is a perfect square.

Now the probability p_s of choosing a perfect square from a fishbowl filled with counters numbered from 1 through x is given by $p_s = ([x^{1/2}]/x) \approx x^{-1/2}$. Thus for $x = 100$, $p_s = 0.10$ and for $x = 200$, $p_s = 0.07$, etc., the decrease being, of course, more than proportional to the increase in x. Finally, $\lim_{x \to \infty} p_s = 0$, thus demonstrating that the comparative size of the set of all squares in relation to that of the set of all integers is zero. The two are very far indeed from being equal. Though like all infinite distinguishable sets they can, of course, be endlessly paired off; that by no means, however, ensures their equality. The method of comparative probability of member selection is a far more powerful and accurate one than the simply empty tautology of endless pairing—a process and result which represent nothing more than the meaning of the phrase "infinite and distinguishable" in another form, and which emphatically do not establish cardinal equality. Any two infinite sets with distinguishable members may obviously be endlessly paired off with each other. To call this fact a "transfinite cardinal number aleph-null" is simply rather elegant nonsense, for the actual comparative cardinality of two denumerable infinite sets, as has been seen, may range all the way from zero of any order through infinity of any order.

Let us now consider all the real numbers between 0 and 1. Clearly, what we find out here will concern all the real numbers, since by prefixing integers to the real proper fractions all the other real numbers may be formed. In different terms, all the real numbers may be uniquely and exhaustively mapped on the points of the straight line from 0 to 1. All these points can in turn be isomorphically mapped on the set of all possible decimal fractions, including those with an infinity of digits. To measure this set irreducibly let us employ the dyadic number system, since all complications of a higher number system in this problem would be due only to the higher base. Using then the base 2, we find that there would be 2^n possible dyadic "decimals" of n digits.

Hence the total number R of decimal fractions between 0 and 1 is given in lowest terms by $R = \lim_{n \to \infty} 2^n = 2^\infty = c$, where c stands for the Cantorian cardinal measure of the set of real numbers. The result follows directly from the number of possible permutations, with repetitions allowed, of two things (namely, the two digits 0 and 1 of the dyadic system) in n possible different places on a line. But this same limit is also the measure in lowest terms (that is, using the base 2) of the infinite set of all integers, our familar aleph-null. Hence we may write, using the equality sign in the Cantorian context,

$$\text{aleph-null} = c$$

showing finally and unmistakably that there is only one type of infinity in this context of "pairing off," and thus the inadequacy of the Cantorian concept of transfinite cardinality.

3.95. The fact that $c = 2^\infty = $ aleph-null also permits us to observe that the real numbers are denumerable since they form an infinite set whose Cantorian ratio with a set of all integers is $\lim_{n \to \infty} 2^n/2^n = 1$. Let us try to observe this fact concretely, recalling here also the remarks made in 2.11. Let us slice the line 0-to-1 at will (with the proviso that no more than the first slice of any given length will be entered on the record, and that in the case of simultaneous equal slices of a new length, only one will be considered as the first slice of that length) and continue to slice the slices, entering the magnitude of each line length so gained on an accruing record. Let the jth act of slicing be termed s_j, and the number of different magnitudes accrued by the jth slicing, m_j. Where ϕ is the recursive quasi-stochastic function satisfying the conditions of the proviso, we may write

$$m_j = \phi\,(m_k)_1^j$$

Clearly now as j approaches infinity, m_j approaches the number of real numbers and becomes at the limit a cardinal measure of the infinite set of all real numbers. Since every s_j can be interpreted as a selection of at least one distinguishable member of the infinite set in question, to which an enumeration may be assigned, the above procedure shows that this infinite set is also denumerable by thus being able to be placed in one-to-one relation with the natural numbers, since a relation of next-ness has been able to be specified. In the Appendix to this paper, in the section on the axiom of choice, it will be shown how this entire basic matter of next-ness or choice-relation devolves upon the more fundamental condition of distinguishability. The following theorem can be proved: If the members of an infinite set are distinguishable, a choice-relation can be found; corollary: If the members of an infinite set are distinguishable, it is denumerable.

3.96. Denumerability in relation to infinity is as important in its way to the theory of biosimulation as the relation of dimensionality to infinity, which was previously discussed. The reason for this importance lies in the domain of what we may call the theory of instruction, which we will next consider, for instructions must be sequentially arrangeable in a discrete manner in order to be intelligible.

4.0. SOME CONSIDERATIONS ON THE THEORY OF INSTRUCTION

4.1. There is a very interesting recursive function which the writer discovered in refining the final text of this paper. It is defined as follows:

(1) n mutually distinguishable objects $a_1, \ldots, a_n$ are in a given linear sequence denoted by the subscripts.

(2) Any two contiguous objects in the sequence may be paired together according to some rule of relation, or left separate, as one pleases, and any number of pairs may be so formed or not, except that a_1, a_2 must always be paired.

The recursive function under discussion is then defined as

$$R_n(a_j) = P_{(1)(2)}$$

where $P_{(1)(2)}$ is the number of possible patterns formable in the given sequence by the application of the above two rules. We were able to show that there is an explicit and computable form for this quite general function, namely

$$R_n(a_j) = F_{(n-1)}$$

where $F_{(n-1)}$ is the $(n-1)$th term of the Fibonacci series, enumerated so that F_1, $F_2 = 1$; $F_3 = 2$, etc.

This function also plays, we found, a primary role in the operationally exact analysis of the fundamental arithmetic process of addition; thus the Fibonacci series lies at the roots of arithmetic and hence of number theory. This conclusion is further illuminated by the fact that all addition is implicitly recursive in the sense that the sum of a sequence of figures is at any stage dependent on all the preceding figures back to the first; and the Fibonacci series is the simplest explicit demonstration of recursivity in arithmetic. It turns out that the above function also represents the number of patterns of possible addition for n numbers; thus 5 numbers have $F_4 = 3$ patterns: $(a + b) + c + d + e$, $(a + b) + (c + d) + e$, and $(a + b) + c + (d + e)$. [One cannot add more than 2 numbers at a time.]*

Also, where M_n is the number of operationally different multiplications (that is, taking three groups of four things is not the same operation as taking four groups of three things) that may be performed between n factors to yield their product, then

$$M_n = 2 \, _nC_2(n-2)! \, F_{n-1}$$

The number of operationally different ways n numbers may be *added* [here $(2+1)+4+3$ is the same operation as $(1+2)+4+3$ but not the same as $(1 + 2) + (4 + 3)$ or $(1 + 2) + 3 + 4$] to give their sum is more complex. If A_n is this number, then

$$A_n = \, _nC_2(n-2)! \sum_{\substack{q=2 \\ p=0}}^{\substack{p=[n/2]-1 \\ q=[n/2]+1}} \, _{(n-q)}C_p \, 2^{-p}$$

*The rule that we first add the first pair does not lose generality, for we are now concerned with combinations of patterns and not, as in the later function A_n, with their permutations.

$[n/2]$ being the integral part of $n/2$, the number of values for both p and q being $[n/2]$.

These numbers increase rapidly, the number of operationally different ways of adding only 7 numbers being 9450, while 6 numbers can be added in 990 ways. The same 6 numbers could be multiplied in 3600 different ways. Five numbers can be added, it turns out, in (5)! ways and multiplied in 360 ways. The number 5 is a point of inflection, as it were, with respect to the number of ways a number of numbers may be added, since if the number of addends is less than 5, the number of ways is less than the factorial of the number of addends; while it is greater than that factorial if the number of addends is greater than 5. (Five is also a privileged Fibonacci number, since only for it does $F_n = n$, and ordinality and cardinality are unified.)

4.2. We have stressed operations because they are instructions. The operation $3 + 2 + 1 + 1$ means add 3 to 2, then add 1 to the result, and finally add 1 again to that result. The operation $3 + 2 + (1 + 1)$ means add 3 to 2, then add 1 to 1, and finally add the two results together. Though the ordinary arithmetical sum is 7 in both cases, the operations involved, and hence the instructions given, are quite different. Thus in the theory of instruction it is the *operational paths* by which a certain result may be obtained that are more important for consideration than the result. This emphasis is, of course, the essence of the idea of programing and program design.

The theory of instruction is broader, however, than simple programing, for we may build machines which can be instructed so as to work out their own programs according to the data they receive from their environments. Thus the theory of instruction includes programing on one or more meta-levels.

4.21. It also includes abstract linguistics.* Language, which

*Which properly should also in turn include the logical and semantic analysis of theories. Such an analysis of some aspects of relativity theory was undertaken by the writer in 1953 with the multiply demonstrable conclusion that the theory was formally inconsistent, since many of its principal results stem not at all from the relativistic assumptions (which lead to and concern simply differing scales of measurement arising from the enforced need to use signals of finite speed as a measuring device). Rather, those results spring from the (pre-Einstein) Poynting-Poincaré developments of Maxwell's electromagnetic field theory. And the inclusion of basic elements of Maxwell is not expressly admitted in Relativity

we have already cursorily mentioned in other connections, is very germane to the theory of instruction, for language of some sort is the substrate of all instructions.

N. Chomsky's work, deeply influenced by the prior and brilliant results of E. L. Post, is one example of the present intense interest in abstract linguistics, which of course has been springboarded by the advent of information theory. For the theory of instruction, however, a more operational rather than what amounts to an ultimately descriptive emphasis is required by practical exigencies as well as by theoretic considerations. We have space here for only a brief outline of the alternative we have in mind for linguistic analysis.

4.22. Let us consider the schema

[Which] WHAT ACTS [How and/or Why and/or When and/or Where]?

The meanings of the words are unrestricted. "Why" includes both the specification of a goal and the specification of a cause in its gamut of meaning, and "Where" includes both place, and conditions or circumstances of place; "When" similarly includes both time, and conditions or circumstances of a time; and "How" includes in its meaning both internal state or external means or extent.* "How is he doing his work?" may be answered by "sadly," "happily," "with a new hammer," "slowly," or "intently," for example. Similarly the "Which" of the schema may refer to physical or psychological contexts, and the question "Which man could do that?" may be answered by "The third man," or by "A good man," or "A man thus-and-thus skilled."

The two sets of brackets in the schema indicate that they belong to and are a part of the more general terms which follow and precede them respectively. "Which (sort of) WHAT" is still a "WHAT." Acting how, why, etc., is still acting.[†] Our schema is offered as basic, and hence most adaptable, to machine instruction.

Theory—or else the entrance of such elements is masked in its formalism, and mention of their existence thus suppressed. The depth of the inconsistency is such that, as shown in [19], ch. IV, even $E = mc^2$ derives directly from Maxwell, not from the relativistic assumptions.

*For "How much, little, long, far, etc.," belong to "How." Compare *"How so?"* Similarly *comment* ("how") in French links with an imperative of *commenter* ("to comment").

[†]To be or to become are also still to act, and are subsumed under ACTS in the schema; for both require actions to maintain themselves. For instance,

We must also mention here another very important context for "How"; namely, the context of what are normally considered objects grammatically, and not adverbs. "He whistled a jig" and "He whistled sweetly" both tell us "How" he whistled. All objects are in a very profound sense adverbs of manner. This is also true of prepositional objects. "In the house" or "in the woods" essentially qualify the in-ness and tell us the kind it is. These considerations clarify the ambiguous grammatical position of adverbial objectives such as "miles" in "I walked five miles," et al. The accusative is primordially an adverb.

4.23. Thus all language addresses itself to events and ultimately answers the question, with almost infinite variety of repetition, "WHAT ACTS?" Another view of the deep connections between language and occurrence is afforded by considering that all sentences are spoken in the present. Thus "He hit the ball" includes a speaker and a hearer engaged in a conversation in some present in which a past act of some third person is being mentioned. We cannot talk about either the past or the future except in the present. In this sense the sentence "He hit" is as much in the present as "He hits." The subject matter being discussed is simply in a different context, in this case a context of time.

In view of the observations (3.62) as to the linear-permutational nature of all expression, and the basis for that fact in the nature of occurrence, we see in the present conclusions but another instance of what we might have expected from our previous findings.

4.3. A glance shows the formula for M_n in 4.1 to be less complicated than that for A_n even though the operational combinatorial situation is considerably more complicated in multiplication. Why, we are now meaningfully able to ask, should the expression of the operations or performance in a less complicated situation be more complicated?

The answer is important to the theory of instruction: Because a more complex task with more uniform construction rules (i.e., fewer generating functions and hence a greater entropy in the generalized sense already defined in 1.5) is easier to perform or realize than a

---

a man cannot be without the blood circulating or without breathing for a certain time interval. A piece of iron cannot exist without the particles of its nucleus moving within a certain distance from each other. If such motions no longer hold, the nucleus fissions and the iron no longer is.

less complex task with more varied generating functions (i.e., a lower generalized entropy), that is, with a more complex conditionality of construction.

Thus to treat sequence always as significant, whether inside or outside a parenthetical pair, as we do in multiplication, is operationally and hence instructionally easier than to treat sequence within parentheses by a different set of rules than sequence outside operational parentheses, as in addition, even though the complexity (in the sense of the number of subpatterns) of results in the multiplication situation is much greater. The force of this principle naturally increases when large numbers of data and hence mass-operations are involved.

4.4. Thus performance, especially *en masse*, prefers uniformity of rules of action. Mass-performance is Procrustean. On the other hand, thinking seeks non-uniformities so as *not* to neglect them in Procrustean fashion, which for intelligence would of course be ruled out as a neglect of data of reality and hence invalid. The criminal tyrants' course of obliterating a part of reality already neglected, and then saying after its destruction that it no longer exists and hence one is no longer neglecting it, is of course a compound of fallacy and blind desire heedless of the reality of others' wishes or welfare, and hence utterly pathological, with past deeds standing contrary to false assertion. But intelligence can afford neither to be invalid nor, what is even more difficult to avoid, to be untrue. Intelligent thinking, seeking ever to test the validities it has gained against further reality to determine their content of truth, thus must ever search for new clues of non-uniformity with its previous conclusions in order to better its premises.

The food of intelligence is as much decreasing entropy, as increasing entropy is the nourishment of controlled performance. The two must remain in fruitful balance, which means that they shall operate within a value system that places the demands of intelligent thinking above those of mere performance for immediate results without the interposition of further thinking. Otherwise, the generalized entropy in the system or situation will increase to the point of purposeless, stagnant monotony, or to some other form of death, such as cessation, below any point of possible life or progress, of systemic action. We have thus arrived at the same conclusion we gained previously by the route of comparing the fate of Shannon information in a situation dominated by cybernetic control to a situation dominated by the decontrolling process of arriving at scientific discovery.

4.5. It is interesting that, like intelligent thinking, deep affection also pays careful attention to non-uniformities: to the least differentiation of behavior or expressed wish on the part of the object of attachment. A mother watches her baby very observantly and a master watches a pet the more closely the more attachment is present, noticing at once the slightest indisposition which passes completely unnoticed by another. It finally appears that mass-treatment, lovelessness, and valuing performance or results above the ways they are gained, all go together; while intelligence, individual treatment, affection, and the valuation of ways of behavior above possible immediate gains also belong together.

Because of these deep interrelations both logical and ontological, we see that the mass-treatment of man by man, with its cognate value system of putting the results of performance above the ways of behaving, ultimately can but lead to degenerate stupidity and the actual inability any longer to distinguish individual differences or fine, vital nuances of thought and feeling.

Brutal and coarse leaders ruling brutish masses is the end result of placing what is gained, rather than how it is gained, first in the human value system. If control or "getting the results I want" (for control is never objective at its root, but always based on what is desired to be gained) is likewise placed first, then cybernetics likewise degenerates.

4.6. If, on the other hand, the theory of instruction is developed and deepened, then it is always seen that if the instructions are less sensitive than the capacity of the system being informed by them, the sensitivity and capacity of the system is either wasted or degenerated by instructions that can in time destroy the unused capacity by either direct interference or by atrophy. The reductively fallacious assertion that man is simply a "device" leads, for example, to such degenerate types of instruction. It behooves us, therefore, in dealing with humans, to frame our instruction theory in the deepest sense, so that our instructions do full justice to the potentiality of a human being.

The applications of the theory of instruction go very far. Suffice it to say here that those applications importantly concern what are known as governments; for systems of law are nothing but instructions for behavior. Hence for the first time an impartial evaluation of political systems and law codes, on the basis of the theory of instruction and the generalized theory of entropy already discussed in this paper 1.50 *ff*, becomes possible.

5.0. CONCLUSIONS

We have seen how the enterprise of biosimulation involves some deep insights. We have also seen that it involves several profound and inherent limitations which have been specified in the foregoing paragraphs; and that in order to discuss that enterprise clearly or adequately, several scientific disciplines must be taken into consideration, the interrelation of which must be fundamentally explored and understood for the discussion. The limitations on the goal of biosimulation are, in fact, part of the nature of the universe in which we live. Hence the understanding of how these limitations operate must shed light on all the rest of our science, as well as on ourselves; and it is in that light that this paper is presented.

REFERENCES

1. W. R. Ashby, "Design for a Brain," 2nd ed., London, 1960.
2. G. Asser, "Normierte Postsche Algorithmen," Zeitschrift Math. Logik, Vol. 5 (1959).
3. M. Davis, "Computability and Unsolvability," New York-Toronto-London, 1958.
4. M. Davis and H. Putnam, "Research on Hilbert's Tenth Problem," Troy, N. Y., 1959.
5. F. B. Fitch, "Recursive Functions in Basic Logic," J. Symbolic Logic, Vol. 21 (1956).
6. H. von Foerster, "A Self-Organizing System and Its Environment," in "Self-Organizing Systems: Proceedings of an Interdisciplinary Conference," ed. by M. C. Yovits and S. Cameron, New York—London—Paris, 1960.
7. K. Goedel, "Die Vollständigkeit der Axiome des logischen Funktionenkalküls," Mh. Math. Phys., Vol. 37 (1930).
8. K. Goedel, "Über formal unentscheidbare Sätze der *Principia Mathematica* und verwandter Systeme," Mh. Math. Phys., Vol. 38 (1931).
9. K. Goedel, "On Undecidable Propositions of Formal Mathematical Systems" (mimeographed), Institute for Advanced Study, Princeton, N. J., 1934.
10. R. Jakobson, Ed., "Structure of Language and Its Mathematical Aspects," Vol. XII in "Proceedings of Symposia in Applied Mathematics," Am. Math. Soc., Providence, R. I., 1961.
11. L. A. Jeffress, Ed., "Cerebral Mechanisms in Behaviour," Hixon Symposium, New York and London, 1951.

12. S. C. Kleene, "General Recursive Functions of Natural Numbers," Math. Ann., Vol. 112 (1936).
13. S. C. Kleene, "Introduction to Metamathematics," Amsterdam, 1959.
14. D. M. MacKay, "The Epistemological Problem for Automata," in "Cerebral Mechanisms in Behaviour," ed. by L. A. Jeffress, Hixon Symposium, New York and London, 1951.
15. D. M. MacKay and W. S. McCulloch, "The Limiting Information Capacity of a Neuronal Link," Bull. Math. Biophys. Vol. . 14 (1952).
16. D. M. MacKay, "Entropy, Time and Information," in the proceedings of the Information Theory Symposium of London, 1950, multilithed, New York, 1953.
17. W. S. McCulloch, "The Reliability of Biological Systems," in "Self-Organizing Systems: Proceedings of an Interdisciplinary Conference," ed. by M. C. Yovits and S. Cameron, New York—Oxford—London—Paris, 1960.
18. W. S. McCulloch and W. H. Pitts, "A Logical Calculus of the Ideas Immanent in Nervous Activity," Bull. Math. Biophys., Vol. 5 (1943).
19. C. A. Muses, "An Evaluation of Relativity Theory after a Half Century," New York, 1953.
20. C. A. Muses, Foreword on chronotopology in J. Rothstein's "Communication, Organization, and Science," Indian Hills, Colo., 1958.
21. C. A. Muses, "The Homeostasis of the Fibonacci Series" and "Inherently Solution-Seeking Processes Irrespective of Starting Values," in Amer. Math. Soc. Notices (see 1959 and 1960 index).
22. J. von Neumann, "The General and Logical Theory of Automata," in "Cerebral Mechanisms in Behaviour," ed. by L. A. Jeffress, Hixon Symposium, New York and London, 1951.
23. E. L. Post, "Finite Combinatory Processes—Formulation 1," J. Symbolic Logic, Vol. 1 (1936).
24. E. L. Post, "Formal Reductions of the General Combinatorial Decision Problem," Am. J. Math., Vol. 65 (1943).
25. E. L. Post, "Recursively Enumerable Sets of Positive Integers and their Decision Problems," Bull. Am. Math. Soc., Vol. 50 (1944).
26. E. L. Post, "Recursive Unsolvability of a Problem of Thue," J. Symbolic Logic, Vol. 12 (1947).
27. F. P. Ramsey, "The Foundations of Mathematics," New York, 1950.
28. D. A. Sholl, "The Organization of the Cerebral Cortex," London and New York, 1956.
29. A. Thue, "Probleme über Veränderungen von Zeichenreihen nach gegebenen Regeln," Skr. Vidensk. Selsk. (1914).
30. A. M. Turing, "On Computable Numbers, with an Application to the Entscheidungs-Problem," Proc. London Math. Soc. (1937).
31. A. M. Turing, "Computing Machinery and Intelligence," Mind, Vol. 59 (1950).
32. A. M. Turing, "The Word Problem in Semi-Groups with Cancellation," Ann. Math., Vol. 52 (1950).
33. M. C. Yovits and S. Cammeron, Eds., "Self-Organizing Systems: Proceedings of an Interdisciplinary Conference," New York—Oxford—London—Paris, 1960.

34. W. Grey Walter, "The Living Brain," 2nd ed., 1957.
35. H. Wang, "A Variant to Turing's Theory of Computing Machines," J. Assoc. Computing Mach., Vol. 4 (1957).
36. N. Wiener, "Cybernetics or Control and Communication in the Animal and the Machine," 2nd ed., New York, 1961.
37. M. Yčas in "Symposium on Information Theory in Biology," ed. by H. P. Yockey, R. L. Platzman, and H. Quastler, Pergamon Press, New York—London, 1958.

NOTE ON BIOSIMULATION

This word was coined by the writer in early February 1960 when he conceived the idea of holding an international conference on what was obviously becoming an increasingly vital field: the imitation or simulation by man of the behavior and functioning of living things, such simulation being effected through man-made devices, i.e., machines in the broadest sense.

Protective mimicry, seen in the white winter fur of the weasel or the amazingly convincing form of the Asiatic leaf-butterfly, is not at all biosimulation, since these creatures are not making devices, but are simply endowed with types of bodies whose morphology and physiology work naturally together—without any conscious intention on the part of their owners being necessary—to provide concealment from enemy eyes, thus increasing the probability of their survival.

In the course of the conference at Locarno, Dr. McCulloch, in mulling over "biosimulation," remarked to me one day that the idea was good, but that he would prefer replacing the word by "biomimesis" since the latter had consistently Greek roots, and not one Greek and one Latin. I regretted to disagree with him then and still do now, on the grounds that 1) there are many examples in the English language where Greek and Latin roots are necessarily combined in a word in order to express an exact meaning. The dictionary is full of them. They provide one of the sources of the richness of the English language, starting with Latin itself which greatly enriched its vocabulary by incorporating Greek roots; and 2) "biomimesis" would imply the protective mimicry or convergent evolution found in nature rather than the design and fabrication of an artificial device by man, which device may suggest or even replace the behavior of some living creature, including man himself.

In view of these considerations, Dr. McCulloch's suggestion was not adopted because it would only contain confusing and contradictory implications and would be a bad word for biosimulation.

C.A.M.

CHAPTER VIII

THE SIMULATION OF LEARNING
AND DECISION-MAKING BEHAVIOR*

GORDON PASK

SUMMARY

In this paper we examine the peculiar difficulties of simulating the learning behavior of man, certain animals, and those mechanical artifacts in which forms of organization evolve.

The basic difficulty is due to the fact that these physical structures are adequately representable to an imperfect observer only as *self-organizing systems* in the sense of a definitive paper by Von Foerster, rather than as *systems* in the rigidly interpreted sense of Ashby.

We consider an underlying mechanism called "conceptual homeostasis" which appears to characterize physical assemblies said to "learn" and, since it is argued that the currently used experimental methods are unsuitable for investigations of learning, we propose alternative methods and illustrate their use in some practical applications.[†]

*The work discussed in this paper has been sponsored, in part, by Wright Air Development Division of the Air Research and Development Command, United States Air Force, through its European Office, under Contract No. AF 61(052)–402.

†The reader's attention is drawn here to the exposition of the Addendum to the present paper: "Comments on Evolutionary and Self-Organizing Systems" following section 5.2—Ed.

I wish to acknowledge my great indebtedness to the other participants in the Symposium, in particular, for prolonged discussion, to W. Ross Ashby, Heinz Von Foerster, D. M. MacKay, and Warren S. McCulloch, and also to Alex Andrew and Stafford Beer, who were unable to attend the meeting.* These gentlemen are in no way responsible, however, for the views expressed in this paper.

THE CONCEPT OF A SYSTEM

1.1. A universe of discourse, denoted U, is a set of abstract and irreducible statements, which are *logically* true propositions for a specified group of experimenters or observers, and which are communicable within this group. Each member of the group knows what conceivably could be the case (whatever is logically true). The discourse is a sequence of comments directed from one member to another, indicating that some of these possibilities are, or are not, apparent.

In this paper we chiefly consider a limited kind of U, suitable for discussing the values of a finite set $v*$ of n variables v_i—where $i = 1, 2, \ldots, n$—and a category of "behavioral propositions" about relations between the v_i and between consecutive expressions (or distinct "comments") in the sequence of discourse.

One form of behavioral proposition (I) asserts an "abstract state" of $v*$, that is, a complete description $V = v_1, v_2, \ldots, v_n$ of the values of the v_i. If the v_i are binary there is a set $V*$ of 2^n "abstract states."

Another form of proposition (II) asserts a relation between successive V, for example, that $V(r + 1) = F \cdot V(r)$, where r is an ordering label for any comment in the discourse, $r + 1$ an ordering label for its successor, and F a function with range $V*$ and domain $V*$. With binary variables v_i there are 2^{2^n} such propositions. We need only consider forms (I) and (II), although others, such as $v_1 = f(v_2, v_5)$, are permissible.

The most fundamental U depends upon the form of proposition that the population of experimenters *can* conceive of (upon concepts or relation, composition, rule, and regularity within the capacity of

---

*Dr. Andrew, though unable to attend because of a prior commitment, contributed a paper which was presented *in absentia* and which forms the first chapter of these Proceedings—*Ed.*

the brain). These limits are moderately determined for intelligent adults. Moreover, Piaget [36] has demonstrated the orderly extension of these limits, as children develop concepts formalized as logical multiplication, closure, linear ordering, and the resolution of components in several dimensions.

Experimenters commonly use a much more restricted U. Scientific convention dictates other and agreed constraints (propositions *agreed* to be true and as a deductive consequence propositions *agreed* to be false or "inconceivable" in the sense that they *are* not rather than *cannot* be conceived). Further, there is a subset of conventions and the corresponding "inconceivable" propositions which experimenters may be prepared to break and which are often determined by tentative theories, which are advanced from intuition, or, as considered in 1.5, on the basis of evidence gleaned from observation.

1.2. An attribute a_1, a_2, . . . is a property sensed by a well-defined instrument or procedure (we may extend this definition to include distinct and communicable percepts experienced by an individual). Kindliness, rate of climb, and length are attributes. A pair a_i, a_j differ as their sensory apparatus (instrument or procedure), and they are defined by the design of the apparatus.

Attributes are "of" the complete environment. The "objects" to which they are related have been well specified by sets of attributes found comparable and, in a sense we shall discuss, evidencing consistent behavior. Thus, we can determine the kindliness or length of a man, or the length or rate of climb of an airplane, but neither the rate of climb of a man nor the kindliness of an airplane. The objects "man" and "airplane" have the status of coherent and distinct entities because some of their descriptive attributes, being comparable, lie in the same subset, $a^*_{(man)}$ or $a^*_{(airplane)}$ as the case may be, and also because some $a_i \subset a^*_{(man)}$ are not included by $a^*_{(airplane)}$ and some $a_j \subset a^*_{(airplane)}$ are not included by $a^*_{(man)}$.

Measurements are definite events that occupy a finite interval, say Δt. A measurement made at an instant t yields the value of an attribute at t. The "measured value" of a_j is an element selected from an index set (commonly the index set of the integers), by evidence from the apparatus characterizing a_i, and ideally this element (or number) determines the property said to be sensed. But the apparatus is imperfect, the evidence is incomplete, and real "measured values" are necessarily uncertain indices of a_i. The apparatus can thus be conceived as a mechanism for selecting at each interval of Δt, but not more often, imperfectly valued indices of $a_i(t)$ or, for a set of a^* of m attributes $a\dagger$, imperfectly valued states $A(t) = a_1(t), a_2(t), \ldots, a_m(t)$.

1.3. A parameter is some experimentally controllable quantity that modifies the behavior of the attributes deemed relevant to the experimental inquiry. Whereas, in the case of attributes, the value is uncertain, the value of a parameter is known and controlled by the experimenter. But the constraint which is modified by the parameter and the effect that changing this constraint will exert upon the behavior of the system is more or less uncertain.

Let $y_1, y_2, \ldots, y_m$ be parameters. $Y(t) = y_1(t), y_2(t), \ldots, y_m(t)$ is the state of the parameters at the instant t (if the y_j are binary there are 2^M possible states). To change the values of the parameters is a definite event. It is convenient to assume that the state of the parameters can be changed each interval Δt, but not more often.

1.4. Let us partition the variables v_i of V^* into relabeled subsets:

$$v_1, v_2, \ldots, v_m = x_1, x_2, \ldots, x_m = X^*$$

$$v_{m+1}, v_{m+2}, \ldots, v_n = y_1, y_2, \ldots, y_m = Y^*$$

$$V^* = X^* \circledast Y^*, n = m + M$$

To observe or to perform experiments it is necessary to map a set a^* of the attributes of the environment onto some of the variables v_i in U^*, in the sense that the values of $x_1, x_2, \ldots, x_m$ become indices of the values of $a_1, a_2, \ldots, a_m$ (this is the simplest arrangement; in fact, we require a mapping between A^* and V^*). Further, the parameters y_i must be functionally related to the a_i (again, we need a mapping between a subset of V^* and A^*). The whole process, which entails selection of these attributes and parameters relevant to the experimental objective as well as the physical embodiment of the abstract mapping, is called identification [16] of the universe of discourse and denoted L. The construct $C = A^*, L, U$ is called a system.

Propositions in U become hypotheses in C. An abstract state in U becomes a state in C. A sequence of states in U corresponds with states $A(t)$ separated by Δt; thus $V(t) = V(t) \rightarrow V(t + \Delta t) \rightarrow$ becomes a behavior in C. A behavioral proposition in U becomes a prediction about the behavior of C.

1.5. A system gains empirical content and becomes of predictive value when hypotheses are verified by experimental test. An inductive procedure has been considered by Ashby [3] as "black box" testing. The experimenter records the behaviors of the "black box" or system for different values of the parameters, and builds up estimates of state transition probabilities p_{ij} (where i, j are used as indices of the states), and if the probability estimates are stationary, it is possible to construct transition probability matrices $P = ||p_{ij}||$. Although the probability estimates can approach arbitrarily close to 1 or 0, such a procedure cannot lead to certainties, for a confirmed hypothesis need not be invariably true. On the other hand, a single negative case can deny a hypothesis. Thus, the scientific method of posing or inferring from the evidence invariant theories of behavior, which experiments will be designed to negate or disprove, is relatively efficient. If this method is adopted U should be chosen with as much structure as the choice of attributes will permit.

Obviously the specification of a *system*, devoid of empirical content, is the structural information (in MacKay's sense [20, 21]) associated with the experiment, while the metrical information (in MacKay's sense) depends upon confirmation or disproof of the hypothesis in the system.

The experimenter tries to discover a coherent and thus describable behavior. In terms of the transition probability matrices $P = ||p_{ij}||$, and state probability distributions which, for initial state X, we shall denote $p_X(t)$, a behavior is coherent and describable either if

$$p_X(t + \Delta t) = p_X(t) \cdot P = X(0)P^t \tag{1}$$

which is the Markovian case (in particular, where P is positive, regular, and for large enough t we have:

$$p_X(t) \to p* \tag{2}$$

where $p*$ is a fixed-point probability distribution, independent of the initial state) or, failing this, if

$$p_X(t + \Delta t) = p_X(t) \cdot P_r \tag{3}$$

where r is the index of P_r in a set $\mathscr{P}$ of Markovian transition probability matrices, defined upon the same states, and is selected as a known function of an average θ that depends upon the states that have previously occurred, $r = g(\theta)$. A slightly more common variant

of this case occurs when P_r can be characterized if the behavior
is observed over an interval T. This entails the restriction that r
shall not be changed by selection more often than T. Finally there
is the case

$$p_x(t + \Delta t) = p_x(t) \cdot P_t[_{Y(t)}] \tag{4}$$

where the current transition probability matrix is selected by some
function $r = f(Y)$ of the parameters.

Of these, equation (1) is a *statistically state-determined* system
in Ashby's [3] sense and becomes a *state-determined* system if the
entries p_{ij} in P approach 1 or 0 when equation (2) reduces to the
equilibrial case. Equation (3) determines a sequence of statistically
state-determined systems which are, as a whole, state-determined.
Thus, if in equation (4) the experimenter is defined as part of the
system, the system as a whole is ultrastable.

1.6. If the behavior of the system, or a subsystem, assumes
one of these forms, the system or subsystem is predictable (at least
in a statistical sense) and determines a model, from which it is
possible to build a simulation of the system, either in the abstract
or in some physical embodiment. Indeed, since assertions about the
system are independent of the particular choice of attributes, the
simulation can be given *any* physical embodiment. One realization,
for example, consists of a roulette wheel with n stable conditions
corresponding to the n states of the system. The roulette wheel is,
for each turn, biased by one of $n \cdot r$ different sets of n weighting
coefficients, each set corresponding to the n entries in a single
row of a single transition probability matrix P_r. The value of r is
selected either by an averager, which delineates the selecting function $r = g(\theta)$, or at the user's discretion [thus simulating $r = f(Y)$].
In each case we accept the convention that each turn of the roulette
wheel occupies one interval Δt. The particular set of n weighting
coefficients (a particular row of P_r) depends upon the outcome of
the last, say the tth, turn of the roulette wheel. Using the bias thus
determined, the roulette wheel is again turned. Sequences of states
obtained in this manner describe the behavior of a *representative
system*, in other words, one of the *statistical ensembles* of state-
determined systems that satisfy the statistical constraints embodied
in the simulation. If the p_{ij} are 1 or 0 there is, of course, a unique
representative system. If $1 > p_{ij} > 0$ there are innumerable representative systems in the ensemble with states determined by the statistical constraints *and also* by the so-called *chance event* which
is the outcome of turning a roulette wheel.

1.7. Recalling the stages needed to arrive at a simulation:

(i) The experimenter sets out some agreed, abstract, logical possibilities, so defining U.

(ii) The abstract states V^* that form the basic data of these possibilities are identified with states of a selected and imperfectly observable subset a^* of the attributes of the environment to form a system C.

(iii) The logical possibilities thus become experimentally testable hypotheses about states of a system. By confirming or denying these hypotheses the experimenter infers the existence of statistical constraints.

(iv) To produce a simulation some device, such as a roulette wheel, is used to exhibit some of the set of behaviors which are admissible, given these constraints. Since any assertions about the system are independent of the fabric of the environment or the particular attributes selected, the system can be simulated in any fabric, for example, on a computer or a special mechanical arrangement.

1.8. Simulations of industrial plants, traffic congestion, chemical reactions, ocean currents, and many other physical happenings are performed very satisfactorily in this manner. We may be more or less ignorant of the detailed events so that the simulation is more or less adequate. But, however crude, we have the impression that the simulation is the right *kind* of thing, based upon the right *kind* of model, and that its imperfections could, in principle, be rectified if more accurate or expensive experiments were to be conducted.

According to our definition *any* part of the environment, supplied with energy, that exhibits some discernible behavior, can be represented as a system and simulated, though the system may be incoherent and uninformative.

The experimenter may or may not know how informative his system is likely to be before he starts performing a set of experiments. His uncertainty, if it exists, comes from ignorance of which attributes can profitably be observed together. In the case of maximum ignorance the experimenter merely tries constructing a system (and we have commented that it is *possible* to construct a system identified with *any* part of the environment) in order to find out, by subsequent testing, whether or not its behavior is coherent (whether or not, in other words, the system has any predictive value). Suppose that this system $C_1 = (A_1^*, L_1, U)$ is *coherent* in the sense of 1.5; then *because* of this the attributes defining A_1^* are comparable. Similarly, if a subsystem had been coherent the comment would have applied to at least a subset of the attributes. On the other hand, if C_1 is incoherent the attributes *may or may not be comparable*. In any case the experimenter will try some other system, say C_2, which differs from C_1 either in the identified attributes or the structure of the universe of discourse, or in both respects.

We should notice at this point the following:

(i) That experimenters *can* build up knowledge about which attributes are comparable and reasonably considered together, merely by trying to construct coherent systems and registering successful attempts. But the process involves a search among an indefinite number of possibilities, is impracticable, and may be disregarded.

(ii) Given that C_1 is incoherent, and ignorant of which attributes *are* comparable, the experimenter must rely upon his intuition in choosing C_2, but:

(iii) If he knows something of the character of the attributes beforehand his choice of a C_2 likely to be fruitful will be rationally guided by these data.

(iv) The data concerned may have been gleaned as suggested in (ii), but this, although it *may perhaps* be the only source, is not *necessarily* the only source.

The fundamental constraints that determine the form of concept that appears in the least restricted universe of discourse, have so far been regarded as imposing a restriction upon admissible descriptive frameworks and the communication of their content. But it is also possible to interpret these constraints as basic empirical truths about the environment; to argue, in other words, that "man" and his "environment" bear necessary relations to one another. According to this point of view, a man cannot be conceived by another man, without the environment which is common to them both. Whether the environment has the status of "reality" or of shared empirical "belief" is an irrelevant and probably undecidable issue. The important point is that the structure of a reality or shared belief changes the experimenter's choice of system in a manner distinct from the effect of the data suggested in (ii), with reference to which it is meta-information. It is this meta-information which directs our hunches and on the basis of which some situations are regarded as necessarily similar, although there are no rational grounds for this supposition.

DISTINCTIONS BETWEEN BEHAVIORAL SCIENCE
AND CLASSICAL SCIENCE

2.1. In classical physics there are "laws of science" or unifying principles that relate the attributes conventionally used in making measurements. Further, any of these attributes may be controlled, as a parameter, by the experimenter.

$$(\text{pressure}) \cdot (\text{volume}) = (\text{constant}) \cdot (\text{temperature})$$

is a rather low-level "law of science," because when expressed in its exact form:

(1) It enunciates a correlation that always occurs between the readings of a manometer, volume measure, and a thermometer in a well-defined (energetically closed) environment.

(2) The relation can be explained in terms of other "laws of science" (such as those governing the motion of particles).

Because there are many "laws of science" in his field of inquiry, the classical physicist leads a tidy life. In his system the identified attributes, being related by some "law of science," are always comparable. Further, his systems are constructed with a common universe of discourse that includes these "laws of science" and if a behavior in C_1 is haphazard, he is immediately guided in his choice of C_2. (Indeed, in classical physics, the word system has acquired a special meaning, "a collection of related physical objects.") But these restrictions that so helpfully guide an investigator also limit the sort of regularity he can contemplate (to the sort admissible in classical physics).

By way of contrast there are few, if any, behavioral "laws of science" and the behavioral scientist has to choose his attributes intuitively and to guess intuitively a C_2 if the behavior in C_1 is incoherent. The absence of "laws of science" is due, in part, to our greater ignorance in fields like biology and psychology, but also it is due to the inquiries that interest and seem relevant to biologists and psychologists. These have a far wider scope than the precise inquiries of physics and as a consequence any unifying principle of behavior would, if it existed, be very elaborate indeed.*

*In another paper I define a collection of comparable systems as a "reference frame." While the behavioral sciences have many different "reference frames," physics has one [30, 32].

It is true that laudable attempts have been made to reduce certain aspects of the behavioral sciences to tidier form, but without exception these have entailed either (i) specialization of the results, or (ii) logical ambiguity in the descriptive model.

Of these, (i) has been considered in detail by Beer who points out that "operational research" is a kind of behavioral science almost wholly concerned with specialized inquiries. In the extreme case the operational research worker wishes to make a statistical model of a factory X at an instant t, in order to build a controller (which, of necessity, embodies this kind of model) for factory X around the instant t (for the next few years maybe). He does not, as a primary objective at any rate, concern himself with the principles underlying all factories. In part this is because, even if the detailed data were available, the model to be made from them could not be expressed in the existing scientific language (this is recognized in the comment that management is an art rather than a science, but Beer [7] more cogently remarks that the science behind management is cybernetics).

2.2. Both (i) and (ii) are manifest in "rat psychology" which is, perhaps, the most tidied branch of behavioral science. A fictional history will illustrate the point. Many years ago, there were many perfectly respectable ways to describe the behavior of a rat and just as many behaviors to describe. Psychologists, of course, were anxious to discuss certain loosely defined aspects of rat behavior like "learning." Now, the investigation lead them to consider situations where it was possible to recognize *adaptations* of behavior. Since the animal did not read or write, but did run about its cage very often, a maze was the obvious choice of situation. Among the behaviors exhibited in the maze one kind amounted to walking along a particular path, and consequently the different paths in a maze became known as the response alternatives open to the rat, or as the set of possible rat behaviors. Now, although the development of rat psychology took place informally, by vague messing around with rats, it could have occurred by a sequence of formal experiments in which variously identified systems were tested and only those with a consistent behavior retained. Perhaps the main reason for retaining the maze was that if the rat were suitably stimulated by adjusting parameters like food supply, it could be induced to move along a unique path rather rapidly, and for certain values of this parameter the adaptation persisted. The effective parameter could, once again, have been discovered by testing a sequence of systems. Once discovered it became known as reinforcement and the process of convergence to one of the possible rat behaviors became mistakenly known as "learning."

Within the conditions indicated, rat behavior is statistically predictable (consider the Estes "Learning Model" or Skinner's reinforcement program). Within these conditions we have an operational research problem like the factory in (i), which is solved by advancing an adequate statistical model. The solution is of considerable value even in practice. Thus animal trainers, perhaps the most advanced of the operational research workers, use the reinforcement techniques proposed by Skinner with remarkable success. But their underlying models (or the more explicit statistical models of Estes) do not, strictly speaking, describe learning. They account very well for adaptive changes in a limited mode of behavior (given also, incidentally, rather specially prepared animals). But the rat maze is only a formal learning situation. Any attempt to interpret this "learning" as learning in general, as the same process that we ourselves call by this name, is open to criticism, for logically, learning in general cannot be exhibited within a restricted field. Ostensive definitions of the process indicate the truth of this contention, for they sample of a necessity a wide variety of situations which, if described impartially by the experimenter, would lead him to identify incomparable sets of attributes with a sequence of different systems. Or consider the minimal criterion embodied in Minsky and Selfridge's learning heuristic [27], where to say an object learns we must agree that it constructs *response alternatives* and *relations of similarity* between situations that are (to the object) different in kind (neither of these activities *can* be *demonstrated* in the rat maze).

The rat, of course, may learn. It is merely that the experimental method is unable to discern whether it does or not. The rat in its maze dithers, dawdles, and blinks, and the action of walking over a path which features so dominantly in the experiment constitutes a minute (through conceivably an important) part of its repertoire. Nor (even if the action of walking along a path is important) is this behavior necessarily separable from a myriad of others. All the evidence suggests that reinforcement has a very elaborate effect, and that the adaptations described by "rat psychology" are a limited facet of learning.

2.3. Much the same comments apply to experiments carried out upon human subjects. In an attempt to determine specific and repeatable conditions the well-attested method of the controlled experiment is carried over from classical physics into the behavioral sciences. The experimental environment is built up from separable categories of discrete elements, namely, stimuli, response alternatives, and reinforcements. In this respect the human subject is more amenable than a dumb animal. For with a dumb animal the experimenter must discern what *is* a discrete stimulus by the kind of rational intuition that Lettvin, Maturana, and co-workers [17] used in the case of the frog (points of light on the frog retina are *not* discrete stimuli, but the motions of small objects and particular kinds of shadow are). With a man, on the other hand, the experimenter can request his cooperation and make certain he agrees to regard events, such as the illumination of one from *n* possible lamps, as symbols for discrete stimulus entities. Similarly, the subject agrees that a set of *m* response buttons, one of which can be pressed at once, are symbols that exhaust the gamut of possible behaviors. Finally, the subject agrees to credit certain distinct "reinforcement" stimuli with a special directive function and to value the approval of the experimenter, which is indicated by the delivery of "reinforcement." (Thus, "reinforcement" modifies the subject's attitude.) Stimuli are instructions given to induce the performances of skill, as necessary data, while reinforcement conveys meta-information *about* the performance of the skill and the experimenter's degree of approbation. (Notice this is "subject's meta-information" or meta-information with respect to the stimuli. It must be distinguished from "experimenter's meta-information," which is meta-information with respect to the subject's behavior.)

For many learning experiments the experimenter chooses a relation *R* to hold between the stimuli and the responses, a sequence in which the stimuli will be presented, and a rule of reinforcement, like "reinforce each response selection that satisfied *R*."

The coherence of the subject's behavior in such a learning experiment is measurable. Because of the agreed interpretation of events in the environment, the set of stimuli are identified with parameters $y_j \subset y^*$, $j = 1, 2, \ldots, M$ and the set of responses $x_i \subset x^*$, $i = 1, 2, \ldots, m$ are well specified, and it is thus possible to compute probability measures such as "variety" and "redundancy." Now redundancy, denoted η, is intuitively acceptable as an index of the coherence (or organization) of a system (since it strictly *is* a measure of coherence if our *expectations* of events tally with the observationally estimated probabilities of events).

Let $p_i(t)$ denote the probability of occurrence of the state V_i, estimated for an instant t. The variety of the system at this particular instant, denoted $\xi(t)$, will be

$$\xi(t) = \sum_i p_i(t) \log_2 p_i(t)$$

If μ is the maximum variety achievable with the constraints of the system, the redundancy $\eta(t)$ is

$$\eta(t) = 1 - \frac{\xi(t)}{\mu}$$

Using any plausible rule of reinforcement, $\eta(t)$ will increase from a value typifying a behavior governed by recognition and acceptance of R at some later instant $t = \tau$, and different rules of reinforcement induce this adaptation more or less rapidly.

From the *experimenter's* point of view, the state V_i of the system depends upon the subject's response. Thus, if the sequence of stimuli is determinate

$$\xi(t) = \sum_i p_{jl}(t) \log_2 p_{jl}(t)$$

where $p_{jl}(t)$ is the probability, estimated for t, that x_l occurs, given y_j, and where $j = 1, 2, \ldots, M$ and $l = 1, 2, \ldots, m$. If stimuli are produced by a chance machine (biased to determine y_j with a probabilistic constraint Π_j), we have

$$\xi(t) = - \sum_j \sum_l \Pi_j \cdot p_{jl}(t) \log_2 p_{jl}(t)$$

The relation R determines a characteristic function defined upon V^*, and such that, for invariable reinforcement of a correct response:

$$\text{Reinforcement} = \left\{ \begin{matrix} 1 \text{ if } v = M \text{ membered set of } V^* \\ 0 \text{ if not} \end{matrix} \right\}$$

or equivalently, since $V^* = X^* \circledast Y^*$:

Given $Y_j(t)$

$$\text{Reinforcement} = \left\{ \begin{matrix} 1 \text{ if } x(t) = R(y_j) = \text{correct response, } R \\ 0 \text{ if not} \quad\quad\quad \text{(one-to-one)} \end{matrix} \right\}$$

Assuming he adheres to the agreed conventions the subject aims to learn R. Initially he must select among M response alternatives when presented with a stimulus, and from the *subject's* point of view, his decision resolves a variety

$$\log_2 \frac{1}{M} = -\log_2 M$$

which is *his* uncertainty, given y_j, or $R(y_j)$. Ultimately, *his* uncertainty will be removed, as suggested behaviorally, by the decrease in $\xi(t)$ or the corresponding increase in $\eta(t)$. But at various stages in this process we assume that the subject has varying degrees of uncertainty about response to the various stimuli. Now, as Hick and others point out, the formal expedient of representing an intermediate uncertainty as a choice between some number of effective response alternatives M^*, less than M, is not unrealistic. We thus remark that at an instant t less than r the subject decides between $M^*(t)$ alternatives, thus evidencing uncertainty of

$$-\log_2 M^*(t)$$

these alternatives being formal constructs that have an incidental and hypothetical psychological reality.

It is safe to assume psychological reality for a slightly less rigid structure which is adequately supported by the evidence. To be specific we shall assume the following:

(1) That the subject behaves as an intermittent decision maker and contemplates a *decision field* which includes a set of possible outcomes (in experiments commonly identified with specific response alternatives) and various possible forms of evidence (substantiating or denying hypotheses that refer to achievement of these outcomes). Each form of evidence constitutes what Miller [26] calls a *"chunk"* of data. In the limit case the chunk is an attribute of the environment, the evidence indicating its momentary value. The number of chunks that can be simultaneously contemplated is, on average, about eight. The subject is said to have a *"decision rule"* insofar as he can demonstrate a *preference ordering* over the admissible outcomes that leads him to use evidence in a rational procedure for achieving certain favored outcomes. ("Preference ordering" is an over-all characteristic of behavior that is modified by the subject's meta-information or reinforcement.)

(2) The subject is adaptable (in particular, satisfying Ashby's requirements for the least specialized habituation). The subject adapts whenever he makes a decision (his characteristics cannot remain invariant). Further, his adaptation depends upon the conditions of reinforcement.

(3) In terms of chunks the subject has a maximum decision rate. Consider the subject's state of uncertainty about securing a preferred outcome. The experimenter is aware of this uncertainty from introspective reports of confusion and the observation that in some conditions an agreed and reinforced outcome is not achieved.

Uncertainty in this decision field is reduced after assimilating chunks of data.

There is a definite rate per chunk at which the uncertainty can be reduced by evidence that leads to making a decision. If he is made to respond at a greater rate the subject exhibits overload. Overload occurs when the subject's decision field is insufficiently organized.

Uncertainty is reduced by chunks of data specifying evidence of different forms. Consider the subject's uncertainty in terms of these chunks. The maximum variety, or state of maximum uncertainty, is determined by the forms of possible evidence denoted by μ chunks. The variety or state of uncertainty is ξ chunks. The redundancy or organization is

$$\eta \text{ chunks} = 1 - \frac{\xi \text{ chunks}}{\mu \text{ chunks}}$$

(4) In terms of chunks the subject has a minimum decision rate. In other words, he must attend to something whether this is a sequence determined by the experimenter or the activity occurring in his brain. In this case $\eta_{max.} \geq \eta_{chunks}$.

Given assumptions (1), (2), and (3) and a self-paced presentation, it is hardly surprising that the behavioral measure $\eta(t)$ increases and that the subject comes to appreciate R. If the experimenter paces the presentation of stimuli the required decision rate must not greatly exceed the minimum, or, invoking assumption (4), be much less that the maximum (if it is, the subject *must* attend to something other than the stimuli). We conjecture also that the subject will actively *look* for relations other than R, and an obvious form of relation is sequential dependency between the stimuli. (Either the subject tries to discern the determinate sequence or, if the stimuli are probabilistically produced, but not independent, he tries to discover the transition probability matrix, $\Pi = || \Pi_{ik} ||$, $k = 1, 2, \ldots, m,$ that governs the stimulus sequence. If Π is Markovian the probabilities $\Pi_i = \sum_k \Pi_{ki}$ are descriptive.) Discovery of any relations, determinate or statistical, alters the chunks that are decided about. Stimuli regarded as independent feature *as stimuli* in a chunk

of data, but those known to have sequential dependencies will feature *as pairs*, perhaps, or in some more elaborate grouping.

Now consider what happens in practice *after* the instant τ:

(I) If R is readily appreciated, the subject revolts at the monotony and his behavior becomes either haphazard or irrelevant. In this
case the measure $\eta(t)$ either decreases or becomes indeterminate
for any value of $t > \tau$.

(II) If R is inconceivable because it is too elaborate, the subject adopts a more or less successful but stereotyped behavior
pattern.

(III) The subject divides his attention, as a motor car driver
divides his attention if he talks to the passengers.

(IV) The subject adopts different strategies in an attempt to
maintain his own interest in the job, even though these strategies
confer no logical advantage.

Factory workers adopt this expedient when engaged in a monot-
onous occupation. Subjects who exhibit frequency matching, bet-
ting against a chance sequence, probably do much the same. For
although the logically optimum strategy is to choose the most probable alternative on each occasion, Seigel [40] has pointed out that
the optimum strategy for a subject who *needs* to secure a *maximum*
variety of response construction would be the frequency matching
behavior which occurs in real life.

It is possible to account for these empirically manifest behaviors, using the assumptions (1), (2), (3), and (4). The crux of the
matter is that the subject must, according to assumption (4), decide
about chunks of data at not less than a given rate. Relative to the
system measure, the amount of information required to make a chunk
of data is decreased by the adaptive process that goes on between
$t = 0$ and $t = \tau$. At the instant $t = \tau$, the experimental environment
cannot satisfy the required rate. Thus, in (I) the subject no longer
attends to the experimental environment. In (II) something similar
occurs, but the subject is forced by the strength of his previous
agreement to make some kind of response and we predict that this
will be the least taxing kind of response, since he does not really
expect it to prove successful. In (III) the experimental system is
coupled *not* to the subject, but to a separable *automaton* which is,
of course, embodied in some part of the subject's brain. In (IV) the
subject reinterprets the situation. He may, incidentally, do so in a
very profitable way that amounts to learning different methods of

achieving success, but the experimenter is unable to describe these methods within the experimental system for the integrity of this system depends upon the initially agreed interpretation of states and relations. Indeed, in each case, the system becomes nonexistent, and measures such as η are indeterminate, after $t = \tau$, because the experimental situation is too restricted for the subject.

To recaptiulate, the system, though well-defined, does not permit the changes of attention or the construction of other than the prescribed relations. But these processes are a necessary feature of the "learning" that interests us. Consequently, any model derived from the system is too specialized to represent learning, for learning is only manifest in a behavior that extends over many apparently incomparable experimental situations, that is, over situations which could be described only by systems identified with incomparable sets of attributes.

2.4. A different approach is construction of a *functional* model, or learning *mechanism* (the model, in this case, represents how learning occurs rather than allowing us to predict the consequence of learning). Commonly, such models entail the idea of intervening variables (such as reaction potential) that *seem* to have the status of intervening variables in engineering or in classical physics. Thus *apparently*, it is much the same to say that various stimuli and internal conditions determine the value of an intervening variable that, in turn, determines a response, as to say that the rate of inflow of various reactants and the pressure in a reaction vessel determine the concentration of a product, which, in turn, determines the rate at which the vessel is emptied. But, if fact, we can really inspect the product concentration. In principle it can be controlled as a parameter. On the other hand, we cannot put our finger on "reaction potential." Nor is it intended that we should, for this intervening variable has the status of a descriptive convenience, not an attribute or a parameter of the system.

Providing it is interpreted in this manner the intervening variable is a useful though uninformative component in the model, but it is often credited with a different status (as part of the learning mechanism) because people *want* to put their finger on this elusive thing. Now unless it is possible to locate some attribute which acts as an intervening variable (it rarely, though occasionally, is possible), this interpretation is false. As a matter of fact the evidence indicates that the intervening variables of a learning mechanism are *not* localized. In particular, except in automatous animals like the frog, the decision function entailed in making a response is *distributed* or, to use McCulloch's telling phase [24], the mechanism has a *redundancy of potential command*. Insofar as that is true the intervening variables, indeed the whole model, must be ambiguous.

A somewhat similar difficulty occurs when describing chemical molecules in terms of the familiar bond models, and in another paper von Foerster and I [13] compared this description with the description of a learning mechanism. To reiterate the analogy, some molecules are described, well enough for a chemist to make predictions about reaction mechanisms, in terms of a stable structure with fixed bonds. This case corresponds with the form of behavioral description in 1.5, equation (1). Other molecules are tautomeric. A number of molecular species X, Y exist in dynamic equilibrium, but, since any of the X, Y species is momentarily stable and may, in certain conditions, be isolated, we can legitimately model the situation, at any moment and for any specified values of parameters, like acidity and concentration of the chemical material, as a probability mixture that is made up from $a\%$ of X-bond model and $b\%$ of Y-bond model in solution. This is legitimate because the stable components X, Y do exist to correspond with the fixed bond models. Tautomerism is thus analogous to the form of description indicated in 1.5, equation (3). But there are other molecules called "resonant" that are not adequately described by a probability mixture of X, Y-bond models. It can be shown that any set of components open to description in terms of a set of bond models would be unstable components in a plausible dynamic equilibrium. So, very cogently, these neat structures do not exist. Some different kind of model is needed to describe resonance which is also true of our descriptions of a learning mechanism.

2.5. Phrasing the matter differently, observation in the behavioral sciences is liable to a necessary structural uncertainty which is distinct from the familiar uncertainty, given a specific system, about the values of the descriptive variables. Structural uncertainty is an uncertainty about the system itself. It is exhibited in the case of learning experiments by the ambiguity about which sort of model to adopt or which sort of behavior to investigate. In the case of functional models that pose a mechanism of learning, it is exhibited by an ambiguity about the status of components in the model which arises because of resonance.

2.6. At first sight, it seems strange that structural uncertainty should exert much influence in the laboratory, because our thinking is closely wedded to the idea of experiments conducted with controlled parameters where, by the logic of the situation, this form of uncertainty must be excluded if the results are to be interpretable. But, on closer consideration, the experiments of classical science are a special case.

To show this we must consider both the *topic* which a scientist aims to study and the *procedure* he adopts in conducting his study. Let us call both of these, when defined, a field of investigation. Classical science is exclusively concerned with fields of investigation with topics that can be studied within a single system from which testable hypotheses are derived and models and simulations constructed. The same is true for some of the topics considered in the behavioral sciences, for example, psychophysics and sensory measurement. On the other hand, the inquiries made in connection with learning and perhaps the great majority of behaviorally interesting topics require the verification of hypotheses which cannot be derived from any one system at the present state of our knowledge, because they refer to apparently incomparable attributes of the environment. Consequently models and simulations of the kind we considered in 1.6 are of little value, even if they are conceivable.

However, we need not conclude that these fields of investigation are beyond the ken of science, although we must admit that an unconventional experimental method is needed.

The essential requirement, in order to obtain coherent images of behavior, is control of the *relation* between whatever is observed and the experimenter who observes it. One method of effecting the controlled conditions (using the phrase in this broad but admissible sense) is to conduct experiments within the framework of *one* system and this method (which reduces to controlling the parameters) is the most *convenient* method in *classical* science. It proves inapplicable because the subject cannot accept the experimental environment when it is so rigidly prescribed. Thus, in the behavioral sciences, a fixed parameter approach does *not* imply controlled conditions, and conversely in order to *secure* controlled conditions, the parameters of the environment must be continually changed as follows:

(1) Supplying in Ashby's sense, as much variety as the subject needs to keep his attention.

(2) Supplying a form of variety that the subject will accept as relevant.

These requirements can be satisfied, as in 3.1, by providing an unrestricted experimental environment in which the subject is allowed to change his attention and the experimenter tries to keep pace with him. Alternatively, as in 3.2, the recommended experimental method entails construction of a variable experimental environment. The variation must, of course, be of a special kind such that coherent behavior is ultimately achieved. Commonly the variations needed to obtain controlled conditions will change the experimental system so that it, or the set of identified attributes, is incomparable from one moment to the next. Thus, as we remarked a moment ago, the conditional simulations of 1.6 do not adequately represent the system.

EXPERIMENTAL METHOD

3.1. Suppose the subject is allowed to have a substantially unlimited environment such as a room with plenty of interesting events to look at and hear. It is common experience that in these conditions he will wander about attending to whatever attributes of the environment intrigue him (the shape of the furniture, the sound of a phonograph record, etc.) and manipulating various objects, apparently in order to alter the attribute values (opening a window, changing the record on the phonograph, etc.). Indeed it would be difficult to avoid the comment that his behavior, like the experimenters, is *experimental*. Further, because the environment is unrestricted, his behavior is exteriorized. When one aspect of the environment becomes tedious, he will be able to choose some other aspect, which is not. He need never resort to personal ruminations which are inaccessible to the experimenter.

Now the experimenter has called the physical assembly that is wandering about the room "a subject," on the basis of meta-information which has little or nothing to do with the observable behavior. But having given the physical assembly this name, he must also credit it with other properties that stem from a belief that "a subject" is something similar to the experimenter himself.

It is assumed that the subject and the experimenter can appreciate the same attributes of the room. Thus it is reasonable to specify a possibly enormous set of states of the environment, say A. The subject is supposed to indulge in much the same sort of hypothesis construction and testing as the experimenter; in other words, he is assumed to construct a system that the experimenter uses in order to describe the subject's behavior.

We shall denote this subject system $G = A_G^*, L_G, U_G$. Its states are $(V_G = X_G \circledast Y_G) \subset (V_G^* = X_G^* \circledast Y_G^*)$. The X_G are determined by evidential or stimulus variables x_i, that are identified with a subset of the attributes $a_i \subset a$. The subject's hypotheses refer to the values of the x_i which, when they change, convey evidence. From the previous discussion the x_i correspond with "chunks" of data. The Y_G are response states, dependent upon response variables, y_j, that are manipulated by the subject and determine the values of the remaining attributes of the environment.

Now, regarded as a "decision maker," the subject has a "decision field" V_G^* with outcomes V_G, and manipulates the y_j in order to achieve some preferred outcomes (that is, within the logic of U_G there exist rational procedures for achieving or approximating a preferred *state*, given certain *evidence*; the set of procedures, and the logic of U_G, characterizes the subject's rationality).

It is important to recognize the status of G. Models derived from it do not *explain* the mechanism of the subject. On the contrary, they only collate the introspective statements which an ideally cooperative and perspicacious subject could make about his own behavior. Rules governing state transformations in G are "decision rules" (and, in principle, the subject can say *why* he adopts a given procedure by citing a "decision rule"). But, excluding omniscience, neither the experimenter nor the subject can *explain* why a given state is preferred (which would be a necessary part of any mechanistic description), and any assertions that such-and-such a perference ordering is the case are statements in a metalanguage talking about G (rather than the language used within G). A similar comment applies to such preference changing operations as reinforcements, which are used by the experimenter. Whereas application of a stimulus is an operation, a change in some evidential variable of G that is completely described in G, a reinforcement, although such change may effect the behavior manifest in G, is not completely described in G.

The experimenter, having credited the subject with these potentialities, expects to observe a coherent behavior. Thus he constructs the experimental system, say $C = A_C^*, L_C, U_C$. Ideally, he would like to secure a C which is isomorphic with G; failing this he

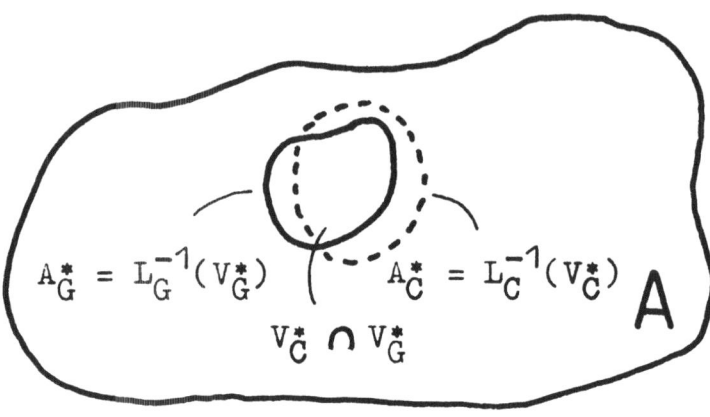

Fig. 1

would like C to be a homomorphic image of G, i.e., a less detailed image in which relations are preserved invariant. If either isomorphism or homomorphism is secured, we write $C = L(G)$.

A prerequisite of $C = L(G)$ is that the subject and the experimenter shall attend to the same states of the environment, $A_C^* = A_G^*$. In Fig. 1 the states in **A** are represented as points in the plane. If there is equality the circles coincide, but a practical approximation is to maximize the measure of the set $A_C^* \cap A_G^*$.

From our definition of an identification, the condition $A_C^* = A_G^*$ is also a sufficient condition for $C = L(G)$. Now, if $C = L(G)$ this does not mean that observations made in C are necessarily informative, but insofar as they are informative, they will be consistent. In particular, the experimenter will be able to construct a transition probability matrix P over the states $V_c \subset V_c^*$ that reflects the constraints governing the state transformation in G. If the subject, confirming hypotheses in G, adopts a coherent behavior, this will be manifest in C as a behavioral adaptation providing the changes are slow enough for the experimenter to discern a trend (thus the entries in P need not be stationary in the strict sense). The crudest index of adaptation is a change in redundancy (over an interval Δt); thus if $\eta_C(t + \Delta t) > \eta_C(t)$, the behavior manifested in C is adaptive and reflects an increase in η_G due to confirmation of hypotheses or the elaboration of probabilistic constraints (the original chunks of data are no longer independent and become aggregated into larger chunks). Commonly, the experimenter is able to make detailed comments about the adaptation. Harlow, for example, can fit rather elaborate trend-predicting functions to the response adaptation curves of apes, providing the apes adopt the same attitude or mental set toward the same kind of problem.

Of course, $C = L(G)$ is unstable. Recalling the assumptions (1), (2), (3), and (4) of 2.3, it *must* be. For, writing η_G in place of $\eta_{(chunks)}$, survival of a "decision maker" entails preserving the condition $\eta_{max.} > \eta_G > \eta_{min.}$. Now for a given system, say, G, the *value* of μ_G is determined. But adaptive changes (or coalesence of chunks into larger chunks, or empirical confirmation of any hypothesis) will reduce the subject's uncertainty ξ_{G_1}, or in particular, the uncertainty $\xi_{X_{G_1}^*}$.

To compensate for this tendency which increases η_G until the limit $\eta_{max.}$ is approached, it is necessary to change the system. Commonly, the change is a change of attention whereby chunks are "redefined," or equivalently the variables of the system are differently identified. Thus, if we express the transformation $G_1 \rightarrow G_2$, the significant change is $A_{G_1}^* \rightarrow A_{G_2}^*$, though conceivably U_G is also altered. In either case it is convenient to dub the process "conceptual homeostasis," for it is a homeostatic change in *system* (and, consequently in the subject's conceptual framework), which comes about in order to maintain the conditions that are necessary for "decision-making" activity according to assumptions (1), (2), (3), and (4) of 2.3. Insofar as the "conceptual homeostasis" entails change in the identification of attributes, we can say it maintains the "decision maker" in a stable *relation* to the environment. When manifested among Harlow's apes, this change is "insight."

Let r_0 be an arbitrary instant, when G_1 is formed, and r_1 the moment at which $G_1 \rightarrow G_2$. Then $G_1 = G(r_0)$ and $G_2 = G(r_1)$, and in general, the subject will change his attention inducing a sequence such as $G(r_0) \rightarrow G(r_1) \rightarrow \cdots G(r_n)$, to which there will correspond a further sequence, $V_G^*(r_0) \rightarrow V_G^*(r_1) \rightarrow \cdots V_G(r_n)$, as indicated in Fig. 2.

An observer, having constructed a system C_1, discovers that hypothesis construction in G_1 (which is reflected as behavioral adaptation in C_1) leads to an increase in η_C in the interval $r_1 > t \geq r_0$. But at $t = r_1$, there is a discontinuity η_C either becoming indeterminate or decreasing. Obviously, in order to maintain a coherent behavior in his system, the experimenter must change his system, as suggested in Fig. 3, to maintain the relation $A_{C(t)}^* = A_{G(t)}^*$.

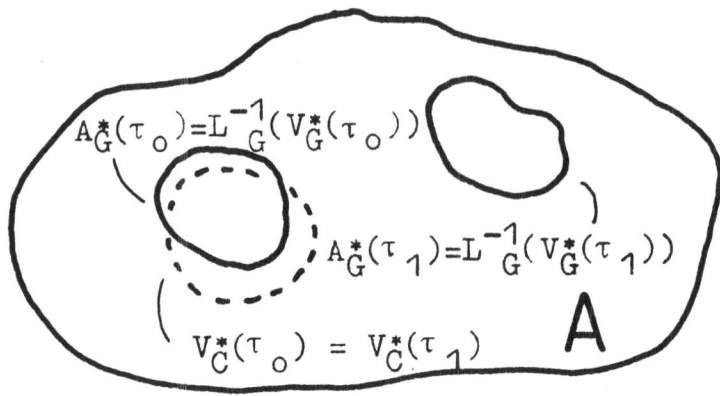

Fig. 2

Contradictory as it sounds, this procedure is not absurd. The fact is, the experimenter can only maintain a constancy in his relation to the subject in a time-extensive system with states that are the disjunction of the states of several time-dependent and meta-stable subsystems. In general, these separate subsystems $C(r_0) \rightarrow C(r_1) \rightarrow \cdots C(r_n)$ are identified with attributes that *become* comparable only because (i) they have been identified with variables in the corresponding subject sequence $G(r_0) \rightarrow G(r_1) \rightarrow \cdots G(r_n)$, and because (ii) the experimenter (on grounds of meta-information unrelated to the behaviors manifest in C) specified "the subject" as a distinct entity, thus implying that systems constructed *by* "the

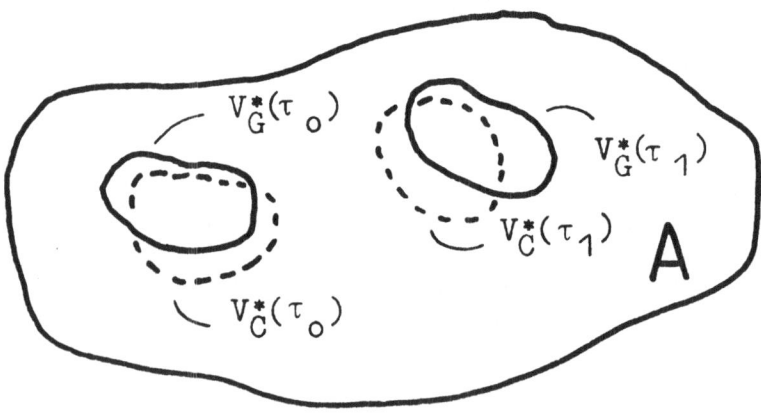

Fig. 3

subject" will be deemed comparable in the sense that the observed *correlation* between the coherent behaviors in the different G will be regarded as an indication that these behaviors belong to the same system. Consequently if it is true that $C(t) = L[G(T)]$ for each value $t = r_0, r_1, \ldots, r_n$, members of the corresponding sequence are deemed comparable, in which case we denote it:

$$\lambda_C = \left[C(r_0) \rightarrow C(r_1) \rightarrow \ldots C(r_n)\right]$$

and for each λ_C there is a λ_G

$$\lambda_G = \left[G(r_0) \rightarrow G(r_1) \rightarrow \ldots G(r_n)\right]$$

such that $\lambda_C = L(\lambda_G)$.

Similarly, for each λ_C there is a sequence of coherent behaviors represented by a sequence of transition probability matrices defined upon the momentarily pertinent states:

$$\phi = \left[P(r_0) \rightarrow P(r_1) \rightarrow \ldots P(r_n)\right]$$

(but notice, the states referred to in P_{r_n} are ordinarily different from the states referred to in $P_{r_{n+1}}$).

Thus, the experimenter's description of the subject's behavior is $[\lambda, L, \phi]$ wherein λ specifies the structural requirements of observation and ϕ summarizes the evidence obtained in each of the different inquiries determined by λ.

A moment's consideration of the conditions in which experimenters construct sequences $[\lambda, L, \phi]$ will convince you that the experimenter could not have specified the components of λ at the outset (unless he had specified all of the states in V which, by excluding omniscience, we have agreed to be impossible). The experimenter may be a child psychologist working in a nursery, in which case λ is determined as he pursues the infant subject and discovers what it *is* playing with—only if he knew beforehand, what the child *would* play with, could he specify λ at the start of the experiment. But this knowledge, if available, stems from the meta-information obtained if the experimenter makes an assumption of similarity with the child. Thus there is a genuine distinction to be made between $[\lambda, L, \phi]$ and the systems, however large, in which we describe gases in vessels, or chemical plants, or any other thing with a behavior we can agree to represent within a well-defined set of states. Less obviously, perhaps, $[\lambda, L, \phi]$ is distinct from an ordinary sequential experimental (for, in this case, there is a well-defined cost criterion that selects the next inquiry from a large but finite set). As an over-all comment, when a physical assembly such as the subject fails to demonstrate a coherent behavior in *any* system, but when it is possible for the experimenter to construct a sequence λ (such that it provides a sequence ϕ of behaviors that *are* coherent), we say that the physical assembly is represented *in relation to this experimenter* by a "*self-organizing system*" $[\lambda, L, \phi]$. The characteristic of being a self-organizing system does not refer to $[\lambda, L, \phi]$ itself, but arises from the relation between the physical assembly and the experimenter (the issue is considered in the Appendix, Part 2, of this paper).

3.2. Now in the experiment we have considered, the experimenter concentrates upon maintaining a relation to the subject that permits observation of a coherent behavior. The topic in this field of investigation is really "the subject" or "all of child behavior," rather than anything so specific as "learning," for the *subject* has *complete* control over the form of relevant inquiry. It may be that this is the only possible kind of experiment.

If so, the experimenter is more of a natural historian than a scientist for he looks, like the natural historian, for the categories of a descriptive framework, rather than determining these categories on his own account. But this need not be his role in practice, provided that he is willing to manipulate the experimental environment. Often it is possible to use meta-information about the subject, and operations such as the promise of reinforcement, to guide the subject in his selection of G, so that λ_G and consequently λ_C refer to more restricted "topics" than "the subject."

There are several techniques which can be adopted by the experimenter or by adaptive automata (one of them, used in adaptive teaching systems, is described in the Appendix, Part 1, of this paper). All of these techniques require certain basic assumptions of which the most important (already assumed in a slightly different form) is a *structure* in the environment that can be appreciated by the subject and by the experimenter. The a_i due to this *structure* are not binary attributes. Inferences can be made by the experimenter or an automaton about many distinct values of the same attribute, not only about its presence or absence.

3.3. To illustrate the method used for varying the experimental environment in order to maintain a constant relationship to the subject, and, in this sense, to nullify the effects of "conceptual homeostasis," assume that the subject is removed from his room and presented with a display:

(i) Of a significant attribute a_I the values of which are *stimuli*. For each *stimulus* there is a "correct response" that is reinforced:

$$Y_0 = R(x_I) = R[L_G(a_I)]$$

where $Y_0 = y_1, y_2, \ldots, y_m$. Each $y_j > 0$.

(ii) The additional attributes a_I indicate the values of the $y_j(t)$ which should appear given $a_i(t)$ in order to achieve a "correct response" Y_0, and consequently reinforcement. These attributes convey what is often called "cue information" because it aids the subject in solving the problems posed by the appearance of stimuli, by reducing his uncertainty about $Y_0 \subset Y_1^*$, even if he is ignorant of R. But the a_I are logically irrelevant to the stimulus. For each value of a_i the remaining attributes a_I can assume any values, without effecting the required response. Thus for each value of a_i there is a subset.

$A^{\#} =$ (given value of attribute a_i) ⊗ (any values of the a_I) and we can assert

$$Y_0 = R(X_G^{\#}) = R[L_G(A_G^{\#})]$$

as the condition for reinforcement.

Suppose (i) that the subject has agreed to *prefer* reinforced outcomes, i.e., to perform the skill and (ii) that the experimenter wishes to discover how the subject distributes his attention about the "cue information" attributes, and how he adjusts his behavior, when dealing with a sequence Π of the stimuli $A^{\#}$. This, in other words is the *topic* in the experimenter's field of investigation.

3.4. The technique consists of a pair of separable procedures.

(I) The experimenter increases the rate at which stimuli appear and responses must be elicited so that, given G, the stimulus variety $\xi_x \#_G$ is maximized. *Increase* in η_C or η_G will thus be due to adaptation and a reduction in response uncertainty which is balanced, as indicated above, by increasing the stimulus variety in order to maintain η_C and η_G between the limits of $\eta_{max.}$ and $\eta_{min.}$. From our previous discussion this expedient will tend to stabilize a given G and if $C = L(G)$ allow the experimenter to construct his transition probability matrix P. Explicitly, the experimenter increases the rate at which stimuli are displayed, until this increase correlates with a decrease in the rate at which the subject makes correct responses. A failure to make the correct response is assumed to indicate an overload, because the subject has agreed to satisfy the rule R.

(II) The experimenter wishes to compare attributes a_l which are incomparable and for this purpose, adopts the expedient of monetary valuation. The subject is provided with a "bank balance" $\theta(t)$, that is continually displayed. He starts off with a deposit. But the bank balance is taxed and, if he did nothing, this deposit would soon be absorbed in taxation. He can earn income by making a correct response (either one unit of money for each correct response or a number of units inversely proportional to his latency on the occasion concerned). The value of $\theta(t)$ is the reinforcement that the subject is asked to maximize (on the assumption of an indefinitely lengthy experiment). But we remarked that in order to make correct responses consistently, and thus to earn money consistently, the subject must make use of "cue information." But, in this "economy" the cue information is made available at a cost that is specified by the experimenter, denoted in the case of the attribute a_l at an instant t as $\rho_l(t)$.

To realize the "economy" in practice the subject is provided with a set of buttons in one-to-one correspondence with the attributes a_l. If he wishes to know the value of the attribute a_l at t, the subject is required to press the lth button. The cost of gaining this knowledge $\rho_l(t)$ is displayed above the lth button. Suppose that $\theta(t) \geq \rho_l(t)$ or, in other words, that the subject has enough money to pay for the data he wishes. When he presses the lth button the value of $a_l(t)$ is displayed and coincidently his bank balance is debited an amount $\rho_l(t)$. On the other hand if it had occurred that $\rho_l(t) > \theta(t)$, pressing this button would have exerted no effect.

The experimenter is thus able to observe which attribute values the subject chooses to inspect and, by varying the cost distribution $\rho(t) = ||\rho_l(t)||$, he can discover how much the subject is willing to pay for the different kinds of data.

Recall (1) that procedure (I) keeps the subject in need of cue information, and (2) only by making correct responses can the subject gain money and since money is needed to pay for cue information a given mode of behavior, entailing some distribution of correct responses, is conditional upon the cue information cost distribution $\rho(t)$. Now (3) the experimenter can (and initially he must) reduce the cost of cue information so that an uninformed subject can gain at least some money (otherwise he cannot do anything coherent). But soon the subject learns to do without some of the originally needed cue information. This tendency is, of course, counteracted by procedure (I). But, broadly speaking, there will be stable modes of behavior (which can be represented, more exactly, by definite strategies) that can be maintained as stable entities only by a particular (not necessarily unique) distribution of expenditure upon cue information. (4) Assume that such a stable mode exists. By definition it leads to a coherent behavior in the experimental system. But, by increasing the cost of cue information, the experimenter can render this mode instable or indeed impossible. Further, there are some strategies of cost adjustment, increasing one attribute cost more or less than another, that most effectively limit the stable mode of behavior. (5) Since the behavior is stable and since he is in a position to discover how much the subject will pay, the experimenter can adopt a most effective strategy. (6) Assume that he does adopt this cost-increasing strategy until the stable behavior shows signs of becoming unstable. (7) Since a discontinuity in $\theta(t)$ is a good indication of instability, assume he adopts the strategy until there is a discontinuity in $\theta(t)$. But, at this point, before the behavior goes adrift, he reverses his proceedure until stability is regained. (8) In these conditions any cue information the subject pays for must be used. For, if the subject wastes money, he cannot maintain the be-

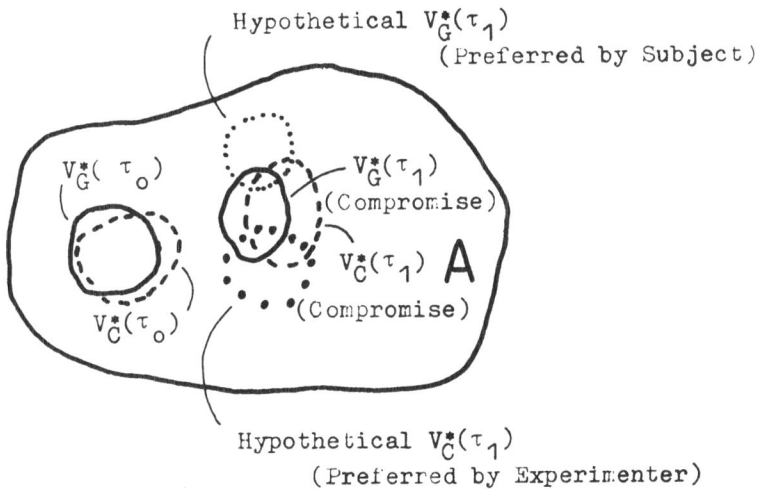

Hypothetical $V_G^*(\tau_1)$
(Preferred by Subject)

$V_G^*(\tau_0)$

$V_G^*(\tau_1)$
(Compromise)

$V_C^*(\tau_1)$ A
(Compromise)

$V_C^*(\tau_0)$

Hypothetical $V_C^*(\tau_1)$
(Preferred by Experimenter)

Fig. 4

havior. Thus the distribution of (cost) · (purchases) is necessarily an indication of the subject's attention and indirectly of G. Similarly, a (cost) · (purchases) distribution conditionally specified with respect to outcomes, as derived from stimuli and response selections, is an indication of the subject's "preference ordering" over the outcomes.

Adopting this strategy, the experimenter reaches a compromise with the subject as indicated in Fig. 4, which has the logical status of a *conversation*. The underlying mechanism of cost adjustment may, very readily, be delegated by the experimenter to an adaptive automaton that learns about the subject's behavior and determines the experimental environment. This kind of adaptive automaton does not dominate the interaction. In contrast, the adaptive teaching machine of the Appendix, Part 1, of this paper, adopts an instructional role, and does dominate the interaction.

THE REALIZATIONS OF CONCEPTUAL HOMEOSTASIS IN VARIOUS ARTIFACTS

4.1. In the Appendix, Part 2, of this paper, we remark that a self-organizing system can be variously realized. Conceptual homeostasis is a special property of some systems of this kind, and, not surprisingly, it appears in a number of artifacts. Within them, the process can be considered at a mechanistic level.

One of the most elegant of these artifacts is an adaptive network of neurone-like elements considered by Beurle [8]. The statistical connectivity between the elements is defined in accordance with the crass histology of the cortex, and there is a precisely specified way in which the network itself is a statistical model of the brain.

The physiological analogy is intriguing and is pursued in papers by Beurle. But for the present discussion we need only consider an indefinitely extensive network of this form* which (for reasons that need not concern us) is viewed as though it were a *decision maker* by some experimenter.

4.2. If the parameters of the elements have been adjusted to satisfy the assumptions (1), (2), (3), and (4), of 2.3, the behavior of active regions in this network will appear (to this experimenter)

---

*These networks are considered in detail in another paper of the Proceedings.

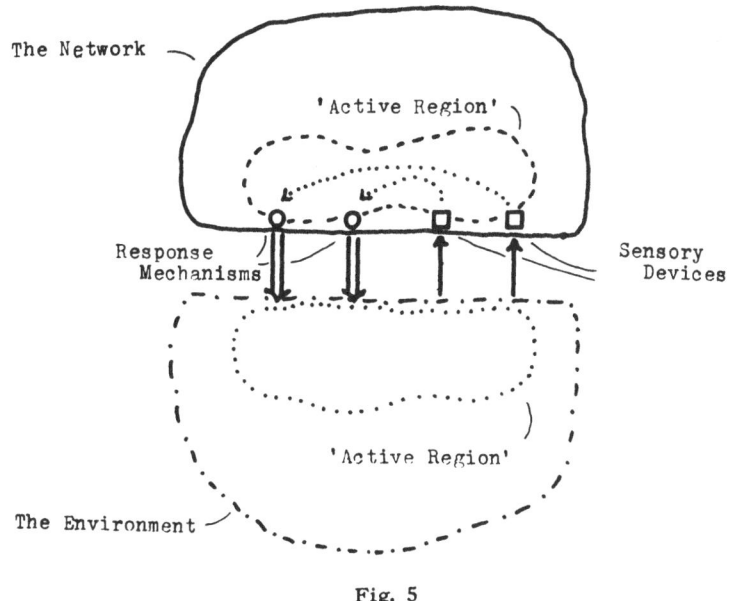

Fig. 5

like self-organizing systems and they will have the special property of conceptual homeostasis.

The network is coupled to the experimental environment by sensory channels and response apparatus, as in Fig. 5. The required parameter adjustments are such that in the absence of a coherent sensory image the sensitivity and the amount of autonomous activity per unit area will increase. If a sensory image is presented, patterns of activity (selectable by reinforcement) arise in the network and are replicated continually (perhaps with variations). Functionals computed over these patterns excite "trial-making" response mechanisms that select states of the environment.

When speaking of the "decision maker" we are not, of course, considering the tangible apparatus of the network, but patterns of activity that are sustained in the network by a cooperative process and limited by a competitive process. The cooperative process can be realized by many physical correlative mechanisms and the competitive process either by energetic constraints or by a suitable inhibitory mechanism. In either case the limitation is interpreted as satisfying the assumption (3) of 2.3 that there is a maximum rate of decision making, a minimum redundancy $\eta_{min.}$ or a limiting informational capacity. The initial connectivity and the parameters of the components will determine the most basic U of the network. It is convenient to assume that the constraints are minimal and activity in a region depends chiefly upon the current activity in adjacent regions and the activity which has previously occurred at the location concerned. Now one consequence of stipulating parameters adjusted to maximize the autonomous trial-making activity of the network in the absence of a coherent sensory input, is that the active regions are prone to expand, possibly also to evolve a characteristic form and, at the boundaries of the network, to engage feedback loops that have some components in the environment. Fancifully, it is as though the network were insufficiently large to sustain the activity it engenders so that stability demands a maximum interaction between the network and its environment. This is much the same concept of a brain that McCulloch advanced in his lecture "Finality and Form" but, in this paper, I wish to interpret the tendency to engulf components in the environment for parts of the system's feedback mesh as a symptom that assumption (4) of 2.3 is satisfied and to regard the active region as a system that "must attend to something." There is a maximum redundancy η_{max}. This decision maker only exists if the network is active. Now, according to assumption (1) of 2.3 the decision maker attends to and decides about "chunks" of data. If the phrases "attends to," "decides about" and "regards as" seem illegitimate, they can be replaced. "Attends to," for example, could be replaced by "is coupled to," which is less contentious. But we have supposed that the decision maker or a subject's brain is deemed *able to decide* and these phrases are commonly used to describe whatever *does decide*. From assumption (2) of 2.3 the decision maker is, in Ashby's sense, adaptable (indeed, according to Ashby, the systems in the network *must* be adaptable for they are large dynamic systems with many stable states [4]).

4.3. Consider the redundancy η_F of the states determined by an active region F (of unspecified extent in the network) that we identify with the mechanical concomitant of decision making. Suppose at $t = \tau_0$, F is adjacent to the environmental boundary so that some feedback loops in the environment, call them E, take part in the activity of F. In this sense, F, E become closely *coupled*. Due to adaptation, ξ_F must decrease and η_F tend to increase. But η_{max}. $\geq \eta_F \geq \eta_{min}$. The only compensation for the decrease in ξ_F is an increase in μ_F, which depends chiefly upon the extension of F in the network. Thus, as adaptation occurs, and pathways (or synaptic impedances) become well-defined and activity from different parts highly correlated, there will be a tendency for F to expand in order to increase μ_F. Or alternatively we could write $F_1 \rightarrow F_2$.

4.4 Suppose that $C(r_0)$ *describes* just the feedback loops E. When F expands the close coupling which existed when $t = r_0$ will be obliterated. Now if we insist upon a constant C we can only interpret E as a fixed set of feedback loops so that μ_E and $\mu_{C(r_0)}$ are also fixed. Due to adaptation in F, η_E and $\eta_{C(r_0)}$ will increase and then, as the coupling is obliterated, will become indeterminate. On the other hand, suppose the experimental environment is a similar network. In this case we are at liberty to interpret E as the name of an active region in the experimental environment, like F, in the artifact, and in this case E will decrease with ξ_F (for being closely coupled E, F are no more than trivially distinct). Similarly, to maintain η_E within its limits, μ_E must increase and E must expand in the experimental environment which we could write alternatively as $E_1 \rightarrow E_2$ (because of the close coupling which, is this case, *is* preserved, it is pointless to ask whether μ_E increases to compensate for increase in ξ_E or ξ_F). In fact, we require $\eta_{max.} \geq \eta_{E \cup F} \geq \eta_{min.}$ and compensate for decrease in $\xi_{E \cup F}$ by an increase in $\mu_{E \cup F}$.·

If we adopt this form of experimental environment E cannot be described in $C = C(r_0)$, any more than F could be described in $G = G(r_0)$. Instead, the experimenter must specify a sequence λ_C to correspond with a sequence of descriptive systems λ_G (which the experimenter could only refer to as "decision maker's descriptions of himself"). For coherence, $\lambda_C = L(\lambda_G)$ when ϕ describes the adaptive changes in the sequence of different systems. But, mechanically speaking, a close coupling is maintained between E and F, and if so, the system that represents E is a relation preserving mapping of the system that represents F and vice versa. In other words, $\lambda_C = L(\lambda_G)$ is secured.

Suppose now a form of experimental environment in between the rigid collection of feedback loops and the large adaptive network. It may be the environment controlled by the experimenter or an automaton.

In the system description, $C(r_0) = L[G(r_0)]$ corresponds with the mechanical condition of close coupling between E and F. This coupling is reduced unless steps are taken to adjust E (for E is no longer a large adaptive system, like the network). There are a couple of extreme possibilities. On one hand, F may be a uniformly expanding, gradually moving region of activity with mean correlation between point activity fairly constant throughout. In this case its behavior, unless matched against an active region in a comparable network, is indeterminate. An observer, such as a *man*, cannot specify momentarily invariant systems like $C(r_0)$ and build up P over a set of states that are, for practical purposes, fixed (nor, for that matter, would it make much sense to talk about "chunks" or "decision making"). At the other extreme, the adaptation in F leads to discrimination of closely related sets of elements.

Thus point activity correlations are highly structured and the abrupt change which occurs at $t = r_1$, when the active region expands, gives rise to a further highly structured configuration in which the constituents are groups of closely related elements that differentiated in the interval $(t = r_1) - (t = r_0)$. In this case, the experimenter *can* adopt momentarily invariant systems $C(r_0)$, $C(r_1)$, ... and describe coherent behaviors. He will also be impelled to say that the network exhibits conceptual homeostasis. MacKay [19] considered a similar process in detail and he called it the development of *hierarchical* structure in which constituents at a higher *level* [in this nomenclature an organization germane to $F(r_1) = F_2$, rather than $F(r_0) = F_1$] stand as symbols for groups of lower-level constituents. Such an organization has the capacity to generalize nontrivially, and in a realistic sense to construct metalanguages.

THE DIFFICULTIES IN SIMULATING
A SELF-ORGANIZING SYSTEM

5.1. Simulation of a self-organizing system in the manner of 1.6 appears to be either impossible or trivial. Of course, each P in ϕ is a statistical model which will determine a simulation like the models of 1.5, where P determines the constraints which any representative system must satisfy and chance events can be used to embody our indifference between representative systems. But the sequence ϕ is entirely distinct from the set $\mathscr{P}$ of 1.5 for, whereas the transition probability matrices of $\mathscr{P}$ are defined upon the *same* set of comparable states, those of ϕ are defined upon *different* and (apart from our meta-information) incomparable states. There is no function to select the P in ϕ as $g(\theta)$ selects among the P in $\mathscr{P}$ and any proposal would be, at best, a neat mathematical fiction. For in selecting the P in ϕ we are selecting between the C in λ, between different forms of inquiry. But the most cogent objection to simulating $[\lambda, L, \phi]$ is that the coherent behaviors are only meaningful in connection with the experimenter. The subject is only a self-organizing system relative to the experimenter. It would be possible, of course, to "simulate" by recording a number of $[\lambda, L, \phi]$, perhaps for the same subject. Recordings could be placed in a machine which, on request, selected one for replaying by reference to a chance event. The basis of this trivial device is a supposed indifference between experimenters. But a self-organizing system is a relational concept and we cannot afford indifference between experimenters (or their experimental environments), without whom the system is not meaningful.

5.2. The only valid simulation is a functional or mechanical model of the entire relationship which yields $[\lambda, L, \phi]$. The artifact must be able to construct metalanguages (but, as noticed, a developing hierarchical structure has this property). Thus, although we encounter the difficulties mentioned in 2.4, the simulation can be constructed (one of MacKay's hierarchically structured artifacts, one of Beurle's networks, a number of ultrastable systems, and a number of evolutionary systems). The difficulty is that this activity may be uninterpretable, and the artifact has the status of a loose analogy or a heuristic or a conceptual toy, although none of these should be despised.

ADDENDUM: COMMENTS ON EVOLUTIONARY AND SELF-ORGANIZING SYSTEMS*

EVOLUTIONARY AND OTHER AUTOMATA

We shall start with a story about two different automata, A and B, which look, at the first glance, like very much the same kind of creature. Each lives in a world where some commodity (money, energy, food, or candy bars, just as you please, providing it is conservable) becomes available in limited supply. To be noncommital we shall call this commodity X. Both A and B are able to collect X, and put it in a bag, and, in each case, the bag leaks. Both A

*This material was presented originally in the form of a second, short paper at the Symposium—*Ed.*

and B behave as if they were programed to maximize the amount of X in their bag, which implies that, on average, they must seek to collect X where its concentration is high.

In saying the supply of X is limited, I mean that although the commodity flows into the world (or is being produced), the automaton can collect X in a given region faster than it is replaced so that the X concentration in the neighborhood of this automaton will decrease. Thus it is pointless for either A or B to sit where they are and collect their X. On the contrary they must move around the world trying to find regions which are not depleted. In order to realize this behavior both A and B are provided with a finite set of possible moves, one of which must be chosen at each instant. Further, they receive sensory data about the concentration of X at more or less distant points, and they select the move they will make at any instant, as a function of their own state and the sensory evidence which they receive.

Although both of these automata move to regions in which X concentration is maximized and, in this sense, can be regarded as hill-climbers [1], the existence and welfare of A does not depend upon its success. This depends only upon its designer, who has assured it of its existence, providing it continues to obey the commands implicit in the function which converts sensory evidence into choice of a move. The function concerned may be, and often is, elaborate. It may involve a whole sequence of previous moves (expressed as the present state), but there is at some stage a limit to the length of strategy which can be inbuilt. Thus, in common with all hill-climbers, the automaton A can reach a position in which it has insufficient sensory evidence to determine a move according to its instructions. In this case it sits where it is indefinitely.

Its designer may guard against this situation by introducing a rule which says that in these conditions the automaton asks for an independent or chance event (for example, it throws a die) and this chance event determines which of the possible moves are made. Without exception practical hill-climbing automata rely upon some scheme of chance perturbation in order to resolve issues which are undecidable within the framework of their instructions.

Unlike A the automaton B cannot exist independently of its world. In the simplest case the substance of which it is made—either its logical structure or its actual fabric—tends to decay and must be maintained by expenditure of X, which can only come from the X in its bag. If the amount of X falls below a critical level, B will literally fall to pieces. This will happen, for example, if the automaton is faced with the dilemma I have just described—it has insufficient evidence on which to base a decision—and as a result remains motionless, depletes the X in its neighborhood and eventually the X in its bag.

Clearly B is an automaton designed to exist (whereas A existed independently of its X-maximizing activities). In a world with automata designed to exist (which stand a chance of ceasing to exist), we commonly have in addition a rule—a "nucleation" [14] rule—whereby automata are created at those points in the world where there is a surplus of X. But an automaton designed to exist is not, in itself, an evolutionary system. In order to be such a thing an automaton must be designed to *survive*. There is, however, a very close connection between the "designed-to-exist" creatures and those which are "designed to *survive*," which merits their inclusion jointly in the category B. It is this. Given a competitive world in which automata can interact (signal to one another and respond), cooperative subsets or "coalitions" may appear. Such coalitions behave like a single automaton and I have (in other papers) [13, 14, 28] described some of the conditions which make this single automaton a creature that is able to survive. For the present purpose we need only note that the simplest way to ensure interaction and aggregation of the primitive ("able-to-exist") automata is to make the fabric of the world use-dependent, so that the act of collecting X modifies the subsequent supply of X at the point where it is collected. More generally (and expressing the requirement in terms of a state description) the primitive automata must be closely coupled to habituable [4] surroundings.

With these comments upon its possible origin, we define automaton able to survive, which is itself an evolutionary system, by adding a rule R of development, to the "able-to-exist" specification. The rule R is applied whenever the "able-to-exist" automaton is imperiled by an undecidable situation. It says:

(i) If the X in the bag exceeds a critical limit, the primitive automaton evolves by transforming itself into a larger, more elaborately structured automaton able to make more moves and to appreciate a greater variety of sensory inputs, for which the (primitively undecidable) situation may not be undecidable.*

*A variant upon this rule, applicable in systems with many interacting

(ii) If the X in the bag is less than the critical limit (less than is needed to maintain the evolved structure), the primitive automaton ceases to exist.

It should be emphasized that:

(i) R is a decision function, the outcome of applying R depends upon the state of the automaton and, in general, its surroundings. There is such a rule, for example, in Selfridge's "Pandemonium" [41], and the R in Rashevsky's [39] evolutionary model is determined by our choice of the network transformation parameters.

(ii) R acts upon the *structure* of the automaton.

Basic Distinction

Thus the chance events that perturbed A when it was presented with an undecidable situation have been replaced in the case of B by:

(1) A rule R which induces a structural modification of the automata.

(2) A nucleation rule which assures a supply of structural elements, namely, primitive and X-dependent automata.

It occurs that an observer looking at a system which either is an A automaton or is made up of nothing but A automata, *need* suffer no *structural* uncertainty (he could examine the essentially finite automaton until its behavior sequence became cyclic, or in the simplest case, he may have constructed the automaton himself). But (because of the chance events) he may, unless he looks inside the dice-throwing machine, suffer uncertainty of a metrical kind about which of several possible outputs will occur. On the other hand, an observer who looks at a system which either is a B automaton, or is made up of B automata, will be liable to a great deal of *structural* uncertainty (unless, perhaps, he constructed the machine and has an entire and detailed history of its subsequent behavior). In other words (because of this) he will not know precisely what kind of structure he is observing.

Additional Points

For clarity I have assumed that the automata have a well-defined form, and might be thought of as Grey Walter tortoises [45]

---

automata, is that evolution occurs by the combination of primitive ancestors one of which is placed in an undecidable situation.

which shamble about the world. In this case their moves are actual motions and their sensory input is derived spatially. But an automaton need not be such a definite thing. Indeed, its basic specification is in terms of "states" and it has the logical form of one of Ashby's "machines" [3], that is, an automaton may be any set of states, related by some well-defined mapping (one or more transformations) such that some recognizable feature is kept invariant (the set of transformations form a group). Thus the automaton might be a mode of oscillation, or a wave of activity in one of the networks described by Beurle [8] (providing this mode or wave tends to survive), or it could be a set of chemical reactions which preserve some cyclic process invariant, or it could be some kind of abstract symmetry which is preserved without reference to any particular physical parts.

Further, the rule R can be variously embodied in the automaton. To cite a pair of less familiar cases:

(1) In Peter Green's [15] analysis of learning, we come across "representations" of data which (in a sense that Green makes explicit) are modes of oscillation in a network. Each "representation" Y includes a number of other representations of different data. In the terms we are adopting each Y is an automaton and the representations included by Y determine R for Y.

(2) A "thread" artifact which I have described (in other papers) [29, 31] gives rise to "automata" in the form of microcrystalline metallic fibrils, overlaid by an oxide coating. The "nucleation" rule for these automata is literally the crystal nucleation rule for the material. The "decay" rule is implicit in a chemical reaction which dissolves the thread. The fibrils develop and ramify according to the prevailing conditions in the system and R is, in this case, determined by the crystal structure of the metal. In particular the dynamics of this system illustrate Stafford Beer's [7] contention that the fabric of an evolutionary artifact is far from irrelevant.

Another important point which I suppressed for the sake of clarity is that it makes sense to talk of an evolutionary automaton only with respect to well-specified surroundings.* The concept of evolution refers to the relation between the *structure* of these surroundings and the *structure* of that which evolves. The particular case we cited—the surroundings in which competition for X took place—

*Similarly it only makes sense, as von Foerster has pointed out, to talk about a self-organizing system relative to a structured world (see [12]).

is valid, but far too specialized. Of course, if there were no restrictions on X the automata could not behave as evolutionary entities, and it occurs also that if they were unable to cooperate by interacting one with another, evolutionary automata (designed to survive) could never be built out of primitive automata (still of the B kind), which are designed merely to exist. However, in general these requirements of competition and cooperation are manifest in a more abstract and less readily extricable form than they are if we think of the automata as tortoise-like machines. I shall not attempt an entirely comprehensive discussion in this paper, but there will be an opportunity to point out a number of ways in which the evolutionary character of an entity depends upon the surroundings in which it is said to evolve.

Evolutionary and Self-Organizing Systems

Having built up a rough distinction between systems which are evolutionary and systems which are not, it will be possible to examine some features—properties of the system—which characterize the evolutionary kind. In doing so I hope to exhibit some consequences of a proposition due primarily to Ashby [5] and to Beer [6], which is (expressed in one way) that any closely coupled dynamic system capable of muliple partitioning will, if made very large, almost certainly be evolutionary.

At this juncture I wish to distinguish "self-organizing systems" from those which are "evolutionary."

To do so I would like to point out that the statement about large evolutionary systems is a consequence of the possible modes of interaction between abstract objects, constrained by the language which we commonly use in describing them, that is to say, by the restrictions of an admissible logic. When it comes to describing some physical assembly, either natural or constructed, we are forced (ultimately on account of various experimental uncertainties) to use descriptive frameworks which are formally incomplete. (A case in point is that experimental hypotheses can be meaningfully posed only within a formal structure, wherein numerical assignments—variable values—are comparable. Such hypothetico-deductive structures are incomplete and in other papers I have called them "reference frames" [32].)

Observers wishing to communicate the precise conditions of an experiment must confine themselves to one reference frame. This

strategy is adopted by those observers who wish inductive valida-
tion of an hypothesis. At least it is used for preference, but, note,
it need not be. There are other descriptions, poetic, discursive,
common-sense, and practical, of a physical assemblage, which are
not included within any one reference frame. In particular we can
and often do adopt a form of description which assumes a measure
of similarity between the observed system and ourselves, and when
we do this I shall say that we look at the system as though it were
a self-organizing system, or if another observer looks on and describes our process of interaction in terms of a metalanguage, he will
say "the system we are observing is a self-organizing system,"
being careful to note that the statement is meaningful only insofar
as he has defined the conditions of the interaction (in this case
that the environment of the system is an observer whom he is looking
at). It thus occurs that it is possible though pointless to look at a
table, or a plant pot, as though it were a self-organizing system.
But when observers look at evolutionary systems they suffer from
so much structural uncertainty that it becomes almost impossible
for them to retain the nicety of strict scientific observation in a
single reference frame, and at the same moment to derive useful information about the state of the system concerned. I thus define the
category of self-organizing systems (in a way which is compatible
with von Foerster's definition [12], and in most respects, is identical with it) as that category of (usually evolutionary) systems
which most observers are forced to look at in this manner if they
are usefully to describe or control what goes on. The property of
being a self-organizing system depends not only upon the behavior
of large assemblies, but upon the way in which, imperfect observers
that we are, we are bound to look at large assemblies when they
occur in the real world. [However, if it so depends, it can properly
no longer be said to be self-organized— Ed.]

COMMENTS ON SOME CHARACTERISTICS
OF AN EVOLUTIONARY SYSTEM

To keep something definite in mind, suppose a large assembly
of nonlinear neuron-like elements with gain greater than one, the
binary impulsive output of any one depending upon an inhibitory
operator (the analogue, in this assembly, to the inverse of local X
concentration), upon the state of the element, and upon impulsive

signals received from other elements through connective pathways with different attenuation coefficients. Let the signal attenuation of a pathway and (since the attenuation may be infinite) the existence of a pathway be "use-dependent" and subject to decay. The network of elements is, in current usage, "plastic" [46]. In general, the neuron-like elements will be, at most, primitive B automata, but given certain rules for the inhibitory operation (roughly speaking, that overlapping regions of mutual inhibition exist), a kind of competition takes place and cooperative subsets of the neuron-like elements will be produced. These *may* have the status of evolutionary automata (they will, for example, if there is a nucleation and decay rule for the elements as well as the connecting pathways and if the mutual inhibitory regions have certain distributions; they *may* if, even in the absence of a nucleation rule, there are sufficient primitive elements, so that a large percentage are almost always inactive). On the other hand, for a different choice of parameters, the network may behave as a conditionable but not as an evolutionary system (its equilibrium behavior, with respect to arbitrary input and output connections, resembling a homeostat [2]—its connectivity changes, one of Uttley's [44] conditional probability machines). Let us call the categories of behavior (induced by these different assignments of parameter values) the "evolutionary" mode and the structurally "invariant" mode.

Invariance of Relations Between Elements, i.e., of Dynamic Structures

In the evolutionary mode cooperative subsets of elements act as evolutionary B automata, having the network as their environment. They are closely coupled to it; thus, the boundary of an automaton is indistinct. For recall that the automaton, by definition, is a dynamic structure and different elements may realize it upon different occasions (the structure is the invariant, but the elements which make it up may change). Usually automata (defined in this way) migrate in the network and interact with one another [28]. Second-order invariants are relations between migrating automata.

Observer Dependence

The relation between an observer (or a set of input and output connections introduced by the observer) and the migrating automata is a special case. (1) The original choice lies with the observer, but (2) if the observations are to be meaningful, the chosen relation must be kept invariant.

The observer calls the system a self-organizing system if he adopts the expedients which we have already mentioned in order to keep this relation invariant. Thus the definition of a self-organizing system in terms of the set of orignally chosen relations for which an *arbitrary* observer can achieve invariance (which is clearly a preferred form) will always be unsatisfactory. Practically important definitions depend upon the *particular* observer or the particular environment he specifies.

Replication, Reproduction, and Stability of Structural Entities

In some special cases it has been shown that dynamic structures will replicate and reproduce and a subset of structures compatible with the network environment will be differentiated as stable. Since Dr. Ashby* will present an argument at this meeting which includes such cases (regarding reproduction as a characteristic of large, habituable, dynamic systems), the subject need not be discussed in this paper.

Redundancy of Potential Command

The network in its evolutionary mode necessarily exhibits McCulloch's "redundancy of potential command" [22]. For, to say where a decision is made, we must locate a subset of elements which makes the decision. But (since the network acts in its evolutionary mode) we have agreed that B automata decide. Although B automata are made of elements, we have also agreed (if the previous argument is accepted) that an automaton is a dynamic structure which may be realized by various elements.† Thus a statement that a particular subset of elements makes a decision is necessarily ambiguous, from which we argue that the network exhibits redundancy of potential command.

The Redundancy of Computation

Such a network also exhibits McCulloch's redundancy of computation [22]. To show this:

*Chapter II, this volume—*Ed.*

†It is possible to argue that an evolutionary automaton is usually a hybrid of several subsets of primitive elements, logically identical with a molecular resonance hybrid. Thus, it is not adequately specified at any instant whatever by indicating a particular subset.

(1) Represent the B automata as computing structures, in relation to input and output connections, so that a set of automata computes some function of the input signal.

(2) Invoke replication to produce parallel connected B automata which are similar (i.e., with respect to the similarity criteria existing in the system). Insofar as our own (external similarity) criteria agree with the internal criteria we shall regard the functions computed by the parallel automata as similar.

REFERENCES

1. A. M. Andrew, "Learning Machines," Symposium on the Mechanization of Thought Processes, Teddington, Nov. 1958. Proceedings published by Her Majesty's Stationer's Office.
2. W. R. Ashby, "Design for a Brain," 2nd ed., Chapman and Hall, London, 1960.
3. W. R. Ashby, "An Introduction to Cybernetics," Chapman and Hall, London, 1956.
4. W. R. Ashby, "The Mechanism of Habituation," Symposium on the Mechanization of Thought Processes, Teddington, Nov. 1958. Proceedings published by Her Majesty's Stationer's Office.
5. W. R. Ashby, "Principles of Self-Organization," Urbana Symposium on Self-Organizing Systems, University of Illinois, June 1960, Pergamon Press (to be published).
6. Stafford Beer, "Approach to a Cybernetic Factory," Urbana Symposium on Self-Organizing Systems, University of Illinois, June 1960, Pergamon Press (to be published).
7. Stafford Beer, "Cybernetics and Management," English University Press, 1959.
8. R. L. Beurle, "Properties of a Mass of Cells Capable of Regenerating Pulses," Phil. Trans. of the Royal Society of London, Series B, Vol. 240 (1956); and communication at the Symposium.
9. Jack Cowan, "Many-Valued Logics and Problem-Solving Mechanisms."
10. Jack Cowan, personal communication.
11. R. Crane, "The Neuristor," Stanford Research Institute Report 1506.1, 1960.
12. Heinz Von Foerster, "A Self-Organizing System and its Environment," in "Self-Organizing Systems: Proceedings of an Interdisciplinary Conference," ed. by M. C. Yovits and S. Cameron, Pergamon Press, New York—London—Paris, 1960.
13. Heinz Von Foerster and Gordon Pask, "A Predictive Model for Self-Organizing Systems," Cybernetica 4 (1960) and Cybernetica 1 (1961).
14. Heinz Von Foerster and Gordon Pask, "Proposed Game Theoretic Model for Self-Organizing Systems," Tech. Rept. 5, Contract Nonr 1834 (21), University of Illinois, Urbana, Illinois.

15. Peter Green, "An Approach to Computers that Perceive, Learn, and Reason," Proc. Western Joint Computer Conference, 1958.

16. N. Goodman, "The Structure of Appearance," Harvard University Press, Cambridge, Mass., 1951.

17. J. Y. Lettvin, H. R. Maturana, W. S. McCulloch, and W. Pitts, "What the Frog's Eye Tells the Frog's Brain," Proc. I.R.E., Vol. 47, pp. 1940-1951 (Nov. 1959).

18. Lumsdaine and Glaser, "Teaching Machines and Programmed Learning," Natl. Educ. Assoc. of U.S.A., 1960.

19. D. M. MacKay, "The Epistemological Problem for Automata," in "Automata Studies" (edited by C. E. Shannon and J. McCarthy), Princeton University Press, Princeton, 1955.

20. D. M. MacKay, "Operational Aspects of Intellect," Symposium on the Mechanization of Thought Processes, Teddington, Nov. 1958. Proceedings published by Her Majesty's Stationer's Office.

21. D. M. MacKay, "Quantal Aspects of Scientific Information," Phil. Mag., Vol. 41, p. 289 (1950).

22. W. S. McCulloch, "Agathe Tyche," Symposium on the Mechanization of Thought Processes, Teddington, Nov. 1958. Proceedings published by Her Majesty's Stationer's Office.

23. W. S. McCulloch and D. M. MacKay, "The Limiting Information Capacity of a Neuronal Link," Bull. Math. Biophys., Vol. 5 (1943).

24. W. S. McCulloch, "The Reliability of Biological Systems," in "Self-Organizing Systems: Proceedings of an Interdisciplinary Conference," ed. by M. C. Yovits and S. Cameron, Pergamon Press, New York—London—Paris, 1960.

25. W. S. McCulloch, "What is a Number, that a Man May Know It, and a Man that He May Know a Number," Ninth Alfred Korzybski Memorial Lecture, 1960, offset in Nos. 26 and 27 of the Bulletin of the Institute of General Semantics; see "Logisticon," Ch. VI of this volume.

26. G. A. Miller, "The Magic Number 7, Plus or Minus 1," Psych. Rev. (1956).

27. M. Minsky and O. G. Selfridge, "Random Nets," Symposium on Communication, London, 1960.

28. Gordon Pask, "Evolutionary Model," Urbana Symposium on Self-Organization Systems, University of Illinois, June 1960, Pergamon Press (to be published).

29. Gordon Pask, "Growth Processes," Proc. Second Cong. Internatl. Assoc. Cybernetics, Namur, Belgium, 1958.

30. Gordon Pask, "The Natural History of Networks," in "Self-Organizing Systems: Proceedings of an Interdisciplinary Conference," ed. by M. C. Yovits and S. Cameron, Pergamon Press, New York—London—Paris, 1960.

31. Gordon Pask, "Organic Control," Cybernetica 3 (1958).

32. Gordon Pask, "Physical Analogues to the Growth of a Concept," Symposium on the Mechanization of Thought Processes, Teddington, Nov. 1958. Proceedings published by Her Majesty's Stationer's Office.

33. Gordon Pask, "The Teaching Machine as a Control Mechanism," J. Soc. Instrument Technol. (June 1960).

34. Gordon Pask, "Teaching Machines," Proc Second Conf. Internatl. Assoc. Cybernetics, Namur, Belgium, 1958.

35. Gordon Pask, "Teaching Machines," New Scientist (May 1961).

36. J. Piaget, "The Child's Concept of Number," Routledge, Kegan Paul, 1951.

37. K. Popper, "Logic of Scientific Discovery," Hutchinson, 1958.

38. J. W. S. Pringle, "Parallel Between Evolution and Learning," in "General Systems Yearbook," Vol. 2.

39. N. Rashevsky, "Topology and Life," in "General Systems Yearbook," 1957.

40. Sidney Seigel, "Decision Making and Learning Under Varying Conditions of Reinforcement," Annals New York Acad. Sci., Vol. 89, p. 65 (Jan. 28, 1961).

41. Oliver Selfridge, "Pandemonium Paradigm of Learning," Symposium on the Mechanization of Thought Processes, Teddington, Nov. 1958. Proceedings published by Her Majesty's Stationer's Office.

42. R. W. Sperry, "Design Principles of Brain," Urbana Symposium on Self-Organizing Systems, University of Illinois, June 1960, Pergamon Press (to be published).

43. E. Thorpe, "Methods of Learning," Symposium on Experimental Biology, 1950.

44. A. M. Uttley, "Conditional Probability Computing in the Nervous System," Symposium on the Mechanization of Thought Processes, Teddington, Nov. 1958. Proceedings published by Her Majesty's Stationer's Office.

45. W. Grey Walter, "The Living Brain," Duckworth, London, 1953.

46. D. G. Willis, "Plastic Neurones Acting as Memory Elements," Lockheed Rept. LMSD 48432.

CHAPTER IX

RANDOM ASSEMBLY OF LOGICAL ELEMENTS*
M. PAUL SCHÜTZENBERGER

The following quotation from page 42 of "Finality and Form" by Warren S. McCulloch (published 1952 by Thomas of Springfield, Illinois) well illustrates the value of the present paper to the theme of this symposium, despite the author's modest insistence that he was not presenting any model.—*Ed.*

"All learning, including the process whereby the rules of induction are perfected, orders step by step an ensemble erstwhile chaotic. And, whenever this, which is a change of state, happens to an ensemble, the statistical variables that characterize it no longer require merely the first few members of the probability-distributions of monads, diads, triads, etc. of the elements of its component systems, but, instead, depend upon the ultimate trends of these distributions of n-ads as n increases without limit. For no task in physics is our mathematics so feeble or so far to seek: Fortunately for us, this change of state in our brains that may happen to water in a moment of freezing, goes merrily on in us as long as we can learn, and some of us may live to share the fun of concocting the required mathematics."

*Because the author was unable, by reason of many demands on his time, to submit this paper in written form, his oral presentation is here given in abridged transcription from magnetic tape. —*Ed.*

Since the notion of random and randomness repeatedly arises in the field we are discussing, I thought that maybe it would be of some interest to build examples of what may happen in certain circumstances when one is using random operations.

What I am about to present is not difficult from a mathematical point of view, consisting as it does not of theorems but simply of statements which I have found to be true to the best of my knowledge. Also, it is not offered as an accurate model for living things nor as one that should be constructed. In other words, it is no model whatsoever. I stress these points because I want to be extremely accurate as to what I am building.

I start with a set of inputs finite in number. The easiest manner of thinking of them is as a set of all words of length n which can be built with "letters" 0 and 1. All the 2^n possible "words" is my set of inputs. A logical element will be any sort of element which, let us say, taking a subset of this set, reacts when the input belongs to this subset and does not react when it does not belong to this subset. So this will be what I shall call a logical element. Now there are very obviously 2^{2^n} possible logical elements.

I shall discuss five examples, and each of these examples will be done in the following manner. I suppose that I am counting the population of logical elements, that is to say, with a probability distribution over this set. If $n = 2$, I have 4 possible inputs and the full complement of 16 logical elements. Let us call this set of all possible logical elements L.

Now what I start with is a reduced collection which contains any of these possible logical elements with a given frequency f_i. Let us start with the first example, as this will prove easier than proceeding abstractly. Suppose now that I am given a fixed wiring procedure. I have this big collection characterized by this frequency distribution, and suppose my wiring procedure is determining a majority organ. That is to say, I will take any piece in the collection, and wire it into a box which is realizing the majority organ, and then I will wire out. The majority organ will react to triple union of intersections of the subsets governed by the logical elements. The majority organ is the rule of the game, so to say.

Now I will take every conceivable triplet of logical elements of my characterized initial frequency distribution, wire them into a majority organ, and get their outputs. Let us consider this as an initial layer, with its own frequency distribution f_t, which is not the same as the initial one f_i. This second frequency distribution also represents an assembly of logical elements. We can again randomly take triplets of wires and repeat the operation, reconnecting always to a majority organ, thus gaining third and higher stage assemblies of logical elements. Let us call the frequency of the third such collection f_r. What I am interested in is continuing *ad infinitum* with respect to this specific wiring procedure, which is randomly wiring logical elements three by three into a majority organ.

Another possibility, and my second example, is to keep exactly the same setup except that now I wire the elements two by two, every possible pair, into, let us say, a Sheffer stroke. This will give another conformation.

A third possibility I want to discuss is to take the elements three by three, and instead of combining them by a majority rule, combine them by an organ which is known as Church's ternary connection. I could choose other logical functions. Another (the fourth example) would be addition modulo 2, wiring the elements two by two into a modulo-2 adder. And there is a last one (the fifth example) that I should like to consider, which is a bit different, and will be done in this way: I will build my second layer with the help of two wiring operations, one consisting in taking two elements and making a disjunctive connection, and then taking the same two and making a conjunctive connection. That is to say I am mixing two types of transform with the same frequency. The and/or wiring system will be used with frequency divided in half.

In each of these examples I am looking for the limiting conditions when the various wiring procedures are randomly continued *ad infinitum.*

There are two extreme pictures of what may happen when such systems go into random evolution. The first, which we may take as typified in Clausius's views, predicts a general leveling; the second, typified in Ashby's conception of a randomly organized ultra-stability, envisions a particularity and concentration rather than a leveling of effect and behavior. These are the two extreme views of what may happen in the long run.*

*To avoid confusion here it is important to remember that the two systems characterized by entropy increase on the one hand (Clausius) and homeostasis on the other (Ashby) are not at all on the same logical and physical footing, for the first is truly random, while the second uses random elements in a carefully contrived manner, with always a necessary stipulation as to the degree to which the environment of the system must be

Usually in most of the cases it is rather impossible to know what will happen, and we must rely on intuition. However, and that is why I have chosen these examples, we can know in some cases and can exactly compute what will happen.

Example 1: In this case, the frequency f_i (of a logical organ)[*] at the limit will be entirely degenerated. This will be an Ashby type of thing. It will degenerate into a probability distribution which at the limit, after infinite time and infinite layers, will consist only of a single subset of the initial assembly. My intuitive interpretation of this is that the minorities in this system are destroyed; it can be proved very easily that this is so.

Example 4: Here the random evolution goes exactly in the opposite direction. In the limit distribution every possible logical organ appears with the same frequency. Here the situation is mathematically completely undegenerate, in that every conceivable one of the $2^{(2n)}$ logical organs is operating with the same frequency. These limiting statements are true "almost everywhere." That is to say, if you offer me a counter-example, I will be able to offer a probability distribution which is arbitrarily near your counter-example, within my wiring rules, and for which my statement is true.

Example 3: Here I am connecting A, the loop which rules a set of responses to the original set, so that $A=B$ or $\bar{A}=C$.[†] This wiring rule produces a system whose random evolution goes much the same way as the previous example, in the sense that it will result in a probability distribution of maximum Clausius entropy and which has the property that the frequency of reacting to any specific word is the same f_i as the original connection, preserving a sort of invariance.

Example 5: The "and/or" wiring rule will behave like the majority organ of Example 1. You can imagine here that I am taking one "and" layer, one "or" layer, and fusing ideally these two layers,

---

protected. If the second system is placed in an environment protected to too low a degree in the special manner required, then the system will break down, and Clausius will rule as usual. The Clausius type of system makes no special demands on the protectiveness of its environment and by Occam's razor is the more logically primal of the two, requiring far fewer special initial conditions. *—Ed.*

[*] Or every subset governed by a logical element. A logical organ is characterized by a subset of inputs. *—Ed.*

[†] This statement refers to a concrete explanation of Church's ternary connection, being written on the blackboard at the time. *—Ed.*

and then repeating the process. It is rather surprising that here I will have a probability distribution that will be such that there exists one chain of subsets out of the set of all my possible input words. Every set that does not belong to this chain will be wiped out, and this one will remain with finite probability under the procedure of the operation.

Example 2: The Sheffer wiring rule is a bit more complicated, because a new phenomenon appears, and the limit does not exist properly, though it does exist in some sort of reasonable sense. It exists in the sense that there will be one type of logical organ which will appear to an overwhelming degree to be tending to one frequency.

In the first example, that of the majority organ, the logical element which will dominate at the end is that element which is such that the probability of every word in it is larger than ½. In the Sheffer stroke wiring rule, this final probability is no longer that, but now has as its limit a form of the golden section, or $0.618 \ldots = (\sqrt{5}-1)/2$. If you present me in this case, by way of vicious counter-example, with a probability exactly equal to this limit ratio, then the system will not be convergent.

Another characteristic of the Sheffer stroke rule is that if at some stage the frequency were low, at the next stage it would be high; and if at first it were high, in the next stage it would be low. *

In conclusion, there is one general statement which is interesting; namely, that whenever the wiring principle—the rule for going from one layer to another—is a logical function which doesn't involve negation, the resulting distribution will be the same as that for the majority organ (Example 1), in the sense that there will be a degenerate convergence. When functions involving negation are employed in the wiring rules, then there is no general way to prove whether or not there is a limit, and in many cases we can thus say nothing.

---

* Such oscillation accords phenomenologically with the convergent oscillation of the Fibonacci series, as it approaches its limit ratio, the golden section, which is intimately related to the Sheffer wiring rule (stroke function).—*Ed.*

CHAPTER X

ON MICROELECTRONIC COMPONENTS, INTERCONNECTIONS, AND SYSTEM FABRICATION*

KENNETH R. SHOULDERS

SUMMARY

Microelectronic data processing systems are analyzed and various requirements for components are considered. The rapid reduction in transmission line cross section upon scaling down causes increased losses in microelectronic systems, thus giving rise to the need for high-impedance components for noncryogenic applications. A new component is proposed that seems particularly suited for microelectronic system requirements and fabrication methods. This component is based upon the quantum-mechanical tunneling of electrons into vacuum, has an estimated switching time of 10^{-10} sec, promises immunity to temperature variations, and seems adaptable to self-forming manufacturing methods giving component uniformity. A method of electron-beam-activated micromachining for film materials is presented in which a thin chemically resistant film is formed with an electron beam to selectively protect the film being machined during a subsequent molecular beam etching. This high-speed process has resolution capabilities of several hundred angstrom units, can process electronically clean materials with minimum contamination, and may ultimately be suited for the economical production of 1-in.^{3} data processing systems having 10^{11} active components.

*Presented in absentia and here printed by permission of the author and the National Joint Computer Committee.

THE OVER-ALL REQUIREMENT

We want to build electronic data processing systems that have the complexity of human neural networks but are capable of operating with electronic speed. These machines should be capable of solving very complex problems such as those that arise in nonlinear systems, magnetohydrodynamics, pattern recognition from the real world, self-organization, and learning, and should in general be very useful assistants in our society.

Having once obtained such a machine, the need will invariably arise to make it highly portable so that it can cope with problems where they exist instead of depending on problems being brought to it. Everyone should have such a personal assistant.

The realization of such a machine requires an extremely high degree of organization of matter and may not be economically permissible unless a high-speed electronic construction process is used for specifying the end product. Admittedly, this is not the next generation of equipment to be expected. Our aims here are to try to achieve what seems possible with electronics and not base our work upon an incremental advance from present devices.

There has been a tendency lately to conceal the need for high-resolution processing methods through the use of such terms as "molectronics," or by talk of distributing "this-or-that." There always seems to be a discrete device, even if composed of distributed parts, which serves our requirements in a data processing machine. It seems likely that this will continue for some time.

Our problem, then, is how to handle material with enough resolution to fabricate 10^{11} devices in a size that is portable, and then to find an interesting configuration for these materials so as to give a desired electronic result.

But before we start building things at random, we might do well to look at some of the properties of electrical devices in the microworld, and thus avoid some lost motion by only working on things that are expected to work. We have picked arbitrarily 10^{11} components for our system. Let us see what this implies in terms of physical size for the machine.

The most highly resolved construction process that we have any control over is what we call "electron-beam-activated micromachining." This process has been shown to give some results in the 100-A region, but let us degrade this to 300 A for the moment and see what we can make with it. If an arbitrary component can be made from about 1000 of these 300-A dots, as seen from the plan view, then the outside dimensions of the component would be about 1 μ. The thickness could be expected to be an equivalent value. If three of these 1-μ-sized areas are used for interconnections for every component, then we have 2 μ of linear dimension per component and 10^4/in. One square inch of area would contain 10^8 elements. If ten layers of components per module were used there would be 10^9 components. One hundred modules, each being 0.010 in. thick for support purposes, would stack to a 1-in. cube having 10^{11} components.

Before we go into the insides of this system, let us look at some external problems. If we wish to pick up optical data, we find that a 1-in. cube made by stacking wafers has just two surfaces available for communication with optical patterns from the outside world. One of these would be expected to receive light images, and the other to generate light patterns for human use.

There will be a noticeable lack of lead wires at the edges of the modules, compared to the number of components on the module. For communicating between modules, wide-band serial techniques could be used for the few wires available at the edge and the surfaces could be used by allowing light coupling between modules. It might be expected that up to 10^4 parallel paths could be achieved in this way without the use of a lens. The bandwidth would seem to depend upon the light detector, and may fall in the 10-Mc range.

In changing the size of things so radically—about three orders of magnitude—we will be well advised to look over old components to see if they can become useful in this size range. For example, we may reconsider a mechanical electrostatic relay because now it could have vacuum contacts and operate at low voltage in the 10-Mc range. We could look again at conventional vacuum tubes and consider the negligible transit time lag and absence of bothersome space charge effects because of the high fields. Thermal devices will be found to have time constants in the microsecond range.

SCALING OF ELECTRICAL PROPERTIES

Not all effects are beneficial when sizes are reduced. One of the most disturbing changes is the increased electrical loss of conventional wires.

The effect of scaling down in size on certain fundamental electronic components can be shown by reviewing the behavior of inductance, capacity, and resistance. The values of inductance and capacity vary directly with their size, while resistance has an inverse behavior. If all dimensions of a standard-sized tuned circuit were reduced by 10^4 to make it about a micron on a side, then the resonant frequency would be raised by 10^4. The Q at this new frequency has been decreased by 10^4, and would be reduced by 10^8 at the original frequency. A search for new filtering methods is in order. RC filters and methods of producing effective inductance could be used, but their stability has never been adequate. This new filter may be the logic of a pattern recognition machine. Serial communication filtering could be handled by sample data techniques coupled with appropriate quantization and logic circuits—in other words, the digital filter. In short, the communication set of the future would become a computer. These techniques would not be thrifty in their use of components and it should be expected that vast numbers of components would be needed.

In addition to an increased loss for tuned circuits, we find that the same mechanisms are at work to cause excessively lossy transmission lines. For example, a 3000-A-diameter line having a length of 1 in. would have 100,000 ohms dc resistance. The added high-frequency loss of the line would be quite severe. A clear dictate for a microcomponent wired to its neighbors in the classical way is that it be a high-impedance component. In general, electric-field-operated devices like tubes and transistors have high impedance while magnetic components have low impedance. This high impedance does not necessarily mean long switching times in microelectronics. Consider that the distributed capacity of a 1-μ device may be as high as 10^{-15} farad, and if this is associated with a 100,000-ohm resistor a 10^{-10} sec time-constant results.

PROPERTIES OF MATERIALS

We should now look into the properties of materials in the submicron region. The resistivity of conductors is very near that of bulk materials for a 3000-A-diameter transmission line [1] but we are encouraged to find that dielectrics can have breakdown strengths several orders of magnitude higher than bulk materials [2]. Breakdown values of 3×10^7 v/cm for a 2000-A film of aluminum oxide are typical. This is primarily because the thickness is near the value for the mean free path of an electron in the dielectric, and an avalanche is not allowed to occur under such conditions and breakdown is forestalled. One should be motivated to look into high-field-strength electrostatic devices in order to take advantage of this effect.

Some of the mechanical properties of microstructures seem to make things difficult for us. For example, it seems much more difficult to grow a highly ordered single-crystal film than a bulk single crystal, especially on an amorphous or micropolycrystalline substrate that may be required for multilayer component construction.

Surface tension forces play a very important role in certain submicron configurations; these powerful forces try to form our carefully shaped parts into tiny spheres which may not be useful [3, 4].

When the quantity of material in our component is reduced to the level required, extreme precautions must be taken to prevent either self-diffusion or diffusion of foreign materials. These microelectronic components can no longer average out the effects of foreign material. "Well, I haven't looked that closely but the thing that does surprise me is that the effects are as big as they seem to be if indeed they are caused by what I suppose" (anonymous contribution to discussion on surface phenomena).

As the size of our device is reduced the surface-to-volume ratio rises and surface recombination effects may become very difficult to cope with.

This increase of surface-to-volume ratio brings with it a fantastic cooling mechanism for individual micron-sized components. It has been found in relay contact research, and particularly by x-ray microtechniques [5], that the power density into a 1-μ area can be 10^8 w/cm^2 continuously without material decomposition. Of course, it would not be expected that many components in the same area could operate at this level without catastrophic effects.

TUNNEL EFFECT VACUUM TUBE

We propose to take advantage of some of the effects found in the microworld and incorporate them into a component based upon the quantum-mechanical tunneling of electrons into vacuum. Fig. 1 shows one configuration that may prove interesting.

The operation of this device may be divided into two parts to help our understanding of it—namely obtaining electron emission and using these emitted electrons.

The cathode properties have been investigated by many workers and there is general agreement that the current density can be 10^7 amp/cm^2 with only very small space charge effects [6]. This is due to the high field strength of a few times 10^7 v/cm. The current from

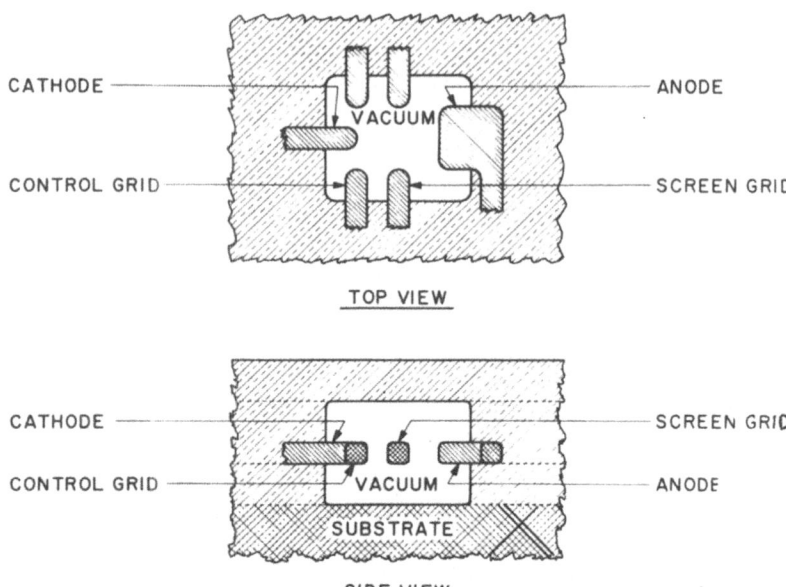

Fig. 1. Tunnel effect vacuum tetrode.

this source can be varied over seven powers of 10 by a change in field of 2 to 1 at the cathode, implying high gain possibilities. Tests at 10,000 Mc have verified that there is no detectable deviation from the dc emission characteristics [7].

The variation of grid voltage would cause the necessary field change at the cathode. A measured velocity distribution of 0.14 ev shows that this is not a noisy source [8].

Our intentions are to form an array of small tips superimposed on the cathode shown in Fig. 1. These tips should be a few hundred angstrom units in diameter in order to obtain emission below 100 v when applied to the screen grid or anode. The cathode shown in Fig. 1 is nominally 3000 A wide.

Electron-optical considerations dictate how the emitted electrons are to be used. A positive control grid would normally be used, but this would not draw appreciable current because it is located away from the electron path between cathode and anode. Negative grids are possible if they are smooth enough or have high work function so as to prevent emission. It is desirable to collect the electrons at a low plate potential, thus avoiding unnecessary heating.

Potentials as low as a few volts would seem possible because the field strength would still be sufficient to allow collection of electron current densities of greater than 10,000 amp/cm^2 without adverse space charge effects.

The screen grid would remain at some level in the 100-v range acting as a bias to help cause field emission, but not collecting an appreciable current.

The upper limit in switching speed for this device would be set by the allowable power dissipation. If an anode voltage of 10 v, a current of 100 μa, and a capacity of 10^{-15} farad is used, this 1-μ-sized device would show a switching time constant of 10^{-10} sec for a power density of 10^5 w/cm^2—well within the allowed value for a single component.

Our complete machine composed of tunnel effect elements could have a maximum input power of 100 w—as determined by heating considerations. The 1 mw of input per device would allow 10^5 devices to operate simultaneously with a 10^{-10} sec switching time, which gives a bit rate of 10^{15}/sec.

The transit time for electrons would be about 10^{-13} sec, and this would seem to remove the need for complicated traveling wave devices to obtain high-frequency gain.

Environment

Tunnel effect cathodes have been found to be insensitive to variations in temperature between 4 and 2000°K. The complete tunnel effect device would seem to be similarly independent of temperature although a high temperature limit is clearly predicted by conduction within the dielectric.

Mechanical forces would not likely affect this microscopic device unless a physical crack resulted in the construction materials.

Ionizing radiation does not affect the cathode properties or other metal electrodes until the dielectric has been severely damaged. The choice of dielectrics for this device is very wide, but materials like aluminum oxide or beryllium oxide, in film form, would be chosen because of their stable characteristics under bombardment.

Reliability

It is obvious that a device is prefectly reliable if none of the material composing it is allowed to move or migrate. This condition for stability is most easily met by using only refractory metals and dielectrics and removing all foreign materials from the system. Tunnel effect devices need only one type of conductor and one type of dielectric; these materials are chosen primarily for their stability, and no compromise has to be made to win some electrical effect. In addition to stable components, it is necessary to have dense layers of encapsulating materials to prevent migration of materials from the outside surfaces into the active areas. Microscopic vacuum and solid-state devices suffer to an equal extent from this migration. To assist the application of dense outer layers it is beneficial to use high-temperature processing for encapsulation.

Several thousand hours of operating life is presently obtained with gross field emission devices operated at 10^7 amp/cm^2 [10]. The cause for deterioration is inevitably due to contamination of the cathode or sputtering of the cathode with ions formed from gas contaminants that migrate into the area. By reducing the area of the container, a large source of contamination is removed. Lower operating voltages reduce the sputtering effects, and a clean construction process would remove the remaining offenders. The field emission cathodes now in existence are the only experimental examples the electronics industry has which operate with the microscopic areas of 10^{-10} cm^2 that we anticipate using. We should be warned that the stability problem for all devices of equivalent area is severe, and then take steps toward clean construction methods.

Reproducibility

Vacuum tunnel effect devices have a very high probability of being self-formed into vast arrays having uniform electrical properties. This seems to be a unique advantage not shared by many types of components. The principal requirement for device self-formation is that a chemical process be effected by a significant electrical property of the component in such a way that the component is altered to a new form. The simplest illustration of this effect is the formation of an electrolytic capacitor in which the voltage controls the dielectric thickness. Additional requirements for self-formation are that all chemical residue may be driven from the component and that the uniformity will not be altered by this material being removed.

Cryogenic devices seem to have a negligible possibility of self-formation; magnetic devices a somewhat higher possibility, but still fairly low; semiconductor devices would be next in line; and then vacuum devices, which would be the easiest group because of the constant accessibility of the electronic surface being formed to the chemicals responsible for forming. It is advantageous to have an electronic device that is insensitive to temperature variations for self-forming methods, because all too frequently chemical action cannot be made to take place at the component operating temperature. Once again vacuum devices, and especially tunnel effect vacuum components, show their advantages.

In the self-formation of our tunnel effect components, the device would be made as near as possible to the final shape by electron-beam-activated micromachining with the many small cathode tips being formed too sharp for use. A voltage would be applied to all electrodes simultaneously in the presence of a molecular beam etchant and at an elevated temperature. The voltage would be raised until the sharpest tips began emitting. These emitted electrons have been found to accelerate the etching of small tips; this in turn tends to increase the tip radius and reduce emission. By gradually increasing the applied voltage up to the operating value, all of the excessively sharp tips are degenerated to a constant emission value. The entire array of components would now be heated under ultra-high-vacuum conditions and sealed with encapsulating layers of materials. This self-forming process has taken into consideration the pertinent spacing variations as well as the cathode properties.

Interconnection

We intend to employ vacuum tunnel effect devices in a system that uses only optical input converters, electroluminescent generators, and a means for interconnecting components. No lumped capacitance, inductance, or resistance seems needed.

Since complete vacuum tunnel effect devices do not exist, detailed electrical characteristics are not known and it would be a waste of time to develop elaborate circuits for this hypothetical device. Still, there are many things that can guide us toward the eventual circuits.

Direct coupling between devices is facilitated by the positive grid characteristics. It has been found that the voltage-vs.-current characteristic of a vacuum tunnel diode behaves like a normal diode with a battery in series with it, thus forestalling conduction until the voltage has been raised appreciably. This bias-battery effect is beneficial for direct coupling.

When an output is sought that takes either one of two states—B+ or ground—two tetrodes are used in series across the power input, one serving as a switchable load resistor for the other. In the type of microelectronics described here, every effort should be made to conserve energy, and the arrangement just described allows the capacity of the switched point between the two devices to be charged or discharged quickly without using a low-value load resistor that requires the constant dissipation of energy for one of the switched states.

If resistors are excluded from our circuits then it will be found difficult to discharge grids under certain conditions. Here we would like to invoke the use of secondary emission [11,12]. The time delay from secondary emission surfaces is so short that it has never been measured. The current density available is arbitrarily high, up to the point that space charge or heating effects set in. The stability for properly cleaned surfaces would be the same as for equally clean field emission cathodes; thus we may feel free to employ this effect in clean microelectronic systems. The effect we seek is to drive a control grid positive when it receives a burst of electrons with enough velocity to exceed the secondary emission one-to-one point. In this way, a floating electrode may be driven positive or negative by changing the velocity of the electrons or by deflecting a beam of constant velocity to either the high or the low secondary emission areas of the electrode.

We would employ active memories of the negative resistance or dynatron type using secondary electron emission in this microelectronics system. A memory device of this type can have an almost arbitrarily low power consumption—limited by the leakage of the dielectric. The storage capacity of this memory must be charged and discharged by very energetic devices such as tunnel effect tetrodes in order to operate in the 10^{-10} sec region.

As an alternate memory method we could use flip-flops having additional tunnel effect tetrodes to replace the conventional plate load resistors. The proper feedback to the variable load resistors serves to provide a low impedance for quick charging and a high impedance for the quiescent period.

These memory configurations reduce the current during the quiescent period to a value just necessary to prevent dielectric leakage from changing the stored value. A large array of these elements in quiescent state would draw a current equivalent to a slightly leaky capacitor of comparable area and thickness. Accidental removal of the voltage source from the system would have no immediate effect.

In future systems we shall want to dispose of some of the wires for interconnecting devices. Besides being a lossy means for conveying information in the microworld, wires are a very inflexible arrangement for connecting components. We would like to have a completely uniform array of low-complexity modules that are not interconnected in the beginning. A "path" should be built as the machine learns, and this path should be built by entirely electronic methods making efficient use of the components. An electrically steerable, periodically focused electron guide, sometimes called slalom focusing [13], seems to answer our needs. This system makes use of the ballistic properties of free electrons and is able to guide bundles of electrons around devious corners, cross beams in the same plane without interference, obtain persistent current loops, and potentially cause certain beam-beam interactions that can do logic.

One configuration that appears useful is to locate our periodic array of modules—capable of launching, receiving, and steering electrons—between two conductive planes at cathode potential. This layer of components would then contain about half as much material as the wired method. Voids, for the potential electron paths, would replace the wires. The potential of the outer electrode of our module would guide the electrons, the potential being determined by an internal memory and past history. The module would be expected to carry out steering functions and logical functions independently so as to increase the logical freedom of the system.

Once again our high field strengths would provide the means for suppressing space charge effects. The transit time for a 100-v beam would be about 1/100 the velocity of light—not a bad price to pay when the dispersion effects on a lossy transmission line are considered.

Having once entered the electron beam realm, we are able to use parametric amplifier techniques and achieve low-noise amplifiers in spite of high lattice temperature [14].

Light Coupling

For coupling light into our system, we will invoke nothing more sophisticated than a photosensitive surface connected to the grid of a tunnel effect amplifier, either directly or through secondary emission electron multipliers.

For output displays, field-emitted electrons can cause dc electroluminescence effects, or in a less advanced scheme simple bombardment of a film of phosphor will suffice. If our systems are to be immune to temperature effects up into the red heat range, blue emission would seem most interesting. A blue-sensitive photo-surface has a high work function and can be stable in this temperature range.

CONSTRUCTION PROCESS REQUIREMENTS

We now need a fabrication method to make our devices. Although vacuum tunnel effect devices have been emphasized, we do not intend to exclude any known electronic component from our repertoire.

It may seem at first that we have taken on some especially difficult problems like vacuum encapsulation, but a closer look reveals that this is no more difficult than filling in unused space in a solid-state system. Present film methods do not see the problem because the edges of the film are so diffuse that a grading effect occurs between adjacent elements. When components are made that have micron dimensions on all sides, high-resolution filling of voids is necessary to prevent a self-induced pin-hole effect. Converting a small closed vacuum cavity can be done as easily as filling voids in one layer so as to smooth the surface, before proceeding to the next layer. This smoothing seems necessary regardless of the component used.

By being able to support a very thin film inside of a vacuum cavity, infrared or thermal detectors could be partly isolated from the lattice. Mechanical devices like electrostatic relays or acoustical filters also need this isolation.

Material Deposition

We have elected to use vacuum deposition methods to obtain our starting materials because this is a convenient method of producing a wide range of clean materials. Thermal evaporation has been used to produce photo-conductors, phosphors, magnetic materials, superconductors, metals, dielectrics, and semiconductors. Reactive deposition methods [15] have produced the same group of materials, but have superior crystalline properties and greater stability. Reactive deposition is usually carried out by reacting some metal halide with a reducing or an oxidizing agent.

These reactions are most conveniently carried out in a high-vacuum system as shown schematically in Fig. 2. For the deposition of molybdenum, one of the evaporation sources becomes molybdenum pentachloride and the other is hydrogen, made by thermally decomposing a material like zirconium hydride. The evaporation rate of these materials is monitored by separate ion gages and adjusted by external regulators. Upon reacting at the heated substrate, molybdenum is deposited and hydrogen chloride is pumped away. By this same method, aluminum oxide films can be formed when aluminum chloride and water vapor are reacted. Pin-hole free deposits are obtained because there are no ash or lumps from the sources that are not immediately volatilized at the surface, and in addition the high mobility of the molecules on the surface does not cause shadowing effects from dust specks. There is less strain in the deposited films since the substrate can be much hotter for re-

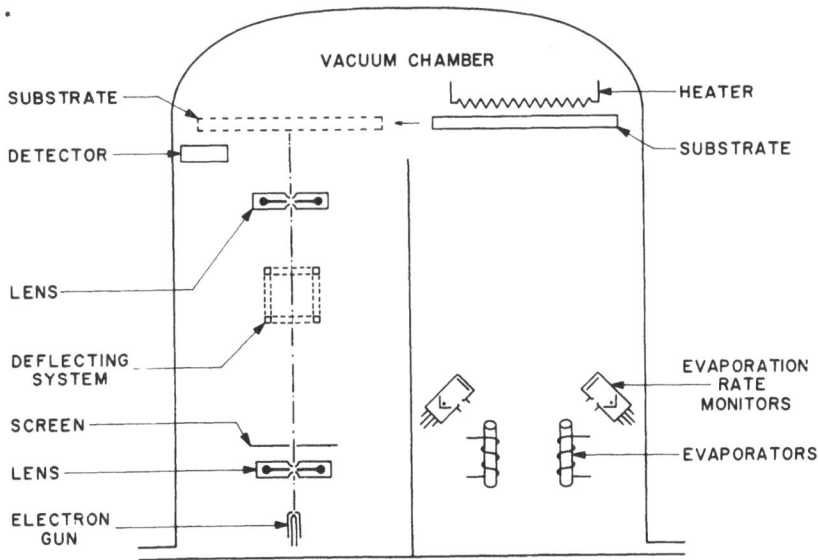

Fig. 2. Processing chamber.

active deposition than for a conventional thermal evaporation. This higher temperature is possible because there is a mechanism for carrying away the energy of the condensing molecule when the volatile product of the reaction leaves the surface. Reactively deposited materials can be graded to the underlying film in an optimum fashion—not so little that the films tear or peel, and not so much as to ruin the sensitive electronic surfaces. Doping can be added to semiconductors with reasonable assurance of going in properly.

Material cannot be accurately localized by masking at the surface with reactive deposition, as it can with thermal evaporation. We are thus led to seek a method of selective removal for the films that are produced.

Material Removal

Any film that can be deposited can be etched away in the same vacuum system by using a molecular beam of the proper compound or element. If one of the evaporators in Fig. 2 becomes a source for chlorine, and the previously deposited molybdenum film is heated to around 500°C, the film will be converted into molybdenum chloride which evaporates from the surface. Aluminum oxide films can be etched in a phosgene molecular beam.

Etching in a vacuum system carries many advantages with it. For example, if etching effects are desired that cannot be obtained with molecular beams, then atomic beams can be used. The lack of surfaces between the source and the substrate prevents recombination of the atomic species. A sputtering etch can be easily carried out in the same apparatus.

It is desirable to have an etching reaction as efficient as possible to produce the cleanest samples. Any excess materials, like carrier gases, coming into contact with the surface raise the possibilities of contamination.

The Resist

It will be found that certain thin layers of material can protect the film below them during etching and thus become a resist. Amorphous silica has been used as a resist for the selective etching of molybdenum and aluminum oxide as well as many others. This silica layer need be only about 50 A thick for the protection of several thousand angstroms of underlying film material. After serving its purpose as a resist, the silica can be removed with a brief hydrogen fluoride molecular beam etch. Many resists are available, and simple chemical selection rules can determine which one is the best choice for any particular requirement.

The resist layers can be thermally evaporated onto a surface through masks, but this would not serve our purposes of having a high-speed, electronically controlled, high-resolution process. We have found ways of producing a silica resist by bombarding certain silicon-containing organic compounds with electrons [16]. The most common example is the bombardment of tetraethylorthosilicate. This substance is a liquid at room temperature and evaporates to the substrate where it probably forms a multimolecular adsorbed layer. When this film is bombarded for about 1 sec with a beam of 10 ma/cm^2 current density, enough silica is produced for our pruposes. The mechanism for silica production is not known in detail, but it is assumed to be a free radical polymerization of the organic followed by decomposition to silica upon heating to etching temperatures.

This gas-like compound is not easy to handle because it tends to enter the electron lens and contaminate the surfaces. An alternate material that also produces silica, but is easier to handle, is triphenylsilanol. This is a solid that is evaporated to the surface and then exposed as described above. Immediately after exposure no change is evident, but heating causes the unexposed areas to evaporate and the exposed portions to remain as a silica-like deposit.

The efficiency of this reaction is such that an average of one molecule of silica is produced for each electron. More sophisticated methods of resist production have given yields of over 10^3 molecules per electron by causing current multiplication within the sample being exposed.

The resolution of resist production has been seen to exceed 100 A. This is observed by exposing a surface of resist-producing material with an oblique flood electron beam in such a fashion that shadows are cast by objects on the surface. These objects are usually polystyrene spheres about 880 A in diameter. An electron microscope is used to view the result.

Electron-Beam-Activated Micromachining

It can be seen that electron-beam micromachining is the combination of certain methods of deposition, resist production, and etching. Our initial requirement for this fabrication process was to economically produce a 1-in.^{3} system of 10^{11} parts being composed of 100 modules; each having ten layers of 10^8 components per layer. How much time would it take to construct the system? Let us find how long it would take to make a single layer of 10^8 components, and then multiply by 1000.

The substrate must first be very carefully prepared by grinding. polishing, preparing terminals, vacuum firing, repolishing, and then final cleaning and smoothing in the ultra-high-vacuum processing chamber. The substrate can be an expensive item.

For each layer of components there may be an average of four depositions and four etchings required. About 5 min per deposition and etching is possible, which includes time for heating and cooling. This totals 40 min so far.

The 10^8 components per layer and their interconnections can be represented as an array of about 10^{11} 300-A dots. This is arrived at by remembering that each component is composed of 10^3 pieces—our basic building blocks. It has been found that high-resolution electron optical systems can easily have 10^8 bits in one field of view—a consequence of the small aperture angles used. A gross image could thus contain 10^5 complete components per field. We will be required to mechanically move the substrate in front of the lens to produce our latent-resist image. A thousand steps are needed to make 10^8 components. Each exposure can be made as rapidly as the electrical and mechanical system is able to servo and register on the preceding layers—about 1/10 sec. The high current density of the electron beam is able to expose the image in a negligibly short time. One thousand steps would take about 2 min per layer or 8 min for four layers. We have now accumulated 48 min to process one layer of components.

The production of an entire machine would take 1000 × 48 min or about 800 hr.

We have elected to use an electron beam to convey information to a surface to describe the patterns of material that will be successively built up to form a module. Besides the obvious advantage of having short wavelength, electron beams have entremely bright sources, i.e., many events per unit time, they are electrically steerable, and they interact well with matter. Beams have been used to analyze the properties of matter such as absorption spectra, crystalline diffraction effects, chemical analysis by x-ray fluores-

cence [17], geometrical arrangement [18], contact potential, and surface cleanliness [19]. In addition, beams have been used in electron mirror microscopes [20] to show voltage, magnetic field, and
resistivity. We intend to integrate all of these functions into a
single electron optical system so that our machine tool becomes an
analytical tool as well.

Electron Optics

The electron optical system employed must integrate the functions of a scanning electron microscope, scanning x-ray fluorescence probe, and mirror microscope. This instrument is required
to operate under ultra-high-vacuum conditions so that conventional
electron microscope designs having many rubber gaskets will not
do. We have elected to make an all-ceramic electrostatic instrument, with metallized surfaces, in order to obtain the necessary
mechanical stability during the vacuum bake-out cycle.

When completed, this instrument should be capable of machining
or viewing structures down to a limit of 100-A resolution. The x-ray
fluorescence probe could measure film thickness to 1/10% accuracy
and be able to carry out a quantitative chemical determination on
10^{-13} g of material to 1% accuracy. The mirror microscope feature
could measure the voltages on any element of our components that
lay on the surface. This voltage measuring method could be converted by simple electrical switching into a very wide-band oscil-
loscope to show the dynamic behavior of the components.

In addition to the functions of magnification, demagnification,
manipulation, and electron and x-ray detection, the electron optical
system must have a pattern generator integrated with it. The simplest means of conveying information to the surface is to use a
scanning electron beam, but it will be found that this method is
severely bandwidth- and energy-limited for complex patterns.

If a perfectly repetitive pattern is required for each of our 1000
exposures per layer, then a simple large-scale mask is needed near
the electron source. If some submodule exists in irregular order
throughout our system then this can be obtained by a mask and then
be deflected electrically to the desired location.

Since this electron-beam machining process requires such a low
current density, purely electrical methods of pattern generation may
be invoked. A slowly scanning input beam can write a charge pattern
on a storage screen which in turn controls the transmission of elec-

trons. Ultimately, we would use a vacuum tunnel effect cathode array for our electron source. The emission from discrete areas would be controlled by local grids connected to micromemory elements which are set by a slowly scanning beam or a microelectronic stepping system to write in the pattern changes that are required. Thus we have components made by electronic micromachining responsible for the building of new systems by the same method. In the end, self-reproduction would be a distinct possibility without the use of a lens system, because all copies would be made on a one-to-one size basis.*

ACKNOWLEDGMENTS

We gratefully acknowledge the support of our work by the Information Systems Branch of the Office of Naval Research on Contract Nonr 2887(00), and the support of the Air Force on Contract AF 19(604)-6114 and the Signal Corps on Contract DA-36-039-SC-84526.

REFERENCES

1. L. Holland, "Vacuum Deposition of Thin Films," John Wiley & Sons, Inc., New York, 1956, p. 233. See sections on "Conduction in Very Thin Films" and "Mean Free Path of Conduction Electrons."
2. D. A. Powers and A. Von Hippel, Massachusetts Institute of Technology Laboratory for Insulation Research. Progress Reports show consistent breakdown strengths between 50 and 200 Mv/cm for film thicknesses between 700 and 4000 A using alumino silicate glass.

*The following note is based on the present editor's visit with the author at Stanford in January 1962. Shoulders, though retaining the conditions of high vacuum and microstructure as a *sine qua non* of his approach, has shifted from a cryogenic emphasis to an automaton and computer concept based more and more upon slalom electron beams looping about fixed positive charges. Such networks have analog properties. His current module is quadruply blocked as "Memory for steering," "Logic for steering," "Memory for logic," and "Logic for logic." Shoulders goes on to envision plasma "brains" path-controlled by electrostatic fields of confined positive ions.

The memory loops of his slalom beams possess very low dielectric leakage and are traversed in a few milliseconds. As references for this newer work can be cited W. H. Bostwick in the *Physical Review* of October 1956, May 1957, and July 1958; also K. R. Shoulders' interim report of September 1960, Stanford Research Institute Project 2863: "Research in Microelectronics Using Beam-Activated Machining Techniques."—*Ed.*

3. W. P. Dyke and W. W. Dolan, "Advances in Electronics and Electron Physics," Academic Press, Inc., New York, 1956, Vol. VIII, p. 153. See the discussion on field emission cathode blunting.

4. E. Mueller, "Handbuch der Physik," Springer—Verlag, Berlin, 1956, Vol. 21, p. 202.

5. V. E. Cosslett, A. Engstrom, and H. H. Pattee, "X-Ray Microscopy and Microradiography," Academic Press, Inc., New York, 1957, p. 336.

6. W. P. Dyke and W. W. Dolan, "Advances in Electronics and Electron Physics," Academic Press, Inc., New York, 1956, Vol. VIII, p. 109.

7. J. P. Barbour, F. M. Charbonnier, L. F. Garrett, and W. P. Dyke, "On the Application of Field Emission to a Two Cavity Microwave Amplifier," paper given at the 1958 Field Emission Symposium, University of Chicago.

8. Russell D. Young and Erwin W. Mueller, "Experimental Determination of the Total Energy Distribution of Field Emitted Electrons," paper given at 1958 Field Emission Symposium, University of Chicago.

9. W. P. Dyke and W. W. Dolan, "Advances in Electronics and Electron Physics," Academic Press, Inc., New York, 1956, Vol. VIII, pp. 102, 121; Appendix II.

10. E. E. Martin, J. K. Trolan, and B. W. Steller, "Research on Field Emission Cathodes," Scienctific Rept. 5, Contract AF 33(616)-5404, Linfield Research Institute, McMinville, Oregon (1959).

11. H. Bruining, "Physics and Application of Secondary Electron Emission," McGraw-Hill Book Company, Inc., New York, 1954.

12. A. N. Skellett, "The Use of Secondary Electron Emission to Obtain Trigger or Relay Action," J. Appl. Phys., Vol. 13, p. 519 (Aug. 1942).

13. J. S. Cook, R. Kompfner, and W. H. Yocom, "Slalom Focusing," Proc. Inst. Radio Engineers, Vol. 45, p. 1517 (1957).

14. C. Burton Crumly and Robert Adler, "Electron Beam Parametric Amplifiers," Electronic Industries, p. 73 (Nov. 1959).

15 C. F. Powell, I. E. Campbell, and B. W. Gonser, "Vapor-Plating," John Wiley & Sons, Inc., New York, 1955.

16. D. A. Buck and K. R. Shoulders, "An Approach to Microminature Printed Systems," Proceedings of the Eastern Joint Computer Conference (Dec. 1958), Special Pub. T-114.

17. V. E. Cosslett, A. Engstrom, and H. H. Pattee, "X-Ray Microscopy and Microradiography," Academic Press, Inc., New York, 1957.

18. V. E. Cosslett and P. Duncumb, "A Scanning Microscope with Either Electron or X-Ray Recording," Academic Press, Inc., New York, p. 12; see also "Electron Microscopy—Proceedings of the Stockholm Conference" (Sept. 1956).

19. H. E. Farnsworth, R. E. Schilier, T. H. George, and R. M. Burger, "Application of the Ion Bombardment Cleaning Method to Titanium, Germanium, Silicon, and Nickel as Determined by Low-Energy Electron Diffraction," J. Appl. Phys., Vol. 29, p. 1150 (1958).

20. Ludwig Mayer, J. Appl. Phys., Vol. 26, p. 1228 (1955); Vol. 28, p. 975 (1957); Vol. 29, p. 658 (1958); Vol. 29, p. 1454 (1958).

APPENDICES

APPENDIX TO CHAPTER V

D. M. MacKay

Contributions to Discussion on Definitions

SYSTEM

I think we must bear in mind that there is a perfectly standard usage of the terms "input" and "output" with reference to a system. This immediately outlaws any "closed" definition that would exclude the possibility of talking about systems in interaction.

DETERMINATE

In discussing determinateness it is important first to draw a line between objectively described systems and personal agents. Then, second, we must clearly distinguish the notion of determinateness from that of predictability. Thus a system may be too complex to be predicted, but it may nevertheless be conceptually defined as determinate if we have reason to believe that an identical system, set up under identical conditions, would always be found to be in an identical state. I am rejecting, in other words, the idea that there is no meaning in determinateness unless we have predictability. If we represent a system by a probability matrix, the distinction to be made is between systems which must be so represented because of our *ignorance*, and those whose matrix represents the existence of *variety in the ensemble* of systems. Variety in the ensemble is something physically different from ignorance of the system. Thus the behavior of complex models of the sort described by Ashby and Grey-Walter is unpredictable in the first sense, whereas the splitting of an atom (according to present-day physics) is unpredictable in the second sense. An ensemble of identical homeostats set off under identical conditions would always be found in identical states.

In connection with the second class of activities, the activities of persons, we meet a fundamental dichotomy between what may validly be believed by an observer, and what may validly be believed by the agent—between the "outside" and the "inside" aspects of personal agency, if you like. I have discussed this at length elsewhere [17], but the essential point is that even if we could write down what a (detached) observer may validly believe in advance about the agent's action, what we have written down could not claim to be uniquely "the truth" about the action, since at least one person, namely the agent, would be wrong to believe it (as ex hypothesi his believing is a new factor which cannot have been fully allowed for in writing it down). In short, a purported description of a choice which he has yet to make can only be classed as logically indeterminate, even though his brain was fully determinate in the physical sense. Let me emphasize that this indeterminateness of an agent's decision is in no way reduced by its predictability to an isolated observer of the decision. This is an irreducibly odd logical situation which is inseparable from (and as far as I can see peculiar to) human agency.

RANDOMNESS

I would like to suggest that we first distinguish between the use of the word "random" as applied to events (e.g., the breakup of atoms), and as applied to states or specifications of states (e.g., the wiring of a homeostat). Having made this division we must further distinguish between (a) the notion of well-shuffledness or impartiality of distribution; (b) the notion of irrelevance or absence of correlation; (c) the notion of "I don't care"; and (d) the notion of chaos. In sense (a) the number 111111 would not be described as a random number, even though it were drawn "at random" from an unbiased population. In sense (b) (in such a case) it would. (b) really characterizes the source, (a) the product.

Both (a) and (b) are technical notions; (c) and (d) on the other hand are more metaphysical notions. Here again, (d) reflects a metaphysical attitude to the source, and (c) to the product. In (d) chaos takes on a quasi-personal role as a kind of anti-God [witness some of the notable debates between scientists and theologians over the theory of evolution, where grievous confusion often arose because purely technical notions of "chance" were taken (on both sides) as metaphysical]. The great majority of debates in this area could, I think, be avoided by making these three distinctions—between events and states, between source and product, and between technical and metaphysical senses of "chance."

TEACHING AND LEARNING

The first distinction I would like to make is again between what can be said about people, and what can be said about things. Teaching and learning are words for describing the activities of persons. There is no opposition between talking about learning in the individual, and talking about an evolutionary process in his *brain*. The one (I believe) entails the other, but the two belong to different conceptual levels. One can of course say that the teacher is a learner, and equally that the learner is a teacher of his teacher, but I don't see that this helps us. The level at which you can say that the teacher learns is not the level at which you claim he is teaching. If I am teaching arithmetic to a child, it may be true in a trivial sense that I am also learning how the child is getting along; but I am not learning *about arithmetic*: in fact it is essential that at this level I must not be a learner, I must *know* the stuff! Relative to the level of arithmetic, any learning I do is "metalearning." The essence of teaching, I would suggest, is a moulding of the pupil's readiness to react. Learning is, if you like, the evolution of such readinesses to match a state of affairs, either physical or conceptual. One can then go on to say that this process of learning has as its correlate at the mechanical level an evolutionary process between competitive organizers in the hierarchic structure of the brain.

To say that "boxes learn" is to confuse categories. It is *people* who learn and teach; so that unless you can give personal meaning to the concept of *dialogue* in relation to your box (in the same sense as we can in relation to the brain of a human person), words like thinking, learning, etc., cannot be applied. Where a box is a substitute for a human teacher, I would perfer to use quotation marks in saying that it "teaches." Even when we speak of a dog as learning, I would maintain as a matter of logic that we are not referring to the box inside his head, but to the "doggy person" whom we talk to as Fido, and like or dislike, etc. Here again the relationship that enables us to speak of teaching and learning is a personal one: the relationship which it is fashionable to describe by "I–thou," as distinct from "I–it." If we ask whether one box can teach another box, this is analogous to asking if one man's brain (the nerve cells, etc., inside his head) can teach another man's brain. The answer is no. *Men* teach other *men*. The most we can say of their brains is that they mediate or embody this process. What is missing in the case of artificial boxes hitherto, is any rational incentive to make the metaphysical commitment implied by addressing it as "thou". This is a commitment which I at any rate would not wish to make in the present state of the art.

Let us be clear that speaking of persons is not a matter of merely *renaming* objects such as brains and bodies. Persons are not objects, but subjects and agents. Personal activity is seen by "reading" the activity of the bodies of persons (as a message is seen by "reading" the ink on a page), when we are prepared or "set" (as most of us are from infancy) to make such a commitment.

SELF-ORGANIZING

The word "self" has in fact no vicious implications here. It means simply "not by others." Its function is purely negative, and gives rise to no logical regress.

I think we are in trouble through confusing *organizing* with *ordering*. To speak of organizing invites the question of "for what." Systems such as threads of crystals that grow themselves are not self-organizing but self-ordering, and it is a matter of very little interest whether one describes them as evolutionary or not, since this depends simply on whether the ordering requires a process of natural selection. I suggest that self-organization might be defined as the development by a system, or the modification in a system, of organization relative to a goal of some sort, without total reliance on the specification of that organization by another.

I do not think that logical dimensionality provides an appropriate yardstick either of organization or of order. The growth of rust on a surface, for example, may increase the logical dimensionality of its description without increasing order.

SELF-OBSERVATION

Suppose that we were able to see the whole machinery of the brain and not only the bodily exterior. When a man said "I see a flash of yellow," this would not only tell us that his muscles had twitched, but also that in his conceptual machinery there was activity corresponding to (mediating) the seeing-of-yellow. Thus his introspective report *could* be good evidence of his internal bodily activity. The extreme attitude Ashby has expressed may perhaps be justified by the very practical limitation of our powers of observation; but I feel that in principle, assuming that we could follow the processes right back from the periphery, no special objection could be raised to the use of evidence attested by introspection. While it may be safest not to trust introspective reports, nevertheless if no other channel of information is available to us, it would seem informationally wasteful to ignore them altogether. Of course this implies that one takes reports (e.g., of seeing-a-flash) primarily as evidence of the neural activity concerned, rather than of the presence of external physical flashes, on which corroborative evidence should in principle be available. In addition, for the theorist himself, his own personal introspection may often fulfill a valuable negative function by providing a check on the experiential correlates of what he supposes to go on in his brain.

INADEQUACY OF DYADIC LOGIC—A NOTE TO WARREN McCULLOCH*

If you mean that at the level of discourse between persons, the logic of objective description, by which we assert the presence or absence of things in the world, is inadequate, then I agree. In particular, to cite my earlier example, the object language in which we may specify the disposition of events in our brains seems incapable of handling the personal relationship mediated through that brain. In other words there are undecidable sentences in that language—logically indeterminate sentences. What is not obvious to me is that the development of a triadic or *n*-adic logic will provide us with any way out of this dilemma.

EDITOR'S NOTE

In the foregoing remarks the writer leaves his field (communication and the psychology of vision) to enter that of philosophy and abstract logic.

*The reader is referred, in this connection, to Dr. McCulloch's reference in his paper (Ch. VI, *post*) to Professor Tarski's work.—*Ed.*

There is an editorial responsibility entailed here, for the flavor of those remarks carries the unmistakable impression that, if not well nigh the final word to be said on the matters treated, the conclusions arrived at could perhaps be refined, but in no way essentially changed.

This impression, we feel, is an unfortunate one for the well-disposed reader, since the conclusions implied in the remarks in question are in fact neither binding nor often even very useful in practice. Thus the writer says at the end of his section on "randomness" that "the great majority of debates in this area could, I think, be avoided by making these three distinctions."

But debate can always be stifled if we make enough arbitrary and *ad hoc* distinctions in the subject matter. (Thus it is not difficult to show that Dr. MacKay's *d*-type randomness proceeds from his (b): or that (c) proceeds from (a), and further that (a) and (b) are neither logically nor materially independent.)

The recurrent trouble appears to be a tendency to draw a subjective, restricting line through a subject, choose one side of the line, and then assert that no one else may discuss the subject's extension to the other side simply because the line has now been drawn. But this is the method of obdurate ideology and not of science, which above all must insist on no *ad hoc* or categorical limitations being imposed upon its scope of inquiry.

The remarks on "teaching and learning" are in cognate ways not quite fair to the points Mr. Pask wished to make and did make, on the basis of existent isomorphisms which if unallowed must also disallow modern group theory. MacKay to the contrary, we can indeed use the terminology of two isomorphisms interchangeably, as long as we indicate that an isomorphism exists and which terminology belongs to which half of it. Pask may conceivably be subject to criticism on this latter ground, but not at all on the grounds MacKay advances.

Again, teaching is not "a moulding of the pupil's readiness to act" – except in the context of a rather paranoid definition of pedagogy, basically motivated by a need to dominate. The essence of teaching is a freeing of the child's mind – an unfolding (the literal meaning of "explanation") of the subject in its richest and most related way, so that the child is free (not "moulded") to make his or her own creative extrapolations validly.

In the note on "dyadic logic" we read at the outset the stipulation restricting logic to descriptions of physical objects. But this is not what dyadic or any other logic is confined to, thus annulling the asserted bindingness of the conclusions that follow the emasculating premise. For logic includes not only a description in discourse of such objects, but also of states of mind and systems of value. And language — as the master dramatists and novelists have well demonstrated in their works — is effectively adequate to handle personal relationships mediated through human intelligent feelings expressing through their neural instrumentalities. With impeccable clarity of logic, they have communicated unmistakably to generations of readers exact personal relationships, states of mind and feeling, and systems of values. MacKay's *ad hoc* distinction is simply inoperative. What language can handle, logic can handle; for they are two forms of the same communication entity.

Similarly, in the section on "determinate," MacKay's "logical indeterminacy of a free choice" (better said, the "linguistic indeterminacy") is seen, when all the dust of the verbiage has settled, to contribute little or nothing to the question of whether freedom of choice exists or not — clearly nothing in the case of any living creature without a syntactical language, e.g., a dog. Rather, MacKay is seen to have confined himself to a semantic question of the minutiae of what can be regarded as evidence or not, in the light of distinctions he has seen fit to draw through the matter. We are reminded of court cases in which perfectly approachable issues are rendered out of reach of decision because of inappropriate, and to that extent invalid, rules of evidence.

The besetting fallacy here seems turning substantive issues into procedural questions, which are then obstructively or arbitrarily handled, the substantive point being allowed to go by the board.

APPENDIX TO CHAPTER VII

C. A. MUSES

The DNA-Protein Code and the Linear
Representability of n-Dimensional
Configurations

A Concept of Integration Furnishing
The Integral of the Heaviside Unit
Function

Proof of the Axiom of Choice

THE DNA-PROTEIN CODE
AND THE LINEAR REPRESENTABILITY
OF n-DIMENSIONAL CONFIGURATIONS*

If we call the primary nucleotides of DNA and RNA n_1, n_2, n_3, n_4, then we have the following triplet-combination rules: In any triplet, where n_q is the second member, (1) n_p can precede n_q only if $p < q$; (2) n_f can follow n_q only if $f \leq q$. This yields 20 triplets, i.e., 44 of the 64 possible combinations are prohibited. Interestingly enough those are the same 20 that F. H. C. Crick, J. S. Griffith, and L. E. Orgel derive from the formal assumption of "sense sites," defined as those triplets which also furnish sense sites only at positions $3m+k$ where $k=1$, 2, 3. The implications of the two above encoding rules for the protein and DNA alphabets not only shed biochemical light on the coding process, but also are sufficient to determine a unique solution to one of the most fundamental coding problems in the genetic and metabolic processes.

M. Yčas [37] said that a unique solution of the coding problem was not yet possible. This problem is to determine how the four nucleotide bases or residues in the nucleic acid polymer control the amino acid order in polypeptide chains running longitudinally along the nucleic acid helices, or more simply put, to determine the code between the protein and DNA alphabets.

For the protein "alphabet" we have an informational "entropy" of $\log_2 20 = 4.32$ bits per symbol and for the DNA (RNA) alphabet, $\log_2 4 = 2$ bits per symbol. Now since 4.32 bits are needed to yield information sufficient to determine 1 protein, 2 DNA symbols are not enough, and hence 3 are minimally required to determine each protein.

*Based in part on a paper filed in December, 1959, with the Society for General Systems Research and presented as an invited lecture before the Medical Faculty of the University of Western Ontario on February 15, 1960.

We shall now show that a unique solution is indeed possible, and that Crick narrowly missed finding it. It seems logically economical to assume that among the primary necleotides there must be a linear order n_1, n_2, n_3, n_4 such that certain linkages, determinable from that order, can never occur. The prohibited linkages point the way to the explanation of lethal mutations as "prohibited" (impossible for continued life) arrangements so that the internal communication system of the organism eventually breaks down. Now if we rule (1) that only n_p can precede n_q where $p < q$ and (2) that only n_f can follow n_q where $f \leq q$, we find that we have only 20 possibilities. These, interestingly enough, are the same 20 as derived formally by the assumption of Crick on the basis of "sense sites" furnishing other sense sites only at positions $3m + k$ where $k = 1$, 2, 3, this also constituting the definition of a sense-site triplet.

But the present rule of selection sheds more light on the relation between the code and the actual biogenetic process as per the evidence. We can verbally summarize our selection rule thus: The second "letter" of an ideal triplet permits only whatever letters can precede to precede it and only whatever letters precede itself, including itself, to follow it. Thus there is an order implied among the four primary nucleotides if this proposed code is valid. This order in turn implies an intersymbol influence between the four primary nucleotides as well as a decision-power in the second or central member of an ideal triplet. Thus there is intersymbol influence in the nucleotides though not among the amino acids governed by or linked to them, and hence not between the triplets themselves.

However, by reason of the controlling decision-power of the central triplet members, the 20 basic amino acids must (on the basis of the n_1, n_2, n_3, n_4 triplet arrays) resolve into subgroups of 2 (n_2-controlled), 6 (n_3-controlled), and 12 (n_4-controlled) members. Note that n_1 can never "control" (i.e., be central). Hence n_1 must be more asymmetrical than the other three. All this follows as the logical consequence of our coding rules.

The selection rule thus gained yields a more logically primal code derivation than Crick's more formal approach, and also provides certain powerful testing criteria, which eventually, will enable us in turn even to supersede them in solving this fundamental biocoding problem. The criteria follow:

(1) There is an arrangement order implied among the four nucle-

otides if our suggested code rules are valid. This order is also shown to be linear.

(2) This order implies prohibited (biologically) linkages, which point the way, with slight modification, to the explanation of lethal mutations as similarly prohibited arrangements. We also can see why they are lethal: they break down the internal biocommunication system, and literally vital information fails to carry. The basis of such prohibitions must be the biochemical impossibility of maintaining certain molecular sequences. The reason for such impossibility is also furnished by this analysis and is seen to lie in the mutual unsaturation patterns existing between two given molecules. The essence of biolinkage is thus electromagnetic in nature. What controls and determines the over-all electromagnetic organization is still not evident. There is apparently a sense context behind the bio-informational language scheme.

(3) The existence of such a primary arrangement order implies an intersymbol influence between the four primary nucleotides. This influence must be sought biochemically in the laboratory. We shall shortly see that the selection rule can establish the direction of this search.

(4) The rule also implies a decisive power in the second or central member of a triplet. (Triplets because of the information-function demand; namely, the information code ratio $(\log_2 20/\log_2 4)$ is minimally included only by 3 units.)

(5) Also it implies that n_1, since it can never be central, is more asymmetrical than n_2, n_3, or n_4. Thus we must search for an asymmetry in one of the four nucleotides not possessed by the other three.

(6) We may think of the nucleotide template models as all with bonding potentials on either side, except n_1 which has such bonds on only one side.

The foregoing bio-informational theoretic discussion is confirmed physically in that the hitherto abstract numbers 1, 2, 3, and 4 emerge as the numbers of unsaturated $C=C$ or $C=N$ bonds in the molecules of the four type-determinants of the primary nucleotides: (1) thymine, (2) cytosine, (3) guanine, and (4) adenine, each nucleotide being the phosphoric ester of a desoxypentose derivative of one of the preceding four, composed of a pyrimidine pair, (1) and (2), and a purine pair, (3) and (4). The biochemical operation of the DNA-protein code thus depends in part on the fact of a basic differ-

ence in function in the molecule between the doubly unsaturated
C=C or C=N bonds and the much more saturated C:O bonds, the former being of course endowed with more potential energy, and hence
operationally associated with less physical entropy. The actual
structures of the four primary nucleotides, with their code numbers,
follow. [If uracil ($C_4H_4N_2O_2$) is used instead of thymine, the number (1) of double C=C or C=N bonds—and hence the argument—remains unchanged.]

$$
\begin{array}{cccc}
\text{N–C:0} & \text{N=C.NH}_2 & \text{N–C:0} & \text{N=C.NH}_2 \\
\text{0:C\ \ C.CH}_3 & \text{0:C\ \ CH} & \text{H}_2\text{N.C\ \ C-NH} & \text{HC\ \ C-NH} \\
\text{HN–CH} & \text{HN–CH} & \text{N–C-N} & \text{N–C-N}
\end{array}
$$

Thymine (1)   Cytosine (2)   Guanine (3)   Adenine (4)

The additional and equally interesting fact emerges that the 20
amino acids, on the basis of these biophysical criteria, arrange
themselves naturally into three groups of 2, 6, and 12 each, as
called for by the code, the groups of governing nucleotides being
encoded as Group I (2 members): 121, 122; Group II (6 members):
131, 132, 133, 231, 232, 233; Group III (12 members): 141, 142,
143, 144 241, 242, 243, 244, 341, 342, 343, 344.

It will be noted that the thio-component provides an unsaturation acceptably equivalent to that of a COOH group, except in the
S–S (more saturated) group (in cystine), where the absence of –S–*
is counterbalanced by two COOH groups, while cysteine and methio-
nine have only one S-component, which provides an acceptable unsaturation equivalent of a COOH group. Here we must remember that
by Dancoff's principle the organism will use as broad a characteri-
zation of protein need as its chemistry permits.

It is now possible to supersede the prior criteria. We do this by
noting first that our assignment of numbers on the basis of potential
bond energy quotas to the 4 nucleotide bases remains a firm and indispensable element in any possible solution of the code. The demonstration of those numbers' direct connection with molecular
structure has already been made. But, in our attempt to save
Crick's suggestion of "sense sites" we were, in the course of our
investigation, forced to see that Occam's razor demanded a better

*The context here being one of the bonding capacity of an organically ef-
  fective group, whether that group be composed of one or more elements
  or repetitions thereof.

solution, and that Crick's idea was not it. Details of the solution
are in the writer's paper (in press) "Systemic Stability and Cybernetic Control" (based on a lecture given on April 30, 1962,) at the
Institute of Theoretical Physics, University of Naples).

The adequate solution follows from the simple rule: 3 "letters"
(DNA bases) per minimal "word," together with the fact that these
letters must be paired (1,4) or (2,3) in the DNA molecule. The
present theory justifies this pairing by the necessity of the same
total (5) of biologically effective double bonds in each pair. The
laboratory confirms this theory. The permutations of 4 things (the
bases or "letters") taken 3 at a time (the minimal "word"), with
repetitions of at least 2 "letters" being necessary, yields 40 possibilities. Since these must be paired by the DNA molecular requirements, we have just 20 "words" of 6 "letters" each, of which,
however, only 3 are necessary to determine each word, since the
other three are formed by reflection *modulo* 5. These 20 words control the amino-acids and hence the protein structure. (A recent
laboratory finding can be interpreted in the light of the foregoing to
suggest that the pair 111-444 controls the amino-acid phenylamine.)
The triplet list of the code itself is thus: 111, 112, 113, 114, 121,
131, 141, 211, 311, 411, 222, 221, 223, 224, 212, 232, 242, 122,
322, 422. (Note: 422, for example, is always linked with its "reflection" 133, *et al.* so there is no need to list the reflections.)

Now there are 5 pairs of nucleotide bases in each helical loop
of DNA molecule, and 3 bases = 1 biological "word." Therefore 3
loops of 5 base pairs each (i.e., 30 bases in all) complete a "sentence" of words (i.e., 10 words, 5 on each of the double strands).
But a permutational unit (4 things 3 at a time with at least 2 repetitions) is 40 bases = 20 pairs = 4 loops. Hence a complete cycle of
biological "meaning" is $3 \times 4 = 12$ loops = 60 pairs = 120 bases =
40 "words" (20 on each strand).

But since there are 4 possible kinds of complete cycles (as any
of the 4 bases may start one) we have for the *total cycle* $4 \times 12 =$
48 loops = 240 pairs = 480 bases = 160 "words" (80 on each strand).
This *total cycle* should, then, as derived by the present theory, be
a complete hereditary unit or gene, each nucleotide base corresponding to what the geneticist calls a hereditary "site" (this is a
laboratory term unrelated to Crick's use of the word).

But there are now, to our knowledge, 373 distinct sites proven
in the laboratory to exist in the gene, with also the proven fact that

researchers have isolated only some 78% of them. That means there is a total of $100/78 \times 373$ which to the nearest integer is 478, almost the 480 we arrived at on the basis of the present theory, thus confirming it in the laboratory. The theory is further confirmed by the fact that the smallest known virus (Japanese encephalitis) is 18 mμ in diameter. It must contain at least one gene or hereditary unit or it would be unable to reproduce. Now one nucleotide base is some 3/8 mμ in diameter and 480 of these make a length of 180 mμ i.e., about 3 coils of 18 mμ diameter—a reasonable picture of a small virus' RNA core—thus again checking in the laboratory the theory here presented, and pointing the way to a method of obtaining the minimal size for a biological organism. Now we can go on to say (since A:B as 3:2) that the A-cistron or larger independent functional unit of the gene contains 288 sites: and the B-cistron, 192, 96 being connected with a sub-unit, of which there are 3 in A and 2 in B. The 480 sites form a linear array.

We now turn to the challenging question of how such a linear coding rule, resulting in essentially (even though helically twisted) linear genetic patterns in chromosomes, can be adequate to contain the full complex of biological instructions for the building (though the living process surpasses incomparably anything that we would call "building") of a three-dimensional body. To answer this question we must turn to what will probably be found to be the substratum of all other mathematics: the theory of arrangements* of elements.

If a "threading" or unique (nonrepeating, non-self-crossing, and exhaustive) linear ordering rule can be prescribed for all m members of some set which is extended in c $(\geq m)$ cells in a space of n dimensions, then the number C all possible configurations of the mem-

---

*Including in the broadest sense both combinations and permutations. Recalling the footnote of 3.62, we may say that combinations refer to cardinality in a very general sense, while permutations refer to ordinality. This complementary dichotomy reaches down into the basic arithmetic processes, multiplication and division being not simply repeated addition and subtraction respectively, but also containing the number of times (an ordinal concept) the same number was added or subtracted. Division is additionally important because it is also isomorphic with measurement. The little wheel of a map-distance measurer is identical in function with the wheel of a simple calculating machine engaged in division. Since mathematics itself is fundamentally concerned with measurement in general, it is easy to see why divisibility dominates the theory of numbers, which is the heart of mathematics.

bers can be mapped on a line as the linear permutations of m and c. If $m = c$, we have simply $C = (m!)$. The expression for C becomes correspondingly more complicated if unoccupied cells and/or repetitions (identical members except for position) be allowed.

The proof of the above theorem is obvious from the geometry of the situation. A similar theorem also emerges; namely the following: For any specification of $c \geq m \geq 1$ members (of which $c > q > 0$ are null) divided into $m \geq g > 0$ classes and distributed with no more than 1 to a cell among c contiguous cells (of which q would hence be empty) in n dimensions, at least one threading rule may be formulated which will transform the n-dimensional set into a linear sequence of c positions, and which would also furnish by its inversion the regaining of the original n-dimensional set by reassembling or refolding the linear sequence contiguously in prescribed fashion in n-dimensional space.

Corollary: All the possible configurations C of the g-fold m in the c cells in n-space can be calculated from an appropriate rule of only linear permutation.

Thus the possible configurations of 8 black pawns and 8 white pawns on a chessboard are given from the theory of linear permutations, after the application of a boustrophedon threading rule, their total number C_p being $(64!) / (8!)^2 (48!)$, or over (a million)^3. Since 64 is also 4^3, this same number C_p gives the total configurations of the 8 black and the 8 white pawns in a cube of side 4 composed of 64 cells.

For more complicated situations the following specific formulation can be gained. The total number of possible configurations C, in a space of $n > 0$ dimensions, of a_1 objects or elements of one kind, a_2 of another kind, a_3 of a third kind, etc...., through a_k, in $c = \sum_1^k a_j$ cells, is given by

$$C = \frac{c!}{\left(c - \sum_1^k a_j\right)! \prod_1^k [(a_j)!]}$$

whence it at once follows that the number of such configurations of k different things is $c!/(c-k)!$ for in this case all the $(a_j)!$ are 1.

The power of the above method of treatment stems from the fact that the value of n is irrelevant for the solution. This fact in turn reveals that the above theorems are logically equivalent to our preceding finding in the footnote to 3.62 as to the fundamental importance of linearity or one-dimensionality. We shall see in the third portion of this Appendix that the first dimension holds a preferred position in the dimensions of extension as well as in the metadimensions of meaning, this fact in turn being at the basis of any possibility of explicitly expressing the nature of the universe. We have already pointed out that man's most powerful systems of expression, words and numbers, are one-dimensional. That this is so is no accident, nor is it one that time, as occurrence, can be treated as a threading rule (through a space of a dimensionality which we previously evaluated as five—see [20], p. xi).*

That one-dimensional representation is adequate to contain the instructions for configurations in any number of dimensions is a pervasive conclusion, enabling us to answer now our initial question as to how the one-dimensional genetic instructions, whose code we above sketched, can be sufficient to enable the biological formations of bodies.

We can finally gain some humble insight into the art of universe building. It is evident that with quite conceivable and comparatively small finite numbers of different groups of elements (an alphabet), the numbers of combinations and configurations thereby producible grow so rapidly as to approach very quickly a practical infinity. This, in the terms of our present context, would mean a well-nigh inexhaustible profusion of forms and possibilities in the universe so being created. That tremendous power of growth, however, can be controlled by an equally great power of restriction in the form of rules of selection. Thus, the number of possible configurations of a given number of pawns (or pawns and chessmen) is drastically limited when only "playable" (i.e., derivable from play according to the rules of chess) positions are considered. With more rules, the limitation becomes still more drastic. Thus universes could be made fertile by permutation and manageable by selection rules, which in a real universe would, of course, have to be rooted in actual forces promoting various kinds of juxtaposition, congruence, and repulsion, all operating together.

*This instructional adequacy of one-dimensional time not only shows that the art of the classical dramatist, who proceeds by a thread of occurrence, is adequate to express all possible situational significances, even when the dimensionality of these may far exceed one, but it concomitantly demonstrates the adequacy of one-dimensional time (the only time of which we are normally aware) for all possible metalevels of subtlety of experience: n-dimensional configurations can be adequately expressed, and recorded, and reproduced from one-dimensional permutation patterns.

A CONCEPT OF INTEGRATION
CAPABLE OF INTEGRATING
THE HEAVISIDE UNIT FUNCTION

Some years ago Abraham and Bloch discovered multivibrator circuits by accidentally connecting output to input in a two-stage audio-amplifier. This feedback type of connection produces a square wave, the physical realization of a succession of Heaviside unit functions. Square waves can then be converted into synchronization or "sync" pulses by an RC filter such that R greatly exceeds the internal resistance of the circuit and C is a low enough capacitance so that the time constant of the discharge interval is much less than the pulse width of the square wave.

Finally, a germanium diode may be inserted to suppress the blunter, shorter, and hence less usable positive spikes, so that only a series of sharp negative sync pulses is left, which now may be used to synchronize two oscillators under the rule that the servo-oscillator which is synchronized must have a frequency lower than that of the forcing oscillator. Multistage operational sequences can thus be formed, and the square wave with its derived sync pulses* lies at the heart of the modern circuitry of servomechanisms, electronic counting, and manifold types of feedback checking.

All these devices are very near to the kind of techniques demanded by biosimulation; and at the mathematical heart of such considerations lies the Heaviside unit function. Before specifically discussing that function, however, it is necessary to introduce at this point a new concept of integration.

The integral has been geometrically interpreted, when it has been so interpreted at all, as the area under the curve (C_1) represented by the function which is the derivative. Such an interpretation lends itself best to approximate and very useful computational

---

*Whether in the form just described, or in the form of tiny dc voltage pulses used, for instance, in cascades of bistable triggering circuits with pentodes.

methods, as well as analogue computation. The limiting process involved may be symbolized as $(0) \cdot (\infty)$.

But when we are able to perform an exact analytical integration we obtain another function which in turn can be graphed as a curve (C_2). Geometrically, there is no simply stateable relation between C_1 and C_2. What is clearly needed is a more geometrically profound interpretation of an integral than as an area.

But now let us consider what in geometrical fact we do when we differentiate a differentiable function $F(x)$. We obtain, by the application of various rules stemming from a limiting process symbolizable as $0/0$, another function

$$f(x) = m \tag{1}$$

which is in fact the variable slope of the tangent to $F(x)$ at any point.

Let us now write the equation of this variable tangent, which will be in the form of a linear equation, with variable slope and intercept. Because the slope, m, derives from the nature of $F(x)$, the intercept, b, will also so derive, yielding the function

$$\phi(m) = b \tag{2}$$

Now we have, as the equation of the general tangent line to $F(x)$, the function

$$T(m) = mx + \phi(m) \tag{3}$$

Obviously now, where $E(s)$ stands for "the envelope formed by the variable tangent of slope s,"

$$F(x) = E(m) \tag{4}$$

therefore

$$\int f(x)dx = E(m) \tag{4a}$$

Now let us try to find this envelope by partially differentiating equation (3) with respect to m and setting this derivative equal to zero:

$$\frac{\partial T(m)}{\partial m} = x + \frac{\partial[\phi(m)]}{\partial m} = 0 \tag{5}$$

Solving, we obtain $m = h(x)$ and, recalling equation (1), we have the identity

$$h(x) = f(x) \tag{5a}$$

Substituting in equation (3) we obtain

$$F(x) = x \cdot f(x) + \phi\left[f(x)\right] \qquad (6)$$

Hence

$$\int f(x)dx = x \cdot f(x) + \phi\left[f(x)\right] \qquad (7)$$

We see that $T(m)$ is a fundamental transform for $F(x)$, thus arriving at the analytical definition of an integral as an envelope, definite integrals being arc lengths thereof. This will be found to be a fundamentally useful and more direct alternative to the ordinary definition as area under a curve whose ordinates measure the slope of a tangent line. In our definition there is no arbitrary shift from "slope" to "ordinate"; but angles are preserved directly as angles, and tangent lines as tangent lines. Integrals thus can be studied as curves, just as derivatives, without the secondary mapping concept of "area" being introduced. This difference in treatment, in some instances, may constitute the difference between being able to integrate a difficult transcendental function or not.

There is a direct application to analogue computers. Clearly $f(x)$ can be analogued to yield $T(m)$ and hence $F(x)$, which would be finally obtained in the geometric form of the actual curve that it is. This is a more informative and straightforward procedure than analoguing $f(x)$ as an area in the usual manner. Moreover, any points of inflection of the integral, as well as any maxima (minima) appear distinctly with their coordinates—a sometimes indispensable requirement in systems analysis.

We must also keep in mind the fact (previously mentioned*) that the integration of a function increases by one unit the dimensionality of the space of that function; for an envelope is one dimension higher than a tangent line. Thus fractional integration—as well as the fractional differentiation which so intrigued its brilliant exponent, Oliver Heaviside—is seen by our definition to be immediately and inherently related to *fractional dimensions*, and hence to the imaginary as a dimensionality operator. A usable and nonarbitrary image emerges for conception, and the basic notion of integration as the inverse of differentiation is nonarbitrarily preserved in both the geometry and the algebra.

To make this concept of integration operational, the formation rules for finding $\phi\left[f(x)\right]$ must be gained in each case. Some exam-

*See [20], pp. liv-lv, *passim*.

ples of such results are shown in Table I (note that $\phi(m)$ and $f(x)$ combine in their relationship some formal aspects of being both reverses and inverses of each other).

Table I

$f(x) = m$	$\phi(m)$	$F(x) = \int f(x)dx = mx + \phi(m)$
arc sin x	cos m	x arc sin $x + (1 - x^2)^{1/2}$
$1/x$	$-\ln m$	ln ex
ln x	$-e^m$	$x (\ln x - 1)$
$(x/3)^{1/2}$	$-m^3$	$2(x/3)^{3/2}$
$-x/2k$	km^2	$-x^2/4k$

This table may be indefinitely extended.

The Heaviside unit function is described in Fig. 1, being zero throughout the range $(t < 0)$, suddenly rising to $+1$ at $t = 0$, and remaining at this value thereafter.

We now may ask ourselves what the envelope would be that would be formed if we consider the ordinates of the Heaviside unit function as the actual slope of a variable tangent line. The solution shows the power of the method, since it is gained in this case even without algebra. Indeed, as will immediately be apparent, the algebra in this instance is comparatively extremely extended. The integral of the Heaviside unit function is given in Fig. 2, with a zero constant of integration assumed. From the foregoing results, it is seen that the explicit integral of the Heaviside unit function assumes the simple form

$$\int u(t)dt = t \cdot u(t) \tag{8}$$

We now proceed to evaluate $u(t)$.

The simplest explicit functional form fulfilling the properties of the Heaviside unit function is

$$u(t) = M \; (\exp it^{1/2}/\text{Re } t^{1/2}) \tag{8a}$$

where $t^{1/2}$ denotes the positive square root and Re "the real part of," and M stands for the modulus-extracting operation. The value of the function at the point $t = 0$ is determined by the fact that

$$\lim_{t \to 0} (t^{1/2}/\text{Re} \, t^{1/2}) = 1$$

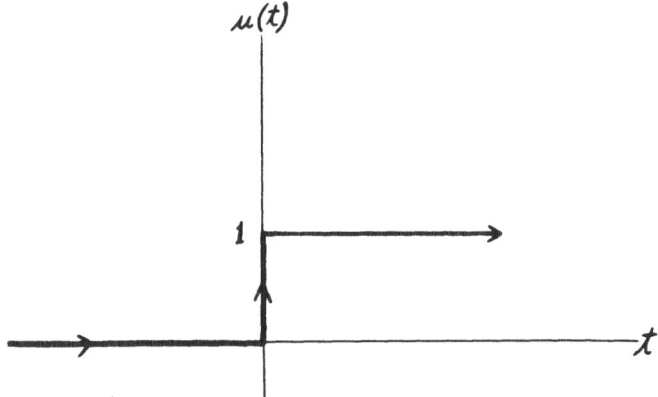

Fig. 1. The Heaviside unit function $u(t)$.

It is worth noting that the amplitude of $u(t)$ is a constant for all $t \geq 0$; namely, $\omega = 1$ rad.

Another functional form for the Heaviside unit function is given by

$$u(t) = M \left(\exp it^{1/2} \mid [t]! \mid^{-t} \right) \tag{9}$$

the brackets indicating "integral part of." The absolute value of $[t]!$ is required to render $u(t)$ zero for all negative values of t, since $(-N)! = \pm \infty$, N being a natural number. Simply $\mid [t]! \mid$ would satisfy the conditions except that the $(-t)$ exponent in equation (9) yields a pulse-type amplitude function with a maximum at 1, which accords

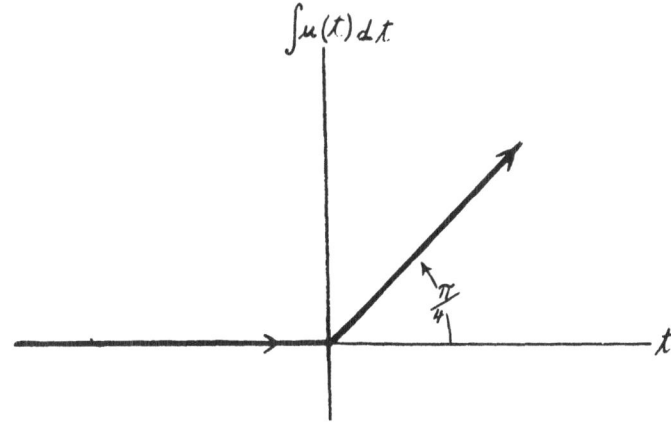

Fig. 2. $\int u(t)\, dt = t\, u(t)$.

better with the concept and physical background of the Heaviside function in relation to sync pulses, than would a nonwave function with compounded exponential increase. Thus for positive time, where $r = [t]$, we may write

$$\omega_r = \frac{r^{1/2}}{(r!)^r} \tag{10}$$

which when taken as a series converges to show a total amplitude at the limit $(r \to \infty)$ of slightly less that $78°$; that is,

$$\sum_0^\infty \omega_r = 1.3616\ldots \text{rad} \tag{11}$$

The form (9) of the Heaviside unit function—which may be the form nature prefers—demands quantized time, and hence a discrete form of ultimately observable reality. We mention this alternative functional form here because the anomalous behavior of the time has already been observed in treatises on quantized field theory in quantum mechanics. The quantization of time as well as of energy is now pointed to as the direction toward the solution of these anomalies. An important relevance, to our theme, of this direction is that with quantized time all processes in time, including thinking, would be atom-like and discrete; and observed temporal reality would not be a continuum. With Gauss we could then reiterate in a deep new sense that Number Theory, as the mathematics of the discrete, is the queen of mathematics and hence of all the other sciences.

PROOF OF THE AXIOM OF CHOICE

From a rather secluded position in the nineteenth century, the theory of sets (which includes group theory) has come to dominate the imagery and notation of modern mathematics and logic. This domination may be partly due to the unscientific but ineluctable forces of fashion, but it is certainly partly due to the increasing attention which a combination of circumstances has brought to bear upon problems involving very great or indefinitely large numbers of elements which are subject to the same constellation of conditions and operations. As we saw in 3.2-3.3, the point holds a key position among all the dimensions; and the notion of a point is essential to the notion of an infinite set. The papers presented by Drs. Beurle and Schützenberger in this volume have also shed light on the relation to biosimulation of considerations of large ensembles.

At the heart of the theory of sets lies the so-called "axiom of choice," which has been shown to be equivalent to several other basic axioms, including Zorn's "lemma" and Zermelo's "theorem," the quotation marks indicating that they are actually forms of the same axiom. After the present paper had been drafted, the writer learned that E. Farah in 1955 (*Bull. Math. Soc. of São Paulo*, vol. 10) had in addition shown the equivalence of the axiom of choice to the general form of the stipulation that intersection must be distributed over union of sets. Examples could be multiplied in demonstrating the fundamental place of the axiom of choice in the present frontiers of thought. What we shall endeavour to show now is that the axiom of choice is actually not an axiom, but a theorem resting on deeper and more general considerations.

The substance of the "axiom" is that every set has a choice function, or that there always exists an exhaustive and unambiguous method of selecting any member of any subset of any given set. As mentioned, this stipulation—regarded as an essential but unproven assumption—underlies the entire theory of ensembles or sets, which in turn bases so much of so many modern investigations, including particularly and pertinently for us the theory of automata, where considerations of sets of internal states are vital.

The very notion of a *set* S means that its $m > 1$ members share at least one common and explicitly specifiable property P by virtue of which one can speak of *membership* in the set or of the relation "being a member of S." We are also clearly given that the number of occurrences of P in S is m. For a given member m_k of S we can now write

$$m_k = P + \bar{P}_k \tag{1}$$

where the property residue $R_k = \bar{P}_k$ exists and is unique for m_k, R_k comprising all the properties of m_k other than P. If the R_j were either null or nonunique the m_j would not be distinguishable and S would not be an aggregate but a single object (m being reduced to 1, and neither P nor $\bar{P}$ existing), and hence irrelevant to the notion of *order*, which begins with the number 2: in this case, with $m \geq 2$. It is also true that

$$S = mP + \sum_{1}^{m} \bar{P}_j \tag{2}$$

where all the $\bar{P}_j$ are nonidentical and mP denotes m identical occurrences of an identical property P. It should be noted that equations (1) and (2) are the least that can be said, for there must be minimally one common property for S to exist.

It is now clear that if a basis for ordering S—that is, a choice function—exists, it must be sought in the $\bar{P}_j$, for such ordering involves necessarily a *rule of differing*. It should be recalled at this point that $\bar{P}_j$ of the set S are never nonexistent and that they minimally must be such that they distinguish at least the positions of the m_j in some space, even if they fail to refer to differing internal properties of the m_j by reason of these latter being indentical except for position. Hence the subset S' is not a null set, where

$$S' = \sum_{1}^{m} \bar{P}_j > 0 \tag{3}$$

This is not an assumption but a conclusion which we have traced directly from the notion "members of a set" which is in turn involved in the definition of "set." The $\bar{P}_j$ must at least refer to differences in some sort of spatial position* even when they do not refer to differing internal properties of the m_j. When we are given a set, we are given at the same time the distinguishability of its members.

But noncoincidence, or difference in position, implies some sort of distance and hence some sort of measurability or method of comparing two or more distances. What now remains to be shown to prove the axiom of choice is that there is always at least one way to order a configuration of m noncoincident points. That there is such a rule is most easily apparent from the following construction.

A random configuration of points (Fig. 3) is presented. Connect all the outermost points of the configuration to form a closed figure. Disregarding for the moment this first "ring," perform the same operation with respect to the remaining points. If we continue to do this, until all the rings so yielded are obtained (Fig. 4), the innermost such ring will contain either 0, 1, or 2 points (more only if those 3 or more points improbably formed a straight line), and the minimum number of points for a "ring" is of course 3. The ordering rule consists in being able to place all the points of the configuration in ordinal relation to a selected point on the outermost ring to which we assign the number 1. We then proceed counterclockwise† on this ring, calling the successive points so reached 2, 3, etc., until the ring is completed, say at p. We then proceed to assign the number $(p + 1)$ to the point on the next outermost ring which is nearest to the point p. If there are two such points (and under the rule there cannot be more than two) then the number $(p + 1)$ is assigned to that one of the two points which is reached from the point p by proceeding inward and counterclockwise. Proceeding in this fashion, one may exhaustively and uniquely order the given configuration.‡ This

*In this connection, and in that of the heuristic *differentia* between "class" and "set," the reader is referred to the footnote in 3.62.

†If the extremely rare configuration occurs of all the points lying on a straight line, then we would proceed from lower and/or left to upper and/or right. This rule also applies to a straight-line formation that may remain within the innermost ring.

‡In connection with our remarks on randomness in this paper, it is interesting to note that the above procedure provides an absolute means of classifying random configurations of points according to their numbers of rings, as above defined, with a subnumber representing the number of points remaining within the innermost ring. A configuration consisting entirely of points forming a straight line would be treated as having zero rings, being thus designated as $0_{2(5)}$ if the line consisted of five points A configuration of three rings having no points in the innermost ring would be typed as 3_0, and so forth.

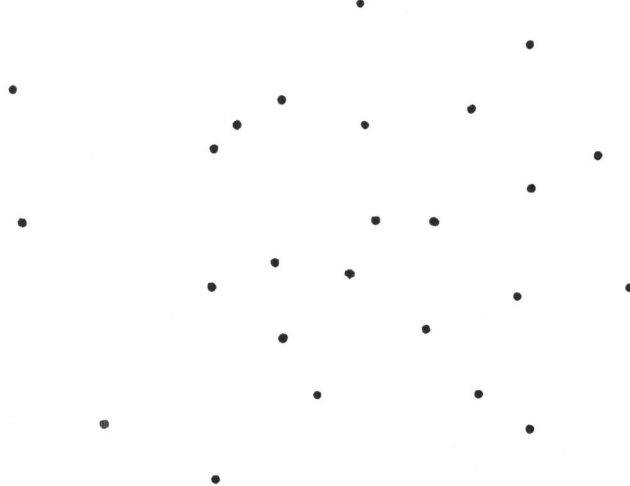

Fig. 3. A random point configuration.

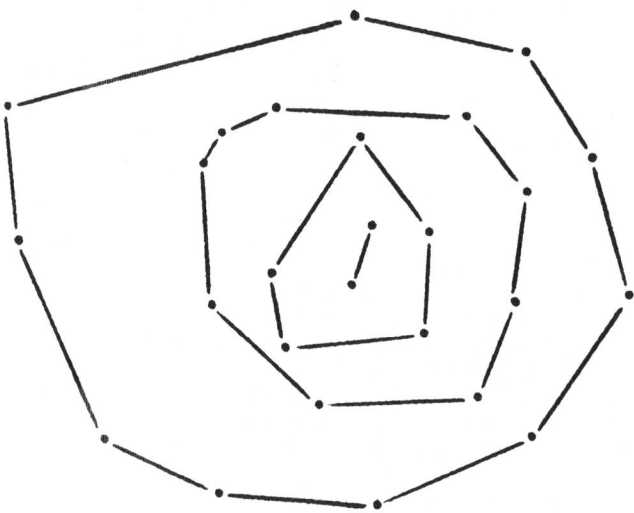

Fig. 4. The same configuration shown to be type 3_2.

ordering rule may be extended, if desired, to "shells" instead of "rings" in a space of any dimension.

An alternative method of proof of the axiom of choice takes its point of departure from the set S'. By the same steps by which we arrived at equation (1) we can write

$$S' = mP' + \sum_1^m \bar{P}_j' \tag{4}$$

where P' is the minimally single common property shared by all the $\bar{P}_j$ of S. Obviously this process may be continued similarly by forming the new set S'', etc., until the point is reached where the members of the thus final subset differ only in position in some space, these differences hence constituting the ultimate basis of the initial distinguishability of the m members of S. The members of this final subset S_f would thus be completely identical except as to position. What keeps them distinguished, then, is intervening distance, and hence distinguishability is ultimately separation, which involves us immediately in the notion of the continuum, as the separation may be to any degree; and there is only a smaller, and no smallest, attachable to this "any." Thus the axiom of choice depends upon the existence of a continuum.

This same conclusion is reached by considering that to order means to ordinate, that is, in any aggregate to assign one element therein as "first"; one as "second"; one as "third," etc.; and that this process involves the concept of a linear sequence or one-dimensionality, which is to say *distance*.

Continuing, it now remains to show that a choice function exists for S_f which, since its members differ only in position, is isomorphic to a set of points. A point may always be chosen outside this set so that no two distances between it and any point (member) of S_f are equal. This yields a set of line lengths, equal in number to the members of S_f, which can be laid end to end in order of increasing length to form a straight line, at the beginning point and at each division of which can be placed one member of S_f, which is now ordered.

To complete this proof of the axiom of choice one further question remains to be answered: how far does distinguishability extend between two line lengths which are approaching the same magnitude? Clearly, this distinguishability—and hence the axiom of choice itself—is sustained for all finite differences of length, however small. This is all the distinguishability we require in this proof, since more would be needed only to distinguish between magnitudes associated with two or more coincident points—a situation not arising here. We thus have arrived at our goal a second time. It is none the less interesting to observe that, given the proper data, it is possible in the context of magnitude to distinguish between two or more coincident points, and that (as we already saw in 3.3) $p/\infty \neq q/\infty$, where p and q are two different magnitudes, though p/∞ and q/∞ are ordinarily both assumed to be identically equal to 0. If $p = 1$ and $q = 2$, the difference between the two zeros is easily seen from the relation

$$1^\infty = (1 + 0)^\infty = (1 + x/\infty)^\infty = e^x \tag{5}$$

where

$$(1 + x/\infty)^\infty = \lim_{n \to \infty} (1 + x/n)^n \tag{5a}$$

x being any number, real or otherwise, and n being positive real. By equation (5) the two zeros in the example given would result in e and e^2 respectively, and would thus be distinguishable by the operation of (5).

There is an even deeper method of proof of the axiom of choice, which is independent of a geometrical point-mapping of a set. With this method we may prove the axiom of choice even if the members of S are assumed to have not even a common space-representation.

Let us first use a lemma which we have already proved previously: Every infinite extension of infinitization of a dimension (n) is explicitly expressible as an unspecified finite content of dimension $(n + 1)$. Just as an infinite line may be represented as a finite area—something which is no longer line—so must infinite dimensionality itself be finitely or conceivably representable by something that is no longer spatial dimension or extension. Let us agree to call what lies thus beyond dimension "meta-dimensionality," using this term also to refer to all finite dimensions taken together.

Re-examining equation (5) we note that 1^∞ represents the content of a hypercube in the infinite dimension, and that this content is expressible as the function e^x. Applying our lemma to dimensionality itself, the infinite dimension must be as much beyond ordinary dimensionality as the $(n + 1)$th dimension is beyond the (n)th. We have also seen that the first dimension, or linearity, is adequate for the mapping of all higher dimensional magnitudes, in the form of numbers. Thus 64 is not only 64 (linear) units, but represents also, among other figures, a (two-dimensional) square of side 8, a (three-dimensional) cube of side 4, a (four-dimensional) hyperparallelepiped of sides 2, 4, 4, 2, a (five-dimensional) hyperparallelepiped of sides 4, 2, 2, 2, 2, and a (six-dimensional) hypercube of side 2. Similar sequences are obtained for all other numbers (though not necessarily with rational sides), 1 itself representing the content of a hypercube of any finite dimension in units of that dimension.

Thus number or magnitude is an adequate representation of extension or dimensionality itself. Hence the infinitization of number can inform us about the infinitization of dimensionality. But by equation (5) the infinitization of number (1^{∞})—and hence of dimensionality itself—is *function* (e^x) or relation. It may help us to see this by realizing that, just as a higher dimension involves an infinitude of elements of the next lower dimension, just so does a function in general involve an infinitude of magnitudes which may satisfy the function. Function is the meta-meaning of number or magnitude, lying one dimension of meaning above number. Thus dimensionality, representable as extension, number, magnitude, or objective actuality (in the sense of "the extended"), infinitizes into function, relation, or operation, which is hence the second metadimension of meaning, the first being magnitude. Among the metadimensions, the meaning of the nth is the $(n + 1)$th. For metadimensionality is meaning, just as dimensionality is extension. The dimensional extension of a square is a cube; the metadimensional "extension" of a magnitude is a function.

It is an extraordinary and invaluable fact that, since the first spatial dimension was as we saw adequate to map all dimensionality, it is hence adequate to map also the first metadimension, which is dimensionality itself. We shall demonstrate in a forthcoming study* the following theorem: Just as the first dimension provides an adequate mapping for all dimensionality, so the first metadimension can map all the metadimensions, of which there are six plus the zeroth metadimension (possibility), which has an intersection with the zeroth dimension, the point. The corollary is that numbers are adequate to map the metadimensions.

However, for the present purpose it suffices to show that the metadimensions can be ordered. They are ordered by a sequence of infinitizations, starting with the first—magnitude to function—which we have already seen in equation (5) and the subsequent discus-

*"Alphabets of Reality" (2 vols.), now in preparation.

sion. The next natural question is: What is the infinitization of function? Whatever this be, it would have to be something which uses relations as a function uses the magnitudes that make the function explicit by substitution in it. Only ends, aims, or purposes so use relations, which in terms of game theory are the ways the pieces move which can be used to realize strategies, which are explicit forms of purposes.

Proceeding, let us ask what so uses purposes. The answer carries us to the fourth metadimension, that of value and value systems. Using again the appropriate language of game theory, the meaning of any strategy lies in what is valuable to win or achieve in the game. A strategy leading to a less game-valuable achievement is a less significant strategy. The value system is represented by the payoff or scoring matrix.

It is worth noting that value systems yield comparatively simply to a one-dimensional mapping: to value means to establish placements of "this comes first," "this second," "this third," etc. The linear permutation defines the value system. Consider, for instance, the value system defined by the order: (1) self-preservation, (2) public recognition, (3) accomplishment, and (4) private pleasure. This system, which seeks recognition irrespective of accomplishment, is obviously inferior to the system defined by 1, 3, 2, 4. A totally different value system is given by 4, 3, 1, 2, *et al*. The linear permutations provide quite precise characterizations, even predictable personal traits following from such mappings. To have a different value system is to play a different kind of game.

The next level of meaning must rise metalogically higher than the payoff matrix. This step is uniquely determined: the player himself has been reached; and entity is the fifth metadimension. By entity we refer to that which uses and gives meaning to value systems, as they use and insignify purposes.

Calling these five metadimensions we have reached in order M, F, P, V, and E respectively, we see that we may write symbolically

$$E = V^{\infty} = (P^{\infty})^{\infty} = F^{\infty^{3}} = M^{\infty^{4}} \tag{6}$$

We shall not consider here the sixth metadimension, which possesses special characteristics related to what might be called interpretation or the "orchestration" of the entire series, and ends the series of metadimensions which, unlike the dimensionality of space, does not have an infinitude of terms, the infinitization of the sixth metadimension leading again to a form of itself, the only thing beyond it* being again the zeroth metadimension, thus closing the series. Suffice it to say, all meanings whatsoever, and hence all logically abstracted properties, are contained in the ring of the metadimensions which is closed under all logical and/or conceptual operations; and the metadimensions are sequentially orderable. That is all on this subject that we require in our final proof of the axiom of choice, which we can now conclude.

We have completed the proof if the property residues R_j are all in the same metadimension. We are now ready to consider the more refractory case where the R_j are distributed over more than one metadimension. First, all the R_j in each metadimension can be ordered, as we have shown. Each of these ordered sets now can be made subsets of their ordered union by reason of the order in the metadimensions. Our final proof of the axiom of choice is thus completed.

Recalling the several paragraphs from 3.62 through 3.7, we are now in a position to see that a universal Turing machine uT_n (3.62) operates in the third metadimension, an ordinary or specialized Turing machine, T_k, operating in the second. We can also now see that, as mentioned less specifically at the end of 3.7, there are further generalizations of a Turing machine, the first being expressible as

$$\lim_{n \to \infty} uT_n = (T)_4 \tag{7}$$

a supra-Turing machine which operates in the fourth metadimension. There would then be two further sequential generalizations of the Turing machine, represented by $(T)_5$ and $(T)_6$. Thus anything isomorphically symbolizable is constructible. Only the possibilities of the symbolizer himself are not symbolizable, those possibilities being the kind that are ever self-increasing and that cannot be observed without being thereby and to that extent actualized, whereupon they are no longer what they were.

---

*In a specific sense for which there is insufficient space for definition here, and which is best illustrated by the zero proved to lie beyond $-\infty$ in the factorial function. (See the writer's abstract in the January 1960 *Notices* of the Amer. Math. Soc.)

APPENDIX TO CHAPTER VIII*

G. PASK

PART 1: Teaching Machines

Any adaptive teaching machine uses the principles outlined in this paper for stabilizing a student's behavior [18, 33]. Indeed, the process of teaching is, in many ways, similar to a behavioral experiment. The teacher, whether a real-life instructor or a machine, must try to maintain the subject's attention so that his behavior is exteriorized in the experimental environment which, being accessible, may be controlled. Then the teacher must ascertain the regularities of behavior, in order to effect control. But, whereas the *experimenter* is anxious to discover any of the rules that govern behavior the *teacher* is chiefly concerned with bringing about the specific modifications entailed in teaching a skill. His interest is more specialized and because there are some forms of behavior he rejects as irrelevant to the skill, the experimental environment he provides is rather constrained.

We shall consider a prototype teaching machine used to instruct card punching. The Solartron SAKI machines were derived from this prototype by introducing technically desirable alterations which would merely confuse the present discussion [34, 35].

A proficient card-punch machinist is required to read sequences of numerical (or, in some cases, numerical and alphabetic) characters, legibly impressed upon documents such as invoices, and to translate the data into sequences of manual selections of keys arranged upon a keyboard (we shall consider the case of a 12-position keyboard so that for a numerical character one key must be select-

*The bibliographic references in this appendix will be found at the conclusion of Chapter VIII—*Ed.*

273

ed, but for an alphabetic character a coded pair must be selected). The material is not very redundant and a mean latency of about 0.2 sec is demanded.

The real-life data supply is simulated by a stimulus display consisting of four alternative lines of exercise material Π_1, Π_2, Π_3, and Π_4* (significantly different sequences of 24 numerical or alphabetic characters), one of which is *selected* for rehearsal by the teaching machine. The job is *paced* by an indicator which moves in steps along the exercise line positions (pointing out which item in the line counts as a stimulus at a given instant) and which rests for a variable interval a_{rl} ($r = 1, 2, 3, 4$; $l = 1, 2, \ldots, 24$) upon the lth position of the rth exercise line. The real-life response facility is simulated by an identical keyboard, having 12 key locations, which, together with the pairs of key locations that specify alphabetic characters and a possibility "0" that no response is made, will be identified with the response alternatives X_i. Thus, $i = $ "0", 1, 2, $\ldots$, 32. The stimuli Y_j are characters in this alphabet. Thus, $j = 1, 2, \ldots, 32$, a stimulus denoted $Y(t)$ is located by the indicator each instant $t = 1, 2, \ldots$, and $X(t)$ is the subject's response (possibly a "no response") to $Y(t)$.

In addition to stimuli, the teaching machine delivers "cue information" by the illumination of lamps arranged as a replica of the keyboard layout in a "cue information" display. For a given arrangement of characters along the exercise lines the "cue information" that accompanies an indicator position is completely determined and specifies that X_i which is a correct response to the indicated Y_j (in practice, the selection of "cue information" is determined as a part of the program which, together with the exercise line character sequences, can be changed from subject to subject, or for a given subject, about once an hour).

Finally, there is a meter, indicating a performance measure θ, but in this teaching system the pace and condition of the machine are adequate indices of the success and the meter itself appears to be redundant.

Although "cue information" always *can* be delivered it is *not* necessarily delivered. It may be withheld to a variable extent β_j so that it only becomes available throughout some of the interval a_{rl} in which the ith character is presented in the stimulus display (the

*In this case the various Π_r signify determinate sequences, not transition probability matrices.

positions in which the ith character, Y_j, appears depend upon the program mentioned a moment ago). The sequences Π_1, Π_2, Π_3, and Π_4 are such that each of the exercise lines is different in some manner relevant to the subject's performance and the entire set of items is unlearnable within about one hour's tuition. Now this teaching machine determines the values of $a_{rl}(t)$, $\beta_l(t)$, and $r(t)$. Thus at an instant $t = t_0$, some exercise line is selected depending upon the value of $r(t_0)$ and the indicator moves along this particular exercise line, remaining for an interval of about $a_{rl}(t)$ upon the lth position, $t > t_0$. If X_l appears in the lth position an amount of "cue information" proportional to $\beta_l(t)$ is presented to the subject.

The basic skill to be learned entails the relation $X(t) = R[Y(t)]$, which is a one-to-one mapping between X^* and Y^*, since some Y_j are in pairs of key locations. Consequently, as $V^* = X^* \otimes Y^*$, the set $V_0^* \subset V^*$ such that for $X \otimes Y = V \subset V_0^*$, $Y = R(X)$ is a subset of correct outcomes. But manifestly R is not the only thing the subject learns. Ultimately he must *anticipate* sequences of responses to sequences of stimuli which are subsequences of the Π_r, in order to achieve a mean latency of about 0.2 sec. At this stage his "chunks" are *sequences* rather than stimuli and he considers relations between "chunks" like $(X_1 \to X_2 \to \ldots) R^* (Y_1 \to Y_2 \to \ldots)$.

We could (bearing the Π_r in mind) define a larger set of outcomes within which the elements were sequences of the elements of V^*. Again, we could have enlarged the outcome set by considering the various modified forms in which any stimulus Y_j may be displayed. Thus, if Y_j is presented (due to a high value of the variable β_j) with "cue information" that completely specifies the relation $X_l = R(X_l)$, the subject is solving less of a problem than he would be, given none of the additional data, and (insofar as he accepts the stimuli as unitary) is deciding about "chunks" less than a stimulus-response pair (rather interesting possibilities arise when the subject decides about sequences in which some items *are* and other items are *not* associated with "cue information").

Initially the machine selects each exercise line with equal likelihood. Plenty of "cue information" is provided and the required pace is modest. At this stage the subject cannot really avoid successful behavior. Gradually and selectively the teaching machine increases the difficulty of the job, making selections of exercise lines that maximally confuse the subjects, increasing the pace and withholding "cue information." The process is partially reversible

if the student's behavior is impaired in terms of accuracy or in terms
of rate. Ultimately the subject will be card punching from material
that is sufficiently representative of real-life data and is performing
the skill at the required rate.

The teaching machine's activity can be regarded at one level
as imitating the behavior of a real-life instructor, but it is also possible to say that the teaching machine performs the pair of functions
mentioned as separable in 3.4, namely, to recapitulate:

(1) To maximize ξ_Y in order to balance the increase in $\eta_{C(r)}$
which occurs due to adaptation, the whole process depending upon
the assumption that the condition $C(t) = L[G(t)]$ is satisfied.*

(2) To approximate $C(t) = L[G(t)]$, which is only possible if the
subject's attention is occupied by the controlled data and if $\eta_{C(r)}$
is determined (for it is necessary to detect a decrease in the rate
of change of the variable as an indication of *when* to change $C(r)$,
even knowing *how* to change it).

To increase the display variety, an adaptive machine paces the
subject's performance (i.e., forces his response, which if $C(t) =
L[G(t)]$, increases his required decision rate). If we assume that
the least considerable chunk of data is a stimulus-response pair
(but appreciating that the subject may come to anticipate sequences
of these outcomes as decidable wholes), the pacing action is performed separately for each position in each exercise line. The variable concerned is a_{rl}, which is the machine's "expectation" of the
subject's correct response latency at the rth, lth position.

Since by initial agreement the subject is *trying* to obey the rule
R, any mistake is construed as a symptom of overload. Thus, for
each presentation (each occasion the indicator comes to rest upon
the rth, lth position) the machine is built to consider the outcomes,
"correct response," "no response," and "error response," of which
"correct response" or "error response" may occur with a latency
greater or less than the value of $a_{rl}(t)$ (the teaching machine moves
the indicator onward at $a_{rl}(t) + 50$ m/sec, and 50 m/sec is sufficient
to register *some* response). The object is to equate the machine's
expectation of correct response latency with the actual value.

Let $J_{rl}(t)$ be the latency, at t, for the rth, lth position. Let

$$\alpha_{rl}(t) = a_{rl}(t) - J_{rl}(t)$$

But the value of $a_{rl}(t)$ which is registered in a separate memory de-

*In the nomenclature of 3.4, to maximize ξ_{X_G}.

vice for each position on each line is changed by an increment $\Delta a_{ri}(t)$:

$$\Delta a_{ri}(t) = - [F(t) + E(t)] \cdot [\sigma_{ri}(t)]$$

where $F(t) = a$ if $X(t) = R[Y(t)]$, and $F(t) = b$ if not, which is a characteristic function on V^*. Further, $E(t) = c$ if $X(t) = 0$, and $E(t) = 0$ if not.

The values of a, b, and c, which are in the interval -1, 1, are set, for the moment, arbitrarily. The over-all effect is to encourage increasingly larger groupings of the data or increasingly projected anticipation of the outcomes. Suppose, on Π_r, at $t = t_1$, that the subject anticipates his correct response to the item $l + 2$, when making a correct response to item $l + 1$; the sequence $(Y_{r,l+1}, Y_{r,l+2})$ will be associated with lower latencies than $(Y_{rl}, \ldots, Y_{r,l+3}, Y_{r,l+4})$, as a result of which $\sigma_{r,l+1}(t_1)$ and $\sigma_{r,l+2}(t_1)$ will be above their neighboring values. Consequently, upon the next occasion at $t = t_2$, that $Y_{r,l+1}$ and $Y_{r,l+2}$ are presented, they will appear in rapid succession, for $a_{r,l+1}(t_2)$ and $a_{r,l+2}(t_2)$ will be below the neighboring values. In this sense, $(Y_{r,l+1}, Y_{r,l+2})$ are perceptually grouped in the display. But the process is cumulative. For, in order to respond at all to this sequence, the subject is bound to anticipate over at least a pair of items, since being a finite-rate decision maker he can only perform the feat of deciding about "chunks" called "sequences" rather than "chunks" called "stimulus" and "response pairs." He may, of course, make no response, or the effort may elicit an error response, and in either case, the grouping will decay (more rapidly in the case of error response). Not all groupings survive. But for those that do, this ξ_Y maximizing process encourages development.

Now, in anticipating and deciding about sequences, the subject is acquiring relations R^*. But maybe he does not recognize R (or, more likely, is unable to make full use of his knowledge). In this case, we need a mechanism for presenting lesser "chunks" than the stimuli; in other words, for reducing the problem difficulty entailed in deciding about a single stimulus and response pair. The "cue information" serves this purpose.

β_i determines the moment, within $a_{ri}(t)$, that the "cue information" about $X_i = R(Y_i)$ is displayed, and thus the extent to which it can assist a pertinent choice process in the subject. The machine has an inbuilt tendency to remove the "cue information" at a rate inversely proportional to a performance measure θ that we shall consider in a moment. This tendency is countered whenever there is error response. In practice whenever error response indicates overload with respect to one of the X_i Y_j pairs, an increment $E = -b$ is registered and averaged on a separate memory device for each character. The accumulated value is reduced at a rate $\theta(t)$ and the standing value determines $\beta_j(t)$, and consequently the amount of "cue information." Commonly, the mechanisms [of $\alpha_{ri}(t)$ and $\beta_j(t)$] interact; for example, the subject may be able to anticipate over a sequence *because* "cue information" is available (or, conversely, an unstable anticipated sequence may be stabilized by delivering "cue information").

Suppose there were only one sequence Π_0. Eventually the subject would learn Π_0 completely and none of the mechanisms we have considered could increase the display variety (increasing the required latency, for example, would only exhibit muscular limitations and lack of manual dexterity). The machine could be reprogramed at this stage (indeed this is what must be done after four sequences have been learned, using *this* teaching machine), but if the system is to remain stable without external interruption, *some* adjustment is needed, for the machine's actions are redundant and control of them will only by accident control the behavior of the subject.

The method used in the card punching system is to change r whenever there is evidence that the subject has adapted to a particular exercise line, say Π_1. We rely upon interference to confuse the subject's detailed knowledge of Π_1 so that after some other exercise line, say Π_2, has been rehearsed, it is possible to return to Π_1 as though it were made up from relatively novel material.

On the assumption that the $\alpha_{ri}(t)$ and $\beta_i(t)$ mechanisms have performed their functions, a weighted correct response rate measure, over Π_r, is a reasonable index of η_{π_r}, providing that it is weighted by an index of the rate at which the "cue information" has been introduced. A suitable correct response rate or "performance measure" is $\theta_r(t)$. Its value at $t = r_2$ is $\theta_r(r_2)$ = average over t, average over l,i of

$$\frac{E(t) + F(t) - \sum_j \beta_j(t)}{\sigma_{ri}(t)}$$

$r_2 \geq t \geq r_1$, i such that $X_i \subset \Pi_r$, and $r_2 - r_1$ arbitrary. Similarly, $\theta(t) = \frac{1}{4} \sum_r \theta_r(t)$.

We are anxious to detect the condition

$$0 \geq \frac{d\eta_{\pi_r}}{dt}$$

and when it occurs to select a different value of r. Further, the value selected should maximize the initial value of η_{π_r} when the subject starts to rehearse the exercise line. Thus the teaching machine is designed to determine (at the completion of each exercise line) if the measure $\theta_r(t)$ which, from the previous argument, we regard as an indication of $1 - \eta_{\pi}$, has increased, and if it has not, to assume that

$$0 \geq \frac{d\eta_{\pi_r}}{dt}$$

In this case, the teaching machine selects that exercise line for which $\theta_r(t)$ is least.

The process can be regarded, once again, as imitating a real-life instruction for (identifying the inverse of $\theta_r(t)$ with the difficulty of the rth exercise line) the device effects the tuitional rule "practice the most difficult material most often."

Now each of the mechanisms we have considered for maximizing ξ_Y is also a mechanism for approximating $C(t) = L[G(t)]$. Perhaps the r adjustment performs this function most explicitly, for it is no more than a matter of definition that, if the exercise lines do exhibit the "relevant differences" required, their attributes will be identified in different systems C. The selection rule is based upon the meta-information that the subject would like to maximize his rate of increase of θ and this machine strategy assists him by choosing the most difficult C as nearest neighbor in the metric on the set of C. More elaborate systems have been constructed in which short sequences of items are metricized [in a measure like $\theta_r(t)$]. The training sequence has been continually built up from these short sequences (choosing the one to be added at t as that with the least $\theta_r(t)$ as the best strategy given the meta-information that the subject aims to maximize the increase in θ).

But the entities selected, whether exercise lines or something smaller, are not invariant. The $a_{rl}(t)$ mechanisms are continually altering the set from which the r-choosing mechanism makes its selection.

Now it is possible to assign values a, b, and c such that the "cue information" is not too rapidly removed and the pace is not too rapidly increased so that the $\theta_r(t)$ reach a stationary value very quickly. A teaching machine is designed with a, b, and c that satisfy the necessary set of inequalities. In other words, with these values of a, b, and c the student learns to perform with full "cue information" is not too rapidly removed and the pace is not a stable performance, say on Π_1, in these conditions, the teaching machine selects say Π_2. In this way, we guarantee that the teaching machine obtains experience of the student's behavior in each of the different exercise lines.

But having satisfied the necessary inequalities, there are many available values of a, b, and c. The best values, so far as teaching is concerned, depend upon the student and may change a little throughout the training routine.

In everyday nomenclature, a, b, and c determine the relative importance, for a given individual, of speed, accuracy, and other facets of behavior, at various stages in the process of learning to to achieve a given standard of speed and accuracy.

In commercial teaching machines, like SAKI, these parameters are predetermined. But in the prototype machines they were adjusted by a "hill-climbing" device to maximize the change of θ. This makes little difference for card punching, but a "hill-climbing" device becomes very necessary when the performance criterion is not related to the criterion of proficiency at a given stage in learning. Thus a, b, and c would have to be adjusted if learning to deal with the material of the first exercise line depended upon the student's accuracy, his speed being irrelevant, while for the second exercise line learning depended on speed, the accuracy being irrelevant, or, even more cogently, if these comments applied not to exercise lines, but to "early" or "late" in the learning process.

PART 2: Self-Organizing Systems

There are many fields of investigation in which information about the *topic* is gleaned at the expense of structural uncertainty (which commonly appears as uncertainty about the form of inquiry that will lead to coherent observations). Normally, coherence is achieved only if qualitatively different kinds of experiments take place. Thus, when studying the development of embryos, qualitatively different procedures are used at different stages, keyed to questions about *cells*, or questions about *tissues*, or ultimately, about *organisms*. Unless the form of the inquiry is changed in this manner, our concept of a developing embryo does not make sense. Now any coherent system of attributes identified with the embryo is a self-organizing system. The same comment applies to species that *evolve* or, as in the present case, to organisms or automata that *learn*. A self-organizing system is not necessarily "alive," although any living thing is a self-organizing system. We say the embryo is "alive" because it is a self-organizing system and because it is made* from the materials that are used in constructing the members of our own species. We say that an artifact is "alive" if it is a self-organizing system with a behavior that entails our particular form of concept.

A number of compatible definitions of a self-organizing system have been advanced by Beer [7], MacKay [19, 20], Pringle [38], von Foerster, and myself. Of these von Foerster's definition is the most useful for the present discussion.

Given a system it is, as in 2.3, possible to compute the functions μ, ξ, and η, if and only if the behavior in the system is coherent.

Von Foerster points out that in a self-organizing system
$$d\eta/dt > 0$$
In terms of varieties
$$\xi(d\eta/dt) > \mu(d\xi/dt)$$
or if
(i) $d\mu/dt = 0$, then $0 > d\xi/dt$

or if
(ii) $d\xi/dt = 0$, then $d\mu/dt > 0$
as special cases.

Now μ depends upon U *in* the system concerned. Commonly its value is altered by changing the identification of a system (Von Foerster considers the case of changing the number of components in an assembly, but in general μ is a function of the states and the logically specified constraints upon change of state). On the other hand, ξ, given a system, depends upon the hypotheses validated in the system or in the case of a mechanism, upon adaptive changes.

*The embryo, it must be pointed out, is not made, but grows—independently of either human skill or awareness: a very different process having little, if anything, in common with man-made constructions. One must ever be on guard against reductive oversimplification in these matters. —Ed.

Thus, in the sense of (i), a conditional probability machine, like Uttley's which has μ invariant, does act as a self-organizing system when its constraints are adaptively modified (thus changing ξ). The case of (ii) is less common, but is approximated when a mushroom, having reached the primordial stage, begins to "grow" (in this case "growth" means expansion only, for the plan of the organism remains the same). On the other hand, in the earlier stage of its development, when part of the hyphal network becomes differentiated into the primordiae, the mushroom is a self-organizing system in which ξ and μ are changing. This seems to be a much more interesting process for, unlike the change of ξ alone, or μ alone, its physical realization is *not* prone to any obvious limit.

Consider the case of $[\lambda, L, \phi]$. We have a sequence of systems

$$\lambda = C_1 \to C_2 \to \ldots C_{n+1} = C(r_0) \to C(r_1) \to \ldots C(r_{n+1})$$

which cannot be determined at $t = r_n$, or any instant earlier than $t = r_{n+1}$.

(1) An observer might say "I am looking at one system which I shall call C, defined in terms of some invariant connections from an automaton that maintains $C = L(G)$, a process that does not concern me." In this case η is sometimes increasing and sometimes indeterminate,

$$0 \geq d\xi/dt$$

whenever determinable, and μ is *very nearly* constant. The system is thus either a self-organizing system, as in (i), or it is undefined. But unless there is "generalization" when

$$d\mu/dt > 0$$

it does not satisfy (ii). On the other hand:

(2) The observer might say "I shall look at all the systems up to $t = r_i$ and call the changing system C." But since

$$[C_i = (A_i^*, L_i, U_i)] \# [C_{i+1} = (A_{i+1}^*, L_{i+1}, U_{i+1})]$$

we infer that

$$^\mu C_i \cup C_{i+1} > {}^\mu C_i \text{ or } {}^\mu C_{i+1}$$

Thus,

$$d\mu/dt > 0$$

and the system is a self-organizing system as in (ii), but also, in the interval $t = r_{i-1}$, $t = r_i$,

$$0 \geq d\xi/dt$$

So it is also a self-organizing system according to (i).